THE JURY

World's most famous representation of "Justice"

Explanatory note: This representation of Lady Justice with her eyes wide open stands atop London's Old Bailey, scene of many famous jury criminal trials including that of William Penn and William Mead in 1670 (then Newgate prison, see page 83 for details of the Penn trial.)

THE JURY

Tool of Kings
Palladium of Liberty

LLOYD E. MOORE

SECOND EDITION

CINCINNATI
ANDERSON PUBLISHING CO.

The Jury: Tool of Kings, Palladium of Liberty, Second Edition
© 1973, The W.H. Anderson Company
© 1988, Anderson Publishing Co.

Library of Congress Cataloging in Publication Data
Moore, Lloyd E.
    The jury, tool of kings, palladium of liberty.
    Includes index.
    1. Jury—United States.   2. Jury—Great Britain.
I. Title.
KF8972.M6 1988   347.73'752   88-16619
ISBN 0-87084-577-2

CONTENTS

ILLUSTRATIONS

FOREWORD

Lloyd E. Moore is a paradox. He looks like a boxer, but is basically a gentle man. Generally he appears in a black suit, black bow tie and white shirt. This man is a professional photographer. He served as the prosecuting attorney and still is an active litigator in Lawrence County, Ohio on the north bank of the Ohio River. In 1971 he closed the doors to a busy law practice and took his family to London, England for one year. In 1973 he wrote a monumental work on "The Jury" based upon these experiences. He spoke not only from the viewpoint of a pure academician but as one who had toiled in the pits. I have met him there as an antagonist and tested his mettle. He knows whereof he speaks. He knows his juries. Lloyd Moore is a trial lawyer. So am I and it takes one to know one. Now he is revising his original work on "The Jury." The revision is an updating and an expansion of the original. It is a work which trial lawyers, and all lawyers are such to some extent be it primary or only secondary, will want not only to read but to treasure as a reference for future use. It is readable and understandable for the lay person as well as the lawyer.

William L. Howland
Attorney at Law
Of Counsel
Bannon, Howland & Dever
Portsmouth, Ohio

April 1, 1988

PREFACE

Since the writing of the preface to the first edition in 1973, trial by jury has remained very much alive in the United States. Things have happened. On May 26, 1979, a jury of Berlin citizens, sitting under a United States District Court judge from New Jersey who had been appointed as judge for the United States Court for Berlin, found Detlef Tiede not guilty of hijacking a Polish plane, not guilty of depriving persons of liberty, and not guilty of doing bodily injury, but guilty of taking a hostage. *Judgment In Berlin,* Herbert J. Stern (Universe Books, New York, 1984, p. 350).

The Supreme Court ruled in *Batson v. Kentucky,* 106 S. Ct. 1712 (1986), that a prosecutor has to have a racially neutral reason to challenge a black, prospective juror. On November 19, 1985, a Texas jury returned a verdict in favor of Pennzoil against Texaco for 10.53 billion dollars, which is the largest jury verdict in history.

On October 22, 1987, a jury sitting in Belleville, Illinois, returned a verdict against Monsanto Co. for 16.2 million dollars in a trial that had lasted over three and one-half years, making it the longest jury trial in history. Several appellate decisions make it clear that the United States Supreme Court will have to decide if the right to jury trial in civil cases can survive the objection that some cases are too complex for the jury to understand.

Dan Dustin of San Diego, California, while recovering from the shock of jury duty, wrote *How To Avoid Jury Duty* (Mockingbooks, La Mesa, California, 1986). I was summoned to appear for jury duty on November 23, 1987; however there was no need to make use of Dustin's book because the case settled. Since 1973, I have completed my four year term as prosecutor for Lawrence County, Ohio, and decided not to seek a second term.

During the intervening years, I have tried a lot of jury cases involving criminal charges and negligence. Over this period of time there have been a number of studies done, books written, and seminars delivered advising lawyers about what works in convincing jurors. I believe that these psychological-social-marketing studies have added very little to the insight that classical writers gave to us a couple of thousand years ago. It was for this reason that a chapter on forensic persuasion was added to *The Jury.*

The chapter on the constitutional jury has been updated and deepened to make it a more valuable tool to the lawyer who needs to brief a jury issue. The addition of a jury chronology provides a quick way to put jury questions into historical perspective. The quotes in the appendix make readily available insightful thoughts on justice and trial by jury.

Lloyd E. Moore
Ironton, Ohio
April, 1988

PREFACE TO THE FIRST EDITION

That a sophisticated people would leave decisions affecting fortune, honor and life to a fixed number of individuals, selected at random, without regard to intelligence, experience or education would seem to defy rational explanation

The reasons lie in history. The first records of institutions ancestral to the jury are coeval with history itself. The ancient Mediterranean civilizations and the Germanic tribes had groups of laymen who participated in judgment. From these early sources to the modern trial jury there are great gaps, but even biological evolution seldom has a complete chain.

From the time of Henry II of England, the record is reasonably clear but no less interesting. We find that our ancestors were tortured to force them to submit to trial by jury. Jurors were starved into rendering verdicts. Distinctive types of juries evolved to try the cases of aliens and business cases. Occasionally, jurors risked their own fortunes by insisting on rendering a verdict in accordance with their consciences and against the direction of judges who were under the influence of the crown.

Revolutionary America took the jury to its heart as a weapon in its struggle with the mother country. The power of the jury increased and was practically unchallenged in nineteenth century America. It is only in the last half of the present century that signs are appearing that indicate the long story of the jury may be coming to an end. The jury's most serious competitors are arbitration and trial by judge alone. Of these two, trial by judge poses the jury's most serious threat. It is for this reason and for the reason that most objections to judges apply to arbitrators that the last chapter is devoted to a comparsion of judges and jury trial. Trial experience and historical research have left the writer with the conviction that the quality of justice and liberty itself will suffer if the role of jury trial is further diminshed. It may be that the reader will disagree with this conclusion but still find the story of jury trial to be a fascinating one.

Lloyd E. Moore
Chesapeake, Ohio
June 23, 1973

xi

ACKNOWLEDGMENTS

The basic research for this book could not have been accomplished without access to the collections of the Institute For Advanced Legal Studies of the University of London, the British Museum, the Middle Temple, the Law Society, the libraries of the Royal Borough of Kensington and Chelsea, the library of the College of Law of the Ohio State University, and the Law Library of Lawrence County, Ohio (where Sharon Bradshaw was particularly helpful).

Helping me from the Anderson staff have been John L. Skirving (since deceased, who got the project started when he was President of the publisher), Jean Martin, Rod Mortimer, William A. Burden, Dale J. Hartig, and President John L. Mason. Special thanks are extended to S. F. Spira of Beechhurst, New York, for furnishing the negative for the first photograph of a jury and to Judge Kenneth B. Ater for permission to photograph a contemporary jury.

John E. Hall, referee of the Probate-Juvenile Division of the Common Pleas Court, Lawrence County, Ohio, was exceedingly helpful with proofreading and preparation of the index. At every step of the production of this book my wife Marilyn has helped by typing, proofreading, and encouragement.

I
Creation of the Gods

i

Odysseus stole a sacred statue of Pallas Athena—patron goddess of the Trojans—leaving the way clear for the Greeks to capture and raze Troy. Upon his homecoming, Agamemnon, commander-in-chief of the Greeks, was murdered by his wife as a solution to her marital problems. This drastic action by Clytemnestra was distressing to her children; so acute was the reaction of her offspring that Orestes, at the urging of his sister and with the approval of Apollo, killed his mother and her latest lover.

This sequence of events could have ended at this point if the Greeks had not held strong views on matricide. The local citizens were supported in their revulsion at Orestes' deadly revenge by three demigods, known collectively as the Eumenides or Furies. The people and spirits gave Orestes no rest, and he finally sought refuge at Athens where Pallas Athena called together twelve citizens of Athens to try him on the charge of matricide. Apollo, to his credit, was the chief witness and advocate for Orestes, while the Eumenides pressed the prosecution.

This first jury trial of a mortal*, having taken place over three thousand years ago, could well have ended in a hung jury, as there were six votes for conviction and six for acquittal. However, Pallas Athena, in her belief that the better part of justice was mercy, broke the tie and voted for acquittal. This story of the founding of the jury by the patron goddess of wisdom is most clearly set forth in the play *Eumenides* by Aeschylus, who died in 456 B.C.[1]

We are on firmer historical ground when we come to the time of

---

* The very first trial held on the Areopagus was that which tried the god Ares for the murder of Halirrhothius, son of Poseidon. The jury of twelve gods split six to six, and Ares was acquitted. The New Century Classical Handbook, Catherine B. Avery, editor, Appleton-Century-Crofts, Inc. (New York, 1962), p. 149.

1

Solon, who probably lived in the last of the seventh and the first part of the sixth century B.C. History tells us this lawgiver reconstituted the court known as the Areopagus (the tribunal described above by Aeschylus) and another court, the Ephetae.[2] This latter court was composed of fifty-one men above the age of fifty and of noble birth. The membership of the Areopagus was drawn from those citizens who had held the office of archon, nine of whom combined to rule the city-state of Athens.[3] It should not be thought that the lateness of this era in history precludes the historical validity of the trial of Orestes as described by Aeschylus. The Areopagus was known to have existed long before the time of Solon, but he was simply the first to definitely arrange and legalize its constitution.[4]

Certainly, the Areopagus and the Ephetae do not appear particularly democratic in their membership when compared to the modern American jury, but there is more to the Athenian story. Existing along with those two courts was the general assembly of Athenian citizens which held the power of appeal over the other courts.[5] By 450 B.C., the supremacy of the assembly was established in all civil and criminal trials. Any Athenian citizen of the age of thirty or older, who was not indebted to the state and whose civil rights had not been forfeited, was eligible to serve in the assembly — the members being chosen by lot. The assemblies were of varying sizes, ranging from 200 to 1,500, with one member always being added to prevent a tie.[6] There was even a mention of one jury in the time of Demosthenes with 2,000 members, plus the usual tie-breaker[7]. The number varied with the importance of the case,[8] and if the party prosecuting failed to get the fifth part of the votes, he was subject to a fine.[9]

The jury, or *dikasteria* as it was called, met in an area enclosed by rope in the face of the sun.[10] The jurors rendered their verdict on both facts and law, voting in secret and their judgment was not subject to appeal. The magistrate was merely a chairman responsible for order. Pericles introduced pay for jury service.[11] When the oligarchy seized power during the period from 411 to 404 B.C., it abolished the jury, but the democratic party immediately restored the jury on its return to power.[12]

According to John Pettingal, the jury of the Athenians was

brought to Rome by the Decemvirs who had been sent to Athens to investigate the laws of Solon around 451-50 B.C.[13] As described by Pettingal, the system provided for Judices (the jurors) who were chosen once a year to try criminal cases. Out of the entire number, 81 were chosen for a particular trial. Of these, 15 were challenged by each side, leaving fifty-one to decide the case under the supervision of a praetor or Judex Quaestionis, who received the vote and declared the verdict.[14] It was Gracchus who, about 122 B.C., engineered the passage of a statute which transferred the membership of the jury from the senatorial class to the equestrian class.[15] The judging was finally restored to the Senate by Sulla in the year 70 B.C.[16] The size of the jury, however, varied, and in the time of Cicero ranged from 51 to 75 members.[17]

The Roman Judices determined the guilt or innocence of the accused, resolving both questions of fact and of law, and could acquit or condemn regardless of the evidence.[18] The Judices voted on tablets which were marked with either an "A", "C", or the letters "N.L." which, respectively, stood for Absolvo, Condemno and Non Liquet, the latter being their verdict when in doubt.[19]

It is the theory of Pettingal that when the Romans subdued Gaul and, under the rule of Claudius (41-50 A.D.), reduced England to a province, they brought their form of the jury with them. The Romans were to remain in England, for the most part, until the fall of Rome to Alaric in 410 A.D.,[20] or possibly until 448 A.D.[21] Evidence has been found that the Burgundians of southeast France had the Roman form of the jury in the fifth century A.D.[22] From this it is reasoned that either the idea of the jury survived in England from Roman days, or was brought over by the Angles and Saxons, emigrating to England around 430 A.D. at the request of the Britons to help control the Picts and Scots.[23] The result of this "good neighbor policy" was that the Angles and Saxons forcibly uprooted Briton civilization, dispersing their hosts into exile in Wales.[24]

Although this account of the Greek and Roman origin of the English jury is considered fanciful by most serious historians, the possibility of a residual Roman influence is not entirely discounted. Pollock and Maitland, citing Brunner, leave open the possibilty that the Frankish *inquisitio,* an ancestor of the jury, was influenced by the Roman procedures.[25] Jerome Frank was able to say in 1949 that the "germ" of the idea was perhaps borrowed from fifth century Roman procedure.[26]

Having gone that far, we might as well agree with Pettingal that the Greeks and perhaps even the Egyptians had a role in the formation of the jury. The Egyptians had a jury (kenbet) of eight members, four from each side of the Nile, which tried minor charges against workmen in the necropolises. A fellow workman presided. This jury existed almost 4,000 years ago — that is, about 750 years before the trial of Orestes. The Myceneans had trade missions in Egypt by at least the fourteenth century B.C.,[26a] and it is possible that the idea of judgment by one's peers may not have been passed by the Myceneans to the Greeks, and so on, as Pettingal supposed.

ii

Odin, the man who became a god,[27] led a Sythian people from the east (perhaps, considering language similarities, from near India[28]) and settled in Sweden, reputedly becoming the earliest settlers of northern Europe.[29] On the authority of the Edda, a collection of Icelandic theogony and cosmogony edited by Snorri Sturluson at the beginning of the thirteenth century,[30] "Odin ordained twelve Asagods to adjudge all causes in the metropolis of Asgard."[31] We are to assume that Odin himself presided as lawman or judge at this court of assessors or jurors.[32] It is also probable that he introduced trial by battle as well.[33]

Be that as it may, this form of jury trial is the oldest "legal", as opposed to "customary", mode of trial known among the Scandinavians.[34] When historical records were first available around 800 A.D., the jury was already in existence.[35] At this early time, trial by battle was considered the nobler mode of trial, with the jury being reserved for the weak, the aged, and women.[36] About the time Christianity was introduced by Bishop Poppo in Jutland (950 A.D.),[37] the jury became more popular and was the normal but not exclusive mode of trial among the northmen for the next two and one half centuries.[38] In addition to trial by jury and battle, they also used trial by wager of law[39] and by ordeal[40], along with the rest of northern Europe.

The number of jurors on Scandinavian juries also varied. Traditionally, twelve was the most popular number, although the Norway *Thing* (assembly of the people), held on the Isle of Guley, had 36 jurors. The Scandinavians had no principle of unanimity, the causes usually being decided by a mere majority.[41]

The code of Magnus, King of Norway, gives some idea of the Scandinavian jury trial. It was promulgated in 1274 and reads in part as follows:

> The thing shall last so long as the lawman chooses, and during such time as he, with the consent of the jury, deems necessary for adjudging the causes which there are to be heard. Their number is three times twelve; their nomination must be so managed that some fitmen be chosen from every district. Those who are chosen to be jurors shall, before they enter the court, swear on oath after the following form:
>
> > "I protest before God that I will give such a vote in every cause, as well on the side of the plaintiff as defendant, as I consider most just in the sight of God, according to law and my conscience; And I shall always do the same whenever I shall be chosen as juror."
>
> This oath, every man is to swear before he enters the court, the first time he serves on a jury, but not a second time, though he should be chosen. Every man must go fasting into court, and make his appearance there while the sun is in the east, and remain in the court till noon. No man must bring any drink into court, neither, for sale nor in any other way. If those who are outside the sacred cords make there such noise and disturbance that the jurors are prevented from hearing or those from pleading who have obtained leave from the lawman and the jurors, they shall pay a fine of one silver, when detected and convicted, having been previously admonished.
>
> Those who are chosen to serve as jurors shall judge according to law in all causes that in a lawful manner and

course are hither (that is, to Gula-thing) appealed. But in all cases that the code does not decide that is to be considered law which all the jurors agree upon. But if they disagree, the lawman prevails with those who agree with him; unless the king with the advice of the most prudent men shall otherwise decide.[42]

This code gave the lawman more power than he had previously when he was only adviser.[43] The jurors on this island were surrounded by cords held by staves as in Greece.[44]

Provisions were made in Sweden for twelve men to be selected in every lawman's district for the purpose of seeking out lawbreakers. These were sworn to "...not make any man guilty who is innocent, nor any man innocent who is guilty." Decision was by at least seven of their number. The Swedish jury combined the functions of the grand and petty juries.[45] In Iceland, twelve judges or jurors tried cases in the first instance with appeal allowable to a court with thirty-six judges which met on midsummer's day.[46] Juries in Scandinavia generally fell into disuse after the fourteenth century, but there is record of a jury being used in Sweden as late as 1665 A.D.[47]

Most modern authorities do not claim the Scandinavian jury as an ancestor of the English jury.[48] Reeves, however, claimed that it came to them through the Normans[49], as does Repp.[50] A more direct route was through the Danes. Aethelred the Unready promulgated a law in 997 A.D. which was applicable only to the Danish district of England. It provided for a <u>moot</u> (assembly) to be held in every *wapentake* (hundred), during which the twelve eldest *thegns* of the community were required to swear upon a relic that the *reeve* put into their hands, that they would accuse no one innocent, nor conceal any guilty person. This early accusing jury did not seem to have any immediate descendants, and we must find another source for the English jury.[51]

iii

The analogies of the English jury with the institutions of

the Greeks, Romans, and the Scandinavians do not exhaust the instances of comparison. We will look more closely at the chief example, the Frankish, in the next chapter. There are other suggestions of origin of the English jury that are of interest and to which we will now turn.

It is not surprising, considering that in the eighteenth century the jury survived only in England and its dependencies, that the English conceived of the jury as being indigenous to English soil. Writing in 1682, the anonymous author of *A Guide to English Juries* said, "Of what date juries be, is the same to say, as when was England first inhabited...."[52] In a work published in 1752, it was said that the jury's "...antiquity is beyond the reach of record of history."[53] In a supposed dialogue between a barrister and a juryman in 1680, the barrister, when asked how long trial by jury had been in use, replied, "Even time out of mind; so long, that our best historians cannot date the original of the institution, being indeed contemporary with the nation itself....That juries...were in use among the Britons, the first inhabitants of this island, appears by the ancient monuments and writings of that nation...."[54] The Welsh claim that their Bishop Aser Whenenensis brought the jury to the attention of King Alfred, who adopted it from them for England.[55] Actually, if all that is required of an ancestor to the modern jury is that it contain the laity as judges, the ancient druids, who preceded the Romans in Britain, would qualify.[56]

Jerusalem is one of the more unexpected locations for a source of the jury. In 1099 A.D., the crusaders captured Jerusalem from the Saracens. The laws they established were generally modeled on the laws of France, whose soldiers made up a majority of the crusaders. Godfrey, Duke of Bouillon, was made king of Jerusalem. He established two secular courts in Jerusalem, the High Court where he was the chief justice, and the Court of Burgesses where the judges were townspeople. In the Burgesses' Courts, an officer (*vescomete*) presided over a court composed of himself and twelve jurors. The jurors, however appointed, sat permanently, but it was not necessary that the entire twelve should sit at one time; two or three were all that were required. If the accused objected to the court's decision, he could charge it with falsehood and challenge the entire bench to mortal combat. If he did not fight them all, one after the other, or if he did not vanquish them all in a single day, he was beheaded in the first instance or hanged in the second. There is no record of a successful appeal. For a time, some looked upon this as the original jury.[57]

Even the Russians, not surprisingly, have some claim as the jury's founding ancestor. In the oldest law of the Russians, it is said, "[T]he thief who denies his guilt and every debtor who refuses to pay must prove his innocence before twelve men."[58] It is possible that since the Normans were instrumental in the founding of the Russian nation, this tribunal may be derived from Scandinavian sources. It is certain, however, that this and other remote examples have only a coincidental resemblance to the English jury and did not influence its development.

With the foregoing history and mythology serving as an introduction to the story of the jury, the workable definition of the jury will be presented so that the reader will have a basis from which to understand the material. Forsyth defined it thus: "[T]he jury consists of a body of men taken from the community at large, summoned to find the truth of disputed facts, who are quite distinct from the judges or court."[59]

Kalven and Zeisel, in *The American Jury*, said:

> "It [the jury] recruits a group of twelve laymen, chosen at random from the widest population; it convenes them for the purpose of the particular trial; it entrusts them with great official powers of decision; it permits them to carry on deliberations in secret and to report out their final judgment without giving reasons for it; and, after their momentary service to the state has been completed, it orders them to disband and return to private life."[60]

Pollock and Maitland put it more simply, "...a body of neighbors is summoned by some public officer to give upon oath a true answer to some question."[61] If this last definition is kept in mind, it will be seen why the Franks have been taken as the starting point of the English jury by Brunner and others.

Chapter I footnotes

1. *Aeschyli Eumenides,* translated by Jernard Drake (MacMillan and Co., 1853).

2. *Id.* at p. 58.

3. *Ibid.*

4. Drake, *op. cit.* at note 1, at p. 67.

5. *A History of Lay Judges,* John P. Dawson (Harvard Univ. Press, 1960), p. 11.

6. *Ibid.*

7. *An Enquiry Into the Use and Practice of Juries Among the Greeks and Romans,* John Pettingal (London, 1769), pp. 29, 36.

8. *Id.* at p. 36.

9. Pettingal, *op. cit.* at note 7, at p. 30.

10. Pettingal, *op. cit.* at note 7, at pp. 33, 45.

11. Dawson, *op. cit.* at note 5, at pp. 11-12.

12. Dawson, *op. cit.* at note 5, at p. 12.

13. Pettingal, *op. cit.* at note 7, at p. 139.

14. Pettingal, *op. cit.* at note 7, at p. 135.

15. Dawson, *op. cit.* at note 5, at pp. 16-17.

16. Dawson, *op. cit.* at note 5, at p. 18.

17. *Ibid.*

18. *History of Trial by Jury,* William Forsyth (John Parker and Son, London, 1852), pp. 12-13.

19. *Id.* at p. 12.

20. Pettingal, *op. cit.* at note 7, at pp. 140-158.

21. *History of the English Law,* John Reeves (Reed and Hunter, London, 1814), I-p. 2.

22. Pettingal, *op. cit.* at note 7, at preface p. vii.

23. *Id.* at I. pp. 2-3; *op. cit.* at note 7, at p. 158.

24. Reeves, *op. cit.* at note 21, at p. 3.

25. *The History of English Law,* Sir Frederick Pollock and Frederic William Maitland (Cambridge Univ. Press, 2nd Ed., 1898), I-p. 141.

26. *Courts on Trial,* Jerome Frank (Princeton Univ. Press, 1949), p. 108.

26a. *Tutankhamen,* Christiane Desroches-Noblecourt (Penguin Books Ltd., Harmondsworth, England, translated by Claude, first ed. 1963), pp. 34, 106.

27. *A Historical Treatise on Trial by Jury,* Thorl. Gudn. Repp (Thomas Clark, Edinburgh, 1832) p. 16.

28. *Id.* at p. 69.

29. Repp, *op. cit.* at note 27, at pp. 16-17.

30. Repp, *op. cit.* at note 27, at p. 72.

31. Repp, *op. cit.* at note 27, at p. 6.

32. Repp, *op. cit.* at note 27, at p. 75.

33. Repp, *op. cit.* at note 27, at p. 17.

34. Repp, *op. cit.* at note 27, at p. 20.

35. Repp, *op. cit.* at note 27, at p. 5.

36. Repp, *op. cit.* at note 27, at p. 9.

37. *History of Trial By Jury,* William Forsyth (John W. Parker and Son, London, 1852), p. 17.

38. Repp, *op. cit,* at note 27, at p. 17.

39. Repp, *op. cit.* at note 27, at pp. 100-02.

40. Repp, *op. cit.* at note 27, at p. 13.

41. Repp, *op. cit.* at note 27, at pp. 76-79.

42. Forsyth, *op. cit.* at note 18, at pp. 18-21.

43. *Ibid.*

44. Repp, *op. cit.* at note 27, at p. 47.

45. Forsyth, *op. cit.* at note 18, at pp. 22-24.

46. Forsyth, *op. cit.* at note 18, at p. 32.

47. Repp, *op. cit.* at note 27, at pp. 76-79.

48. Pollock and Maitland, *op. cit.* at note 25, at I-p. 140; *A Preliminary Treatise on Evidence,* James Bradley Thayer (Sweet and Maxwell, London, 1898), p. 129; *The Origin of Juries,* Heinrich Brunner (Berlin, 1872). (The copy read by the writer was a handwritten translation at the Institute of Advanced Legal Studies, University of London, translated, W.H. Humphreys, 1951; see pp. 29-30 for his claim of Frankish origin); *A History of Lay Judges,* John P. Dawson (Harvard Univ. Press, 1960), pp. 119-20. The author accepts the Frankish origin of the English jury as urged by Brunner, tempered with the observation that this may not be true of the Jury of accusation; "The Origin and Development of Trial by Jury", H.H. Grooms, 26 Ala. Law 162 (1965).

49. *History of the English Law,* John Reeves, Esq. (London, 1814), p. 84.

50. Repp, *op. cit.* at note 27, at pp. 48, 162.

51. Pollock and Maitland, *op. cit.* at note 25, at I-142-43.

52. *A Guide to Juries,* By a Person of Quality, attributed by Forsyth to Lord Somers (London, 1682), p. 1.

53. *The Complete Juryman,* anonymous (London, 1752), p. 3.

54. *The English Man's Right,* Sir John Hawles, 6th Ed. (London, 1771, being a reprint of the 1680 ed.), p. 4.

55. Brunner, *op. cit.* at note 48, at p. 13.

56. Brunner, *op. cit.* at note 48, at pp. 21-22.

57. Forsyth, *op. cit.* at note 18, at pp. 114-20.

58. Brunner, *op. cit.* at note 48, at p. 25.

59. Forsyth, *op. cit.* at note 18, at p. 8.

60. *The American Jury,* Harry Kalven, Jr. and Hans Zeisel (Little, Brown & Co., Boston, 1966) p. 3.

61. Pollock and Maitland, *op. cit.* at note 25, at I-138.

II
Charlemagne's *Inquisitio*

By 253 A.D., the Franks occupied extensive holdings in Europe, including the Netherlands and most of Gaul. Much of their success in conquest was attributable to the rule of the Merovingian family, whose rulers formed a strong central government by the seventh century,[1] and continued in power until they were replaced by the Carolingians in 751 A.D.[2] Charlemagne (Charles the Great) became king of the Franks in 768 A.D. and created the greatest empire that western Europe had known since the fall of Rome. By 780 A.D. Charlemagne had established these reforms in the Frankish legal system: (1) Ordinary freemen were relieved of the burden of attending court (Germanic peoples had generally conducted their trials through an assembly of the people whose approval of the judgment was necessary to validate the result); (2) A permanent group of lawfinders was appointed by the central authority with a vague requirement of local consent. This was intended to make the law more uniform by giving one group of justices greater decision-making power[3]; (3) An *inquisitio* was established for the resolution of disputed factual situations in which the crown had an interest.[4]

By 800 A.D. the decision in the ordinary courts was decided by the royal presiding officer and the law-finder (a local legal expert) alone, without the consent of any popular assembly. The administrative officer of a royal district, the count, was also authorized to give judgment in less important matters without reference to an assembly. General meetings of the people were held in conjunction with the courts three times a year, and at these hearings the assent of the assembly was required.[5]

Our interest in Charlemagne's legal reforms is in the *inquisitio*. Brunner defines this institution as follows:

> Its distinctive feature consists in the fact that the judge may summon, at his discretion, a number of men from the neighborhood in whom he can assume a knowlege of the matter in question, and demand from them the

13

promise to declare the truth upon the question to be submitted by him. After the promise comes the judicial putting of the question, "*Inquisitio.*"[6]

The *inquisitio* of the Franks had its accusatory aspects (which anticipated our modern grand jury) and its civil aspects, which was a mode of proof by inquisition or interrogation. The next step in the evolution of the trial jury was the Anglo-Norman jury of proof. The jurors themselves were the witnesses and they were the mode of proof, as they were in the ordeal, deed, or compurgation. The final step in the jury's development was the judgment jury which came into being in England in the fourteenth century. In this last step, the jury, instead of being a mode of proof, chose between the proofs or evidence offered by the parties.[7]

It is important at this point to refer once more to the Pollock and Maitland definition of the jury, written in 1898: "...a body of neighbors is summoned by some public officer to give upon oath a true answer to some question."[8] If the reader will keep this definition in mind and heed Edmund Burke's suggestion not to expect to find that modern juries "...have jumped, like Minerva, out of the head of Jove in complete armor..."[9], he will be better able to recognize the beginnings of the jury as found in the *inquisitio*.

The *inquisitio* was a royal prerogative, and available only upon royal command.[10] At first, it was generally used only in fiscal affairs of the crown, but gradually the right to use the *inquisitio* was extended to the church.[11] In a capitulary (ordinance) of Louis the Pious in 826 A.D., the church gained the privilege of calling the *inquisitio* for any land question concerning church property ceded to the crown. (This did not hold true for land transferred to the church from the state.)[12] However, in 829 A.D., this prerogative was extended to the church with respect to any property where it could demonstrate thirty years of unbroken possession. Generally itinerant judges (*missi*) had the authority to use the *inquisitio*,[13] but an ordinary or local judge did not.[14] Royal mandates were issued to agents of the crown directing them to undertake *inquisitios*,[15] although these agents might be ordinary judges.[16]

An ordinary judge could conduct an *inquisitio* when: (1) a party entitled to it demanded it; (2) the king entrusted the count (administrative head of the county) with the privilege of jurisdiction (this was rare in the early years of the Frankish administration; i.e., from 780-830 A.D.); (3) a Jew was a party (under formal witness proof, a Jew needed six Christians to prove a case against a Christian, whereas a Christian only needed three Jews and three Christians to prove a case against a Jew); and (4) the party was a person entitled to the special protection of the king by reason of unfitness to participate in the ordinary proof, e.g., orphans, widows, and incompetents.[17]

The royal mandate ordering an inquisitio to be undertaken was sometimes delivered by a royal agent (missus who may or may not have been a judge) to the officer charged with holding the hearing.[18] At other times the party who had petitioned for the inquisitio delivered the mandate to the presiding officer.[19] Thus, in 890 A.D., Bishop Gilbert petitioned the king and obtained an inquisitio-mandate and laid it before the judge.[20] As it would be inconvenient for a large number of witnesses to travel a long distance, the officer charged with holding the inquisitio generally went to the place where the majority of the witnesses lived.[21]

The officer undertaking the inquisitio chose his witnesses from the neighborhood where it could be assumed they would have knowledge of the matter in dispute. Only the most trustworthy, the best of the freemen, were chosen. The number of witnesses was largely within the discretion of the officer. A minimum number was never fixed.[22] There is an example of an inquisitio with 200 members,[23] but usually the number of members would range between 13 and 66.[24] For example, 20 members were selected to decide hunting and fishing rights in Abersee.[25] Under a mandate of Charlemagne issued in favor of the church of Lorsch, 14 men whose names were recorded were appointed. Only in exceptional cases would the number of the members of the inquisitio be permitted to fall below 12, the number required for formal witness proof.[26] (In like manner, the number 12 probably came to be the standard number of members for the English trial jury.) The officer had the authority to enforce the attendance of the witness-members of the inquisitio.[27] The Frankish people may have been an intemperate lot, hence the capitulary of Charlemagne forbidding anyone under the influence of liquor to plead his cause.[28] Pettingal suggests that this is the origin of the later English prohibition against juries having meat or drink.

The oaths taken by the members of the inquisitio were promissory; that is, they promised to speak the truth without reference to the subject of the dispute.[29] After the oath was administered, the question was stated by the officer in charge. He could put the question to them one at a time or all at once,[30] and the witnesses could give testimony helpful to either side.[31] This procedure contrasts sharply with the formal witness proof of the Franks, where a party selected his own witnesses who were questioned only as to identity. In formal proof, the witnesses took an assertive oath; that is, they swore that the oath of the party who called them was true.[32] Some jurymen were exempted from taking the oath; e.g., priests could be employed in the inquisitio, but not generally in witness proof. They therefore were not sworn but made a declaration according to the vows of their particular priestly office.[33]

A party before an inquisitio had no burden of proof. In an earlier time, although the presiding officer had the authority to undertake the inquisitio, he needed special authority to decide the matter in dispute.[34] In civil matters the inquisitio came to a be a means of proof by which a party could obtain a conclusive judgment.[35] The parties could not challenge the verdict of an inquisitio by resort to a duel, as was the practice in formal proof,[36] but the court could order the ordeal against a member of the panel suspected of perjury. There were benefits in finding for the crown, as was to be true of later English panels. In 802 A.D. Charlemagne decreed protection for members of inquisitios that found in favor of the crown. But, in 845 A.D., there was a verdict against the crown in favor of a church, and church revenues were restored.

If the members of the panel were unable to reach a definite conclusion, another jury might be ordered, although the members of the first panel that had definite information might be retained. (This is similar to the early Enlgish technique called "afforcement.") If the second inquisitio produced no result, the parties were relegated to formal proof.

There were complaints about jury duty even during this period. The procedure was regarded with suspicion, and the people strove to limit its employment. In 855-56 A.D., King Louis held court in Pavia, and his subjects complained of being overburdened by jury duty. The king promised that its use would be limited to the levels that had existed during the days of the early Frankish administrations.[37]

This, then, was the earliest ancestor of the modern trial jury. That it existed in Neustria (the Frankish name for the province of Normandy) is certain. The circuit of the itinerant judges had been re-established there by Charles the Bald in 853 A.D.[38] However, the Northmen raided the northwest coast of France in the second half of the ninth century, and they established permanent settlements in the lower Seine in the last decade of that century. After having gained a reputation as an adventurer in Scottish and Irish raids, Rollo the Walker, son of Rognvald of Norway, came to the lower Seine settlements where he was the outstanding leader by 911 A.D. In that year he defeated the forces of Charles the Simple, and, by the resulting treaty, most of modern Normandy was ceded to the Northmen. The rest was gained as the result of further aggressions by 933 A.D.[39]

The territory thus surrendered by the Frankish king did not cease to form a component part of his empire; the province was only "assigned" to the Normans. In matters of what we now call foreign policy, the Normans associated themselves with the Frankish throne. We can further assume that they substantially adopted the customs of the Franks, including law, faith, and language.[40] It is even said that the treaty with Charles the Simple was conditioned upon the Normans adopting Christianity.[41]

Although the history of Normandy was somewhat unclear for the following two or three centuries, there seems to be good reason for accepting Brunner's conclusion that the tradition of the Frankish jury had considerable influence on the courts of William the Conqueror in the following centuries. The widespread use of this type of fact-finding institution required a strong central government. In the remnants of the Frankish empire, strong central authority was maintained only in Flanders and Normandy, while elsewhere the powers of the central government were lost or granted strictly to local strong men.[42] Strong central government did not exist in England under the Anglo-Saxons.

As we shall see in chapter four, William the Conqueror made use of the *inquisitio* almost as soon as the fighting had subsided. Then, as with the Franks, the jury was exercised solely for the benefit of the crown and exlusively at its prerogative. Although certain characteristics of Anglo-Saxon culture were conducive to the reception of a more sophisticated jury system, nothing comparable to the Frankish system was in existence in England at the time of William's invasion. Perhaps the sole exception to this was the isolated instance of an accusing jury. The limited nature of that jury will be noted in chapter three.

Brunner, by comparing language and procedures as contained in documents of the Frankish and Anglo-Norman eras, demonstrates that it is unlikely that the English jury and the Frankish *inquisitio* had independent origins.[43] The most convincing example offered by Brunner is the suggestion that both Normandy and the Franks gave their respective churches the prerogative to decide land questions by *inquisitio,* as discussed earlier in this chapter. This was a prerogative that the churches of Normandy were still struggling to maintain throughout the twelfth and thirteenth centuries.[44]

It has been over one hundred and fifteen years since Brunner published his work on the origin of the jury. During that time, no scholarship has been able to disprove his conclusions. Pollock and Maitland said in 1898, that "...but for the conquest of England it [the jury] would have perished...." This work went on to say that this belief overcame the English unwillingness to admit that the "...palladium of our liberties..." was not "...English in origin but Frankish, not popular but royal."[45] Holdsworth said the inquisitio was "...the root from which the English jury springs."[46] Whereas Brunner investigated the earliest origins of the present-day jury, it was James Thayer's intention to continue this discussion through the English tradition.[47] He agreed with many of Brunner's contentions, although W.R. Cornish reasoned that it was more likely that the Normans inherited the jury as an already existing English institution, noting the shift by the Normans to the practice of group inquest after coming in contact with England.[48] However, Dawson, in his work, *A History of Lay Judges,* after weighing the evidence available in 1960, said, "It still seems true, as Brunner contended, that the jury as it entered English law was in all essential respects a royal institution."[49] This is tantamount to saying that the right did not grow up from village assemblies but down from the power of the crown. The *inquisitio* of Charlemagne may be the father of the jury, but English influence is very apparent. It is to this English preparations that we will now turn.

Chapter II Footnotes

1. *A History of Lay Judges,* John P. Dawson (Harvard Univ. Press, 1960), p. 37.

2. "The Origin and Development of Trial By Jury," H.H. Grooms, 26 Ala. Law. 162 (1965).

3. Dawson, *op. cit.* at note 1, at p. 38.

4. *The Origin of Juries,* Heinrich Brunner (Berlin, 1872), p. 98.

5. Dawson, *op. cit.* at note 1, at p. 38.

6. Brunner, *op. cit.* at note 4, at p. 84.

7. Brunner, *op. cit.* at note 4, at pp. 36-37.

8. *The History of English Law,* Sir Frederick Pollock and Frederic William Maitland (2nd Ed., Cambridge Univ. Press, 1898), Vol. I-138.

9. *The Works and Correspondence of Edmund Burke,* Ed. by Charles William and Sir Richard Bourke (London, 1852), Vol. VI-138.

10. Brunner, *op. cit.* at note 4, at p. 87.

11. Brunner, *op. cit.* at note 4, at p. 92.

12. Brunner, *op. cit.* at note 4, at p. 94.

13. Brunner, *op. cit.* at note 4, at p. 95.

14. Brunner, *op. cit.* at note 4, at p. 97.

15. Brunner, *op. cit.* at note 4, at p. 99.

16. Brunner, *op. cit.* at note 4, at p. 101.

17. Brunner, *op. cit.* at note 4, at pp. 104-105.

18. Brunner, *op. cit.* at note 4, at p. 100.

19. Brunner, *op. cit.* at note 4, at pp. 100-01.

20. Brunner, *op. cit.* at note 4, at p. 99.

21. Brunner, *op. cit.* at note 4, at p. 103.

22. Brunner, *op. cit.* at note 4, at pp. 108-10.

23. Brunner, *op. cit.* at note 4, at p. 111.

24. Brunner, *op. cit.* at note 4, at pp. 111-12.

25. Brunner, *op. cit.* at note 4, at p. 111.

26. Brunner, *op. cit.* at note 4, at p. 112.

27. Brunner, *op. cit.* at note 4, at pp. 84-85.

28. *An Enquiry Into the Use and Practice of Juries Among the Greeks and Romans,* John Pettingal (London, 1969), p. 188.

29. Brunner, *op. cit.* at note 4, at pp. 85-86.

30. Brunner, *op. cit.* at note 4, at p. 119.

31. Brunner, *op. cit.* at note 4, at pp. 85-86.

32. *Ibid.*

33. Brunner, *op. cit.* at note 4, at p. 116.

34. Brunner, *op. cit.* at note 4, at p. 103.

35. Brunner, *op. cit.* at note 4, at p. 84.

36. Brunner, *op. cit.* at note 4, at p. 86.

37. Brunner, *op. cit.* at note 4, at p. 114.

38. Brunner, *op. cit.* at note 4, at p. 155.

39. Encyclopaedia Britannica (1970), XVI-577.

40. Brunner, *op. cit.* at note 4, at pp. 127-28.

41. Encyclopaedia Britannica, *op. cit.* at note 39 at XVI-577.

42. Dawson, *op. cit.* at note 1, at p. 42.

43. Brunner, *op. cit.* at note 4, at pp. 92 and 118.

44. Brunner, *op. cit.* at note 4, at pp. 96-97.

45. Pollock and Maitland, *op. cit.* at note 8, at I-141.

46. *A History of English Law,* Sir William Holdsworth (Sweet and Maxwell, 7th Ed. 1956, 1st Ed. printed in 1903), I-312.

47. *A Preliminary Treatise on Evidence,* James Bradley Thayer (Sweet and Maxwell Ltd., London, 1898), p.3.

48. *The Jury,* W.R. Cornish (Penguin Presss, London, 1962), p.11.

49. Dawson, *op. cit.* at note 1, at p. 120.

III
The Age of Fire, Water and the Morsel

When the Angles and the Saxons came to Britain they brought with them Germanic legal procedures which they continued to develop until the Norman conquest. The following description of the Anglo-Saxon system relates principally to the two and one-half centuries before the conquest by the Normans in 1066 A.D. The legal procedures were not constant from time to time or from place to place, and only rarely did a king of this period exercise authority over more than a single section at a time. It should also be kept in mind that the inhabitants of England at this time were divided into slaves and free men[1]; the legal procedures largely related to the free. Still, the picture of the legal situation that emerges has a strong claim of authenticity.

The judicial system of the Saxons, vertically, had four possible levels of jurisdiction: (1) the tithing (also decenary; i.e., a rural subdivision pertaining to ten); (2) *wapentake* (pertaining to one hundred); (3) court of the shire or county; and (4) the court of the king or the *wittenagemote*. This was not necessarily a system whereby appeals were had from the lower to the high courts, but the king's court could function in that manner. The jurisdiction of the particular court depended upon many circumstances, including the importance and notoriety of the case.

Every inhabitant was required to belong to a tithing. The members were responsible for crimes committed by any of their number. In the event a member of the tithing was accused of a crime, the others were required to arrest him and bring him to justice. If they considered him innocent, they cleared him by their oaths. If he was convicted and sentenced, they had to pay the *wergild* (man-lot or value, first mentioned in reign of Ethelbert, 568-615 A.D.), essentially the compensation imposed for the crime plus other penalties. If a member of the tithing fled upon being accused or suspected of a crime, the members of the tithing had to make an oath that they were not accessories to his flight. Failure to clear themselves again resulted in the members having to pay the *wer-*

21

gild.[2] If a stranger sojourned with a family for three days, they were presumed to have made a pledge for him. If a crime took place within the venue of the tithing and it failed to produce the offender within 31 days, the *fribourg* (head of a tithing) took two principal persons from his own tithing, plus the *fribourg* and two principal persons from each of the three neighboring tithings. These 12 were to purge the *fribourg* and his tithing of responsibility for the crime. If the tithing failed by this procedure to clear itself of complicity with the offender or his flight, they had to make compensation to the injured party.[3] On the other hand, if a member of the tithing was injured and received *wergild* in compensation, the other members of the tithing were entitled to a share.[4]

There were pecuniary values established for injuries, varying according to the time and place committed and the part of the body involved: the ear, 30 shillings; hearing, 60 shillings; front tooth, 8 shillings; canine tooth, 4 shillings; grinding tooth, 16 shillings; a common person bound with chains, 10 shillings; beaten, 20 shillings; or hung up, 30 shillings; damage to an ox's horn 10 pence; to a cow's horn, 1 pence; fighting in the courtyard of a common person, 6 shillings; or drawn sword only, 3 shillings (if the person who owned the court was worth 600 shillings or more, the amends were tripled and further increases were allowed according to the rank of the person whose premises were violated).[5]

In assessing penalties for other injuries, the starting point was the value set on every man's life, the *wergild*. In the reign of Aethelstan (924-940 A.D.), these values were as follows: the king, who ranked only as a superior person, 30,000 *thrymsae*; archbishop or earl, 15,000 thrymsae; bishop, 8,000 *thrymsae*; priest or thegn, 2,000 *thrymsae*; common person, 267 *thrymsae*. The slayer had to make the compensation to the relations of the deceased. If the deceased was a stranger, one-half went to the king and one-half to the companions of the deceased. If the amounts were not paid, the slayer's relations were not required to aid him if a feud was instituted against him by the relatives of the deceased.

The right of sanctuary in churches was a necessary part of the system because it allowed for time to make arrangements for the payment of the *wergild* while the feud was held in abeyance. Those violating sanctuary were punished. According to King Alfred the

Great, initiating the feud before showing a willingness to accept the *wergild* was punishable. Also, a person injured by an inanimate object was entitled to claim it if he acted within 30 days from the time of injury. His heirs had the right to the object if their relative had been killed, for example, by a falling tree.[6]

Besides the penalties due the injured party, the guilty person had to pay amounts to the king.[7] For the commission of certain crimes, the guilty person was required to redeem himself by personal pains. For example, a thief often lost a hand or a foot, was banished, or sold into slavery. Housebreaking, open robbery, manifest homicide and treason against one's lord were inexpiable.[8]

Keeping in mind that the above principles were applicable to all courts, it was the court of the hundred, the *wapentake*, that made the biggest impact on the average person of Anglo-Saxon times.[9] It met once a month and had both civil and criminal jurisdiction. The presiding officer, the elder, was the head man of the hundreds. He had coordinate authority with the bishop. This court had cognizance of ecclesiastical matters which were entitled to first preference and which were decided by the bishop.[10]

The county court met two times a year or more as required. It was presided over by the shire or reeve, later known as the sheriff, who was assisted by the bishop. This court had cognizance of causes affecting several hundreds,[11] particularly civil causes.[12] The real judges of this court were the suitors of the court (*sectatores*), who were freemen or landholders who met as in assembly. The *sectatores* varied in number; in the time of Aethelred I, (866-871 A.D.) for example, there were approximately twelve or more freemen acting in this capacity. They decided both law and fact but were not sworn to the truth.[13] One month after Michaelmas (September 24), the sheriff, accompanied by the bishop, held the most important criminal court of the year. Also, once a year, during the month after Easter, the sheriff held the *tourn* (or circuit). Together with the bishop, he held a view of the frank-pledge; that is, he determined that all persons above the age of 12 years had taken the oath of allegiance, and also found freemen who were pledged to stand responsible for the youth's peaceable demeanor.[14]

The *wittenagemote*, or king's court, sat with the king, travelling with him whenever necessary. The court was composed of high officers of the state, and it held concurrent jurisdiction with other courts. Generally, its litigation involved causes having to do with the great lords, crimes of a heinous or public nature, and fiscal affairs of the state.[15] This court also served as a court of appeal from the county court and the other courts of a more limited nature.[16]

The system of law and police regulation as described in this chapter was more or less complete at the time of King Alfred the Great (871-899 A.D.).[17] Apparently, King Alfred took the quality of justice rendered in his courts quite seriously. The *Mirror of Justices*, written no later than 1290 A.D., relates that the king ordered no fewer than 44 of his justices to be hanged as murderers in one year for false judgments. One judge was hanged because he gave the death sentence as a result of testimony by 12 men who had not been sworn. Another judge met his fate because his jurors* were in doubt of their verdict and in "doubtful causes one ought rather to save than to condemn."[18]

Before the conquest of England, a charge or claim had to be supported by an oath (after the conquest, it had to be supported by witnesses or the *secta*.)[19] The coroner's office existed before the conquest, this being mentioned in connection with a matter concerning the Monastery of Beverly in 925 A.D. during the reign of Aethelstan (924-940 A.D.).[20] The system of canon law was well developed by 1100 A.D., and although it was no doubt much advanced by the time of the conquest, it was not established as a separate court until the time of the conquest. The written procedure for canon law ordinarily commenced with a statement of claim, followed by a counterclaim. Interrogatories were drawn up by the parties in preparation for questioning by the judge of witnesses. Lastly, the judge's written record of his findings and judgments was included. The witnesses were sworn.[21]

The English claim to have originated the jury is founded on the legislation of such rulers as Aethelred I (866-871 A.D.), Alfred the Great (871-899), and Aethelred II, the Unready (978-1013 A.D.). Good examples of this legislation were the statutes of Aethelred I:[22]

---

* [The reference to "jurors" above was not intended in the modern sense, but rather refers to a type of secratore or compurgator in the various kinds of witness proof that will be mentioned hereafter.]

> Let doom stand where thanes are of one voice: if they disagree, let that stand which seven of them say; and let those who are there out voted pay each of them six half marks.

The following statute applied to Wales:

> Twelve laymen shall administer the law (or explain it) to the British and English; six English and six British. Let them forfeit all they possess if they administer it wrongly, or let them clear themselves that they know no better.

King Alfred issued this statute:

> If a royal thane be accused of homicide he shall purge himself with twelve royal thanes. Any other man shall purge himself with eleven of his own rank and one royal thane.[23]

Aethelred II issued a law which affected only the Danish district of England. In essence it declared that a *moot* would be held in every *wapentake* in which the twelve oldest *thegns* would go out with the reeve and swear upon the relic (which he would put into their hands) that they would accuse no innocent person and conceal no guilty man.[24]

The courts instituted by the two Aethelreds are best understood as accusing bodies. They differed from grand juries in that the appointments were more or less permanent and the members served more as lay assessors than as jurors.[25] The law of Alfred clearly relates to compurgators.[26] Generally, the statutes creating these accusing courts fell into disuse, and thereafter accusations were usually made by the voice of the communty; i.e., at the assemblies held in connection with the local courts.[27]

There is yet one more example of something similar to a jury trial before 1066 A.D. During the reign of Edward the Confessor (1024-1066 A.D.), the parties to a boundary dispute voluntarily submitted the settlement of the matter to a group of neighbors who were sworn.[28] This comes as close to the civil jury as we are likely to find in England before the conquest, but it does not appear to be the result of any general statute. Also, this group does not necessarily seem, on the basis of the information available, to have been summoned by royal authority. When we examine the jury after the conquest we will find that it was invariably summoned by a royal writ.

The various courts that we have been examining were generally accusing bodies as far as criminal matters were concerned (except when charges were brought by individuals). In both civil and criminal matters, although both were occasionally decided by the voice of the assemblies, the courts generally directed the mode of proof that would finally determine the litigation. The four different modes of proof were: (1) oath; (2) official witnesss; (3) compurgation; and (4) ordeal.

The trial by oath, apparently used in less serious matters, might be resorted to after a defendant's testimony was challenged or contradicted by the plaintiff or accuser. The defendant was required to repeat his denial under oath according to an exact formula. Oath came to be piled upon oath, the slightest deviation resulting in the defendant losing his case. This became so risky that many avoided this type of trial by choosing the judgment of God —that is, the ordeal.[29]

Official witness proof first appeared in Anglo-Saxon law in 924 A.D. during the first year of Aethelstan. Witnesses were appointed to attest to bargains, much as notaries did in later English history. (This was perhaps the origin of that institution as far as England is concerned.)[30] King Eadgar the Peaceful (959-975 A.D.) decreed that thirty witnesses for each town, or twelve witnesses for small towns and every hundred, should be appointed to swear to make true depositions. From their number, two or three were brought to witness all commercial transactions. When there was a dispute, the party attempting to prove the transaction had to produce these persons as witnesses. The testimony of commercial witnesses was conclusive.[31] This law is also suggested as another possible precursor of the modern jury by reason of the mention of the number 12. It is said that this type of proof died out after the conquest,[32] but it is probably an ancestor of the deed witness.

In trial by compurgation, as in other Anglo-Saxon actions, the matter was initiated by the fore-oath of the person bringing the action. The defendant would prove his innocence by taking this oath: "By the Lord, I am guiltless both in deed and counsel of the charge of which N. accuses me."

His compurgators would support him with this oath: "By the Lord, the oath is clear and unperjured which M. has sworn."

The value of the oath of the compurgators varied according to the defendant's rank, as measured by the *wergild* or by the hydes of land he possessed (a hyde was equal to 33 acres). A person of bad character might be required to obtain three times the ordinary number of compurgators or undergo the ordeal. A person caught in the very act of his crime could not clear himself by compurgation. In such an instance, the ordeal was necessary, if a trial was held at all.[33] Compurgation in regular cases, if successful, was a complete acquittal.[34] For the mildest crimes, three compurgators sufficed; for more severe matters, six were required; to the most atrocious charges, the defendant had to produce 11 compurgators, with his own oath making the twelfth. Unanimity was naturally required of these witnesses inasmuch as the compurgators were all chosen by the defendant himself.[35]

More popular as a mode of trial was the judgment of God, called the ordeal. It is said that this method of finding truth was given by God to Moses around the year 1450 B.C. The detailed account of the founding of this institution is recorded in the Bible in Numbers, chapter five, verses 12 to 31. Moses was told that a man who suspected his wife of being unfaithful, but having no proof, should bring her to the priest together with an ephah of barley meal (a little over a bushel) with no oil or frankincense on it. The priest was to set the woman before the Lord, take clean water in an earthen vessel and add to it dust from the tabernacle floor. He would then uncover the woman's head and place the grain offering in her hands. The priest would hold "...the water of contention that brings out the truth..." and put the woman under oath. The priest would then say to the woman:

> If no man has had intercourse with you, if you have not gone astray and let yourself become defiled while owing obedience to your husband, then may your innocence be established by the water of contention which brings out the truth. But if, while owing him obedience, you have gone astray and let yourself become defiled, if any man other than your husband has had intercourse with you (the priest shall here put the woman under oath with an

adjuration, and shall continue), may the Lord make an example of you among your people in adjurations and in swearing oaths by bringing upon you miscarriage and untimely birth; and this water that brings out the truth shall enter your body, bringing upon you miscarriage and untimely birth.[36]

The woman answered, "Amen, amen," and the priest wrote the curse on a scroll and washed the scrolls in the water of contention, making the woman drink the water. The priest then took the grain offering for jealousy from the woman and presented it as a gift before the Lord at the altar. A handful of grain was taken and burned at the altar, and the woman again drank of the water of contention.[37]

Charlemagne is sometimes credited with having instituted the ordeal with the words, "Let doubtful cases be determined by the judgment of God."[38] However, the ordeal is more popularly attributed to Bishop Poppo. It is recorded that he preached to the Jutlanders of Denmark, having little success. The bishop asked them if they would believe that the message he preached was divine if he could touch hot iron and suffer no harm. Having obtained agreement to this, he had prepared an iron glove which was heated until it was red hot. He thrust his hand into the glove, withdrew it uninjured and the Northmen were suitably impressed.[39]

However, it would seem that the ordeal was present in England before this time. We do know without question that the ordeal was common in England before the conquest, principally in the forms of fire and water. Ordeal would be required when a party had insufficient compurgators, when he had previously been guilty of perjury, or if he was not a freeman. Of course, the accused had to swear to his innocence before undergoing the ordeal.[40]

In one form of ordeal by fire, hot iron of a pound weight had to be carried nine feet. The hand was then wrapped and sealed. On the third day the accused came to the altar and the hand was unwrapped. If it was not in some way festered or infected, he was innocent, otherwise he was guilty.[41] In a variation, the accused would walk blindfolded and barefooted over nine red-hot plowshares.[42] In addition, the ordeal could be simple, double or triple, known as the threefold judgment of God. In the double ordeal, the weight of the iron was increased to two pounds and, in the triple, to three pounds. Whether the ordeal was to be simple, double, or triple depended upon the trustworthiness of the accused as determined by the accusing thegns.[43]

Ordeal by water was either hot or cold. In the hot water version, the hand was put into boiling water up to the wrist, elbow, or shoulder, depending on whether the ordeal was simple, double, or triple. A variation of this was the requirement that the accused pick a stone out of the boiling water. After that, the same procedure was followed as in the ordeal of hot iron. If the accused was adjudged to undergo the cold water ordeal, he was bound thumb to toes and thrown into water. If he sank, he was innocent. If he floated, the water was considered to have rejected him, and he was guilty.[44] Of course, if he sank, he was retrieved.

These were not the only types of ordeal. One ordeal that was popular among priests, perhaps because it was the safest, was the ordeal of the accused morsel (sometimes a piece of consecrated bread of the Eucharist). The accused would say a prayer asking that he choke while swallowing the bread if he had not sworn the truth concerning his guilt. Godwine, Earl of Kent and Wessex, is supposed to have died in the attempt of this ordeal in 1053 A.D.[45] If the ordeal of the cross was selected as the mode of trial, the accused was blindfolded and given the choice of two sticks. One had a cross carved on it. If he chose that one, he was innocent.[46]

The ordeal was essentially a religious ceremony. Three days before the trial, the accused sought help from the priest, was constantly at mass, made offerings, and lived only on bread, water, and onions. On the day of the trial he received communion, and both he and the accuser came to the place of the trial in the company of not more than 12 persons each. If the accused appeared with more than 12, he was convicted automatically. At the time and place appointed, both the accuser and the accused renewed under oath, respectively, the charge and denial. The accused the proceeded to the ordeal which had been adjudged, as described above. The priest was present during the entire ceremony for the necessary religious rituals; for example, before the ordeal of hot iron, the priest would sprinkle the hot iron with holy water.[47] After 1066 A.D., these modes of trial continued, some lasting for centuries in varying degrees, while others died out. This, then, was the state of Anglo-Saxon law as it existed prior to the time of the Norman conquest.

Chapter III Footnotes

1. *History of the English Law,* John Reeves (Reed and Hunter, London, 1814), I-5.

2. *History of Trial by Jury,* William Forsyth (John Parker and Son, London, 1852), pp. 56-57, 60-61.

3. Reeves, *op. cit.* at note 1, at I-13.

4. Forsyth, *op. cit.* at note 2, at p. 61.

5. Reeves, *op. cit.* at note 1, at I-13.

6. Reeves, *op. cit.* at note 1, at I-15-17, 19.

7. Forsyth, *op. cit.* at note 2, at p. 59.

8. Reeves, *op. cit.* at note 1, at I-16.

9. *A History of Lay Judges,* John P. Dawson (Harvard Univ. Press, 1960), p. 182.

10. Forsyth, *op. cit.* at note 2, at p. 63.

11. *Ibid.*

12. Reeves, *op. cit.* at note 1, at I-7.

13. Reeves, *op. cit.* at note 1, at I-22-23; *The Origin of Juries,* Heinrich Brunner (Berlin, 1972), p. 400.

14. Reeves, *op. cit.* at note 1, at I-6-7.

15. Reeves, *op. cit.* at note 1, at I-7-8.

16. Forsyth, *op. cit.* at note 2, at p. 64.

17. Reeves, *op. cit.* at note 1, at I-13.

18. *The Mirror of Justices,* Andrew Horn, translated from the French by William Hughes in 1646, original written about 1285-90 (His Majesty's Law Printers, London, 1768), pp. 239-40.

19. Brunner, *op. cit.* at note 13, pp. 428-29.

20. Forsyth, *op. cit.* at note 2, at p. 225.

21. Dawson, *op. cit.* at note 9, at p. 45.

22. Forsyth, *op. cit.* at note 2, at p. 67.

23. Brunner, *op. cit.* at note 13 at p. 402.

24. *The History of Enlish Law,* Sir Frederick Pollock and Frederic William Maitland (Cambridge Univ. Press, 1898), I-142-43.

25. Reeves, *op. cit.* at note 1, at p. 23.

26. *Ibid.*

27. Forsyth, *op. cit.* at note 2, p. 194.

28. Dawson, *op cit.* at note 9, at p. 120.

29. Brunner, *op cit.* at note 13, at p. 398; *A Preliminary Treatise on Evidence,* James Bradley Thayer (Sweet and Maxwell Ltd., London, 1898), p. 24.

30. Forsyth, *op. cit.* at note 2, at p. 84.

31. Forsyth; *op. cit.* at note 2, at p. 89.

32. Brunner, *op. cit.* at note 13, at p. 399.

33. Forsyth, *op. cit.* at note 2, at pp. 73-79

34. Reeves, *op. cit.* at note 1, at I-20.

35. *Trial by Jury,* Thorl. Gudn. Repp (Thomas Clark, 1832), pp. 38-39

36. *The New English Bible* (Oxford Univ. Press and Cambridge Univ. Press, 1970), Numbers V-19-23.

37. "Origin and Development of Trial by Jury," Robert H. White, 29 Tenn. L. Rev. 8, 9 (1961-62).

38. *Ibid.*

39. Forsyth, *op. cit.* at note 2, at p. 17.

40. Forsyth, *op. cit.* at note 2, pp. 63, 80.

41. "Early Opposition to the Petty Jury In Criminal Cases," Charles L. Wells, 30 Law. Q. Rev. 97, at 98 (1914).

42. "The Origin and Development of Trial by Jury," H.H. Grooms, 26 Ala. Law. 162, at 163 (1965).

43. Brunner, *op. cit.* at note 13, at p. 404.

44. Forsyth, *op. cit.* at note 2, at pp. 80-81; Brunner, *Ibid;* Wells, *op. cit.* at note 41 at p. 98; Reeves, *op. cit.* at note 1, at I-20.

45. Forsyth, *Ibid.;* Wells, *Ibid.;* Reeves, *op. cit.* at note 1, at I-21-22.

46. Reeves, *op. cit.* at note 1, at I-22.

47. Reeves, *op. cit.* at note 1, at I-21.

IV
William the Conqueror—
Henry the Administrator,
1066-1205 A.D.

Harold's defeat by William the Conqueror at the Battle of Hastings 1066[1], was highly significant in both short and long-range, in consequences for British cultures and law. William's intentions, however, had been to rule the English by their existing law and in 1070 he conducted an inquest to discover their laws.[2]

He also began a vast series of inquests in every county of England. These inquests began as early as 1083, and were completed in the year 1086. The king's justices summoned a jury in every county consisting of the sheriff, the bailiff of each manor, the reeve of each hundred, the priest and some villeins. This jury was required to determine under oath the value and manner of holding of all property within the county in the time of Edward the Confessor, at the time it came into the present holder's hands, and at the time of the inquest.[3] The result of these surveys was known as the Domesday Books, the extensive records of population and landholdings throughout England.

An instance of something closer to a modern trial jury was the inquest summoned to determine what lands were held by the church at Ely on the day of the Confessor's death. A dispute had arisen when a sheriff had treated certain lands as belonging to the king which were also claimed by the Bishop of Rochester. The moots of several shires from the neighborhood were summoned to decide the dispute, with the Bishop of Bayeaux presiding over it. The jurors, fearing the king, found in his favor. The bishop was not satisfied with the verdict and thus directed the jurors to retire and select 12 of their number who would confirm the verdict under oath. They returned the same verdict, but recanted when a monk gave new testimony and they were subsequently questioned individually by the bishop. The land, or at least that part of it which was not claimed by a specific order of the Conqueror, was restored to the church.[4]

King William was the first to generally appoint professional justices. He separated the ecclesiastical courts from the secular courts and introduced the duel.[5] He replaced the foreoath with plaint witnesses. An unsupported claim had been insufficient under both Norman and Anglo-Saxon law to require a defendant to call a witness or produce proof. The Anglo-Saxon claimant supported his cause with an oath, the Norman with a plaint witness. The number of plaint witnesses required by William were two. These witnesses, called the secta, were persons who supported the plaintiff's claim in advance of an answer by the defendant. The secta were not sworn, but the judge would examine them, both for purposes of identification and to make certain that they were in agreement with the claim of the plaintiff. The burden of proof remained with the defendant. The use of the secta faded out in the thirteenth and fourteen centuries.[6] In fact, although it had been the intention to keep Anglo-Saxon law in practice, Norman law nonetheless made a deep impression on English society.

Henry I reigned from 1100 to 1132 during which time there are recorded at least two inquests by juries. The first took place on the order of Henry's son, William, sometime prior to 1120. The writ was directed to the sheriff of Kent who was ordered to summon an inquest to resolve a conflict between the Abbey of St. Augustine and the king's treasury, concerning the rights to a vessel which had been taken. A second writ ordered the vessel restored to the abbey on the basis of the results of the inquest.[7]

In 1121, Henry I commanded that a dispute between the monastery of St. Stephen and the Exchequer be decided by an inquest of neighbors. Sixteen men served on this inquest, although attempts to avoid jury duty were still prevalent.[8] It should be noted that an individual mandate was required for each case, as was true in the time of the Franks.[9]

Henry II ruled England from 1154 until 1189, introducing more far reaching legal changes than any other monarch that ever held that throne. If a single person could be thought of as creating the jury, he would be that person. The first of a series of great enactments which have come down to us from this period was the Constitution of Clarendon (1164). One provision was directed at powerful individuals who were attempting to intimidate others in order to escape prosecution. It provided, ". . . The sheriff shall cause 12 legal men of the neighborhood, or of the *fill*, to take an oath in the presence of the bishop that they will declare the truth about it."[10] This jury was also empowered to declare a verdict of guilt or innocence, thus going beyond the duty of older accusatory courts.[11] Another provision provided for an inquest (jury) to decide whether land was subject to the jurisdiction of the king's court or was church property and therefore subject to the ecclesiastical courts. Apparently the language of this statute indicated that the custom of holding an inquest on this subject was ancient; the churches of the Franks and the Normans also struggled for a similar right.[12] These passages contain the first suggestion of something similar to the modern jury that has come down to us in the English statutes,[13] although the text has not survived completely intact.[14]

Of all the legislation of Henry II, the Grand Assize (Assize of Clarendon, 1166) proved to be the most far reaching in terms of establishing the jury. It is set forth most clearly in *A Treatise on the Laws and Customs of the Kingdom of England*, by Ranulph de Glanville.[15] Whether Glanville actually wrote the treatise is immaterial; what is significant is that the work was written in 1181 and is the earliest treatise that has come down to us on English law. Glanville was the chief justiciar of England under Henry II from 1180 until the king's death in 1189, and thus it might be interesting to note the highpoints in the career of this man who came to be King Henry II's chief judge and executor of his will.

Glanville was sheriff of Yorkshire from 1163 until the Sheriff's Inquest in 1170, when Henry II removed all sheriffs and instituted an inquiry into their administrations. Glanville supported the king during the great rebellion of 1173, and as a result was made sheriff of Lancashire. Glanville and two other leaders won a great victory over the Scots on July 13, 1174. He was made judge in 1176, the Count of Flanders in 1177, and Chief Justiciar ("the king's eye") of all England in 1180. In 1182 he again took to the field leading an army against the Welsh. He was also present at the coronation of Richard I (the Lionhearted) in September, 1189, and accompanied

King Richard on a crusade to the Holy Land in 1190. Although Glanville was rather old for campaigning, Richard had no desire to leave such an influential individual behind in England during an extended absence. Glanville died at the siege of Acon in 1190 either "fighting valiantly," according to one report, or according to another, as a result of the eastern climate.[16]

The Grand Assize, as described by Glanville, was a court designed by Henry II. It was intended to give a person whose possession of land was challenged (the tenant) the alternative to put himself on the Grand Assize (an inquest of four knights and 12 neighbors) or to decide the issue with a duel. When the tenant elected the Grand Assize, the demandant (claimant to the land) was bound to consent to it unless there was a special reason why the Assize was not appropriate; for example, if the parties were descended from a common ancestor from whom they both claimed title.

If the matter of the relationship was disputed, the relatives of both parties were consulted. The question would be settled if the relations were in agreement; if not, the question was referred to the vincinage, or neighborhood, whose decision was final. If no relationship was shown, the demandant lost his case for wrongfully attempting to deprive the tenant of his right to the Grand Assize. If the matter of relationship was confirmed, the Assize was completed and the verdict was determined verbally by the court as a matter of law as to which of the two parties was the rightful heir.

It was necessary for the tenant to obtain two other writs while the Grand Assize was in progress. The first required the demandant to keep the peace, and the second prohibited other courts from proceeding with the action otherwise. At this point, the demandant would cause the following writ to issue:

> The King to the Sheriff, Health.
> Summon by good summoners, four lawful Knights of the Vincinage of Stoke, that they be at the Pentecost before me, or my Justices, at Westminster, to elect on their oaths, twelve lawful Knights of that Vincinage, who better know the truth, to return, on their oaths, whether M. or R. have the greater right in one Hyde of land in Stoke, which M.

claims against R. by my Writ, and of which R. the Tenant hath put himself upon my Assize and prays a Recognition [inquest] to be made, which of them have the greater right in that land. . .

At the time set, the knights appeared and elected the jurors. Both parties had a right to be present at the election and challenge for good cause members of the proposed jury. If the tenant did not appear, the selection of the jury was not interrupted, but it did not continue if the demandant failed to appear. After the election of the 12, they were summoned ". . . to apppear in court, prepared upon their oaths to declare, which of them, namely, whether the tenant, or the demandant, possess the greater right to the property in question."

A key word in understanding the role played by the jurors at the trial was "prepared." It was usual for the jurors to inform themselves about the dispute before appearing in court. The writ also provided for the jurors to view the land before coming to court. If it developed that the jurors testified under oath that they were unacquainted with the facts, other jurors were summoned until there were 12 who had knowledge and who agreed. Knowledge did not mean first-hand knowledge, but declarations of a juror's father or other equally reliable sources were sufficient. The jurors of this court were knights, and their decision was conclusive of the dispute.

Glanville referred to the Grand Assize as a ". . . certain royal benefit bestowed upon the people, and emanating from the clemency of the Prince. . . ." He listed the following as among its benefits: (1) The owner possessed his right to the land in safety pending the outcome of litigation; (2) It avoided the uncertain outcome of the duel; (3) It avoided unexpected and premature death; (4) It avoided the ". . . opprobrium of a lasting infamy, of that dreadful and ignominious word [craven] that so disgracefully resounds from the mouth of the conquered champion;" (5) It was less expensive and more efficient; and (6) The verdict was necessarily more just than the result of a duel.[17]

The Assize of Clarendon of 1166 also provided that those accused by the public inquest (grand jury), as established by the

Constitution of Clarendon (1164), should be tried by ordeal. This
eliminated trial by compurgation and duel in a great many cases.[18]
A statute of 1176, however, provided that if one accused of murder
or a felony passed the ordeal, he would nonetheless be banished.[19]
The term "Assize of Novel Disseisin" is often used synonymously
with the Grand Assize, but it would seem that Novel Disseisin
ought to be reserved for those causes in which there was a claim
that the dispossession was recent. For example, note the writ to
the sheriff under Novel Disseisin from Glanville:

> . . . summon by good summoners, twelve free and lawful
> men of the neighborhood of such a Vill, . . . prepared on
> their oath to return, if T., the father of the aforesaid G.,
> was seised in his Demesne as of fee, of one yardland, in
> that Vill, on the day of his death — if he died after my
> first coronation [Oct. 20, 1154], and if said G. be his nearer
> heir, and, in the meantime, let them view the land and
> cause their names to be imbreviated. . . .[20]

Another example of recent dispossession under the jurisdiction of
Novel Disseisin was when the dispossession had occurred after a
voyage of the king into Normandy.[21]

This is only a sample of the various uses of neighborhood
inquests during the reign of Henry II. Aside from those mentioned,
there was the Assize of Northampton in 1176 (including the Assize
of Uttrum and the Assize Mort d' Ancestor);[22] the Assize of Darrein
presentment at the Council at Windsor, 1179;[23] the Assize of Arms,
1181;[24] and the Assize of the Forest, 1184.[25] However, this list does
not exhaust the use of the inquest during the reign of Henry II.
Clearly the jury was by this time a substantial legal remedy.

All the above uses of the jury were held by reason of a royal
writ. Along with the development of these formal procedures,[26]
there developed trials where the parties, by their own consent,
submitted for arbitration some question of fact to an inquest of their
neighbors. This form of the jury was called the *jurata*. The jurors of
this court were not sworn with regard to a particular dispute, and
had no chance to gather facts about the dispute before being sworn.
The view of the scene, if had, was held after the taking of the oath.
Since the parties had consented to the tribunal, the jurors could not

be attacked by attaint; that is, for rendering a false verdict.[27] It was felt that since the jurors had not had a chance to inform themselves of the situation prior to the trial, it would not be fair to punish them if their verdict miscarried.[28] This form of tribunal, however, was used only for a short time.[29]

The trial jury in criminal cases was brought into use after the civil jury.[30] The criminal jury was present in England in the time of Glanville (i.e., before 1190) but it was little used.[31]

There has been much speculation as to why juries consist of 12 members. Devlin plausibly suggests that this was the number most traditionally used in the wager of law or compurgation.[32] Through the reign of King John, however, 12 was not invariably the number; e.g., Brunner found the numbers of jurors ranging from 6 to 66. Specific examples are given of juries of six existing in a part of Cornwall and also in Wales during the reign of Henry VIII.[33] Thayer found a jury of nine in 1199, and juries of 9, 36 and 40 between the years 1217-1219.[34]

Curious speculation on the origin of the use of 12 members for a jury is contained in a 1682 guide to juries:

> It seems as if very anciently the number on a jury was indefinite, but it was all the persons present, come as would come. . . . But in analogy of late it's reduced to the number of twelve, like as the Prophets were twelve, to foretell the Truth; the Apostles twelve, to Preach the Truth; the Discoverers twelve, sent into Canan to see and report the Truth; and the Stones twelve, that the Heavenly Hierusalaem is built on: And as the Judges were twelve anciently to try and determine matters of Law.
>
> And always when there is any waging Law, there must be twelve to swear in it; and also as for matters of State, there were formerly twelve councellors of State. And any thing now which any Jury can be said to do, must have the joynt consent of twelve. . . . Else it's in construction of Law, not the doing of the Jury, but of Private Persons, and void.[35]

The basic qualifications of jurors involved being free and a property owner, although the statutory inquests mentioned above required that the jurors be knights. As has also been noted, the jurors were witnesses summoned from the neighborhood.[36] As the duel fell into disuse, the official witnesses came to be included on the jury panel.[37]

The jury at this point seldom held the power to actually decide questions of law,[38] although jurors did not have to rely solely on evidence presented in court; e.g., in a case in 1200, the members of a jury rejected a deed given in evidence, ruling contrary to it and relying on their own knowledge.[39] Jurors could be objected to for a previous conviction of perjury, serfdom, consanguinity, affinity, enmity, or close friendship. There could be an objection to the entire array if it had not been selected by a disinterested person. In early times, it was even permitted to challenge the judge, although this right was soon lost. Eventually, the jury of the Grand Assize was sworn by having one member take the oath, while the others promised to uphold it as it applied to them.[40]

The principle of unanimity was not firmly established before the thirteenth century, although in the Grand Assize, 12 of 16 had to agree.[41] The knights on the early juries could render a special verdict if they chose not to render a general verdict, and leave it to the judges to apply the law to those facts. One of the reasons for using the jury during the reign of Henry II was that it saved the time of trained judges.[42]

As the jurors were considered to have personal knowledge of the truth of the matter in dispute and were not, like modern jurors, responsible for judging the credibility of witnesses who presented conflicting testimony, they were held guilty of perjury for rendering a false verdict.[43] The first notice of the punishment rendered for a false verdict in the legal literature of England is found in Glanville. He said those jurors who confessed to or were convicted of perjury would lose all their "chattles" (moveable property) which were forfeited to the king, "although by the great clemency of the Prince; their freehold tenements are spared. They shall also be thrown into prison and there detained for one year at least." They were also held incompetent as witnesses.[44]

The procedure of punishing jurors for false verdicts was called attaint. The issue was tried by another jury, usually consisting of 24 members, who heard only the evidence presented to the first jury. If the first jury had heard additional testimony they might have reached a different result. There was no attaint in criminal matters,[45] and, in the fiscal affairs of the king, attaint was only used if the verdict was against the king.[46] The attaint was not used in the Grand Assize because it replaced the duel which, by its nature, allowed no appeal.[47]

The jury appeared in Scotland during the reign of King David (1124-1153) and spread outward from his court in much the same manner as in England.[48] Coroners were making use of juries for inquests from at least the early thirteenth century.[49] The Court of Common Pleas was taking distinct form by the late twelfth century.[50] Along with the jury, William the Conqueror had brought the trappings of feudalism to England, which included courts of lords responsible for deciding causes between the lords and vassals.[51] The sheriff became a crown agent and held hearings in the shire courts, but his power gradually declined.[52] As has been noted above, the ecclesiastical courts were separated from the secular courts by the year 1100.[53] These courts dealt with matters of status such as birth, death, marriage, and bastardy. They also heard causes where it was alleged that an oral contract had been broken, on the theory that it was a question of broken faith.[54]

Compurgation continued to play a limited role after the conquest, but it was replaced to a large extent by the duel which was the ordinary mode of proof in the twelfth century until the Constitution of Clarendon.[55] The duel was not suitable for some parties; e.g., women, minors, relatives, the blind, deaf, or a person who had become incompetent to be a witness by reason of having been convicted of perjury.[56] The duel was restricted as early as Henry I (1100-1135) to cases in which the property in question was of small value.[57] The assizes of Henry II did not eliminate trials by combat but only restricted the occasions for their use.[58]

Andrew Horne, the author of The Mirror of Justices[59], attributed the origin of trial by battle to the biblical David and Goliath. Noting that no one may substitute for another in combat, he proceeded to describe the duel. At the place of trial the priest first delivered a benediction and then a malediction. The defendant then swore that he was not guilty, and the accuser swore that the defendant was a perjurer. The combatants had their heads, arms and hands uncovered, but their legs and feet were protected with iron, and they carried a shield of iron. Their weapons may have been staves.[60] The accuser was the first to "come into the list," entering from the east. The defendant entered from the west, and they both swore that they had not eaten or drunk anything whereby the truth might be "disturbed and the devil enhanced."

A judge would then make a proclamation warning, under threat of punishment, against the disturbance of the combat by observers. Then the combatants came together. They fought until one was killed, uttered the word "craven", uncovered his left foot, or until the sun went down. If there was no decision by the time the sun set, the defendant had judgment. According to Glanville, "champions" were permitted, although they could not be paid,[61] and if the duel was lost by a champion or by the party in person, there was a fine imposed in addition to the suit being lost. The defeated champion was not permitted to appear as a witness thereafter in court. In the Grand Assize, there was an exception to the rule that a party was allowed to appear in person. The demandant could not appear in his own peson because of the need of a witness who had seen and heard the fact. The tenant, however, could appear in person as well as by a champion.[62]

This was the world of the jury into the early thirteenth century and before the Magna Carta. In 1205 Phillip Augustus, King of France, invaded Normandy and, finding little resistance, conquered the province.[63] The result was that the jury died in Normandy, while continuing in England. From this point forward it is correct to speak of the English jury as opposed to the Anglo-Norman jury.

Chapter IV Footnotes

1. *A History of Lay Judges,* John P. Dawson (Harvard Univ. Press, Cambridge, Mass., 1960), pp. 116-17.

2. *The Englishman's Right,* Sir John Hawles (first printed 1680, 6th Ed. in London, 1771), p. 5.

3. *Domesday Book Relating to Essex,* translated from the Latin by T.C. Chisenhall-Marsh (London, 1864), p. 2.

4. *History of the English Law,* John Reeves (Reed and Hunter, London, 1814), I-84; *History of Trial By Jury,* William Forsyth (John Parker and Son, London, 1852), pp. 100-03; *The History of English Law,* Sir Frederick Pollock and Frederic William Maitland (Cambridge Univ. Press, 1898) I-143. The version in each of these three authorities varies, but they have reference to the same incident.

5. Forsyth, *op. cit.* at note 4, at pp. 96-98.

6. *The Origin of Juries,* Heinrich Brunner (Berlin, 1872), p. 430, and *A Preliminary Treatise on Evidence,* James Bradley Thayer (Sweet and Maxwell, London, 1898), p. 13.

7. *Id.* at p. 219.

8. Brunner, *op. cit.* at note 6, pp. 354-55.

9. Brunner, *op. cit.* at note 6, pp. 218-19.

10. "The Origin of the Petty Jury," Charles L. Wells, 27 Law Q. Rev. 347 (1911).

11. Forsyth, *op. cit.* at note 4, at p. 195.

12. Pollock and Maitland, *op. cit.* at note 4, at I-145.

13. Forsyth, *op. cit.* at note 4, at p. 136.

14. Brunner, *op. cit.* at note 6, at p. 300.

15. *A Translation of Glanville,* John Beames, Esq. (London, 1812).

16. *Id.* at pp. xiii-xviii of the preface; *Dictionary of National Biography* (London, 1890), Vol. XXI-413-14.

17. Beames, *op. cit.* at note 15, pp. 37-66.

18. "Early Opposition to the Petty Jury In Criminal Cases," Charles Wells, 30 Law Q. Rev. 97, at 98 (1914); *Trial By Jury,* Sir Patrick Devlin (Stevens and Sons Ltd., London, 1966), pp. 8-9.

19. Wells, *op. cit.* at note 18, at p. 98.

20. Beames, *op. cit.* at note 15, at p. 306.

21. Beames, *op. cit.* at note 15, at p. 335.

22. Forsyth, *op. cit.* at note 4, at p. 136.

23. Pollock and Maitland, *op. cit.* at note 4, at I-148.

24. Thayer, *op. cit.* at note 6, at p. 57.

25. *Ibid.*

26. Forsyth, *op. cit.* at note 4, at pp. 135, 143; Brunner, *op. cit.* at note 6, at p. 260.

27. Brunner, *op. cit.* at note 6, at pp. 416-17.

28. Brunner, *op. cit.* at note 6, at pp. 421, 423.

29. Brunner, *op. cit.* at note 6, at pp. 421-22.

30. Brunner, *op. cit.* at note 6, at pp. 42-43.

31. Forsyth, *op. cit.* at note 4, at pp. 64-65.

32. Devlin, *op. cit.* at note 18, at p. 48.

33. Brunner, *op. cit.* at note 6, at pp. 273-4, 364.

34. Thayer, *op. cit.* at note 6, at p. 86.

35. *A Guide to English Juries,* by a Person of Quality (Forsyth attributed this work to Lord Somers) (London, 1682), pp. 9-11.

36. Devlin, *op. cit.* at note 18, at p. 17.

37. Forsyth, *op. cit.* at note 4, at p. 151.

38. Brunner, *op. cit.* at note 6, at p. 286.

39. Thayer, *op. cit.* at note 6, at pp. 90-1, 105.

40. Forsyth, *op. cit.* at note 4, at pp. 137, 176-77.

41. Brunner, *op. cit.* at note 6, at pp. 366, 369.

42. Dawson, *op. cit.* at note 1, at p. 293.

43. Devlin, *op. cit.* at note 18, at p. 67.

44. Beames, *op. cit.* at note 15, at pp. 67-68.

45. Devlin, *op. cit.* at note 18, at pp. 67-68.

46. Brunner, *op. cit.* at note 6, at p. 424.

47. Thayer, *op. cit.* at note 6, at p. 156.

48. Pollock and Maitland, *op. cit.* at note 4, at I-144.

49. Pollock and Maitland, *op. cit.* at note 4, at II-643.

50. Dawson, *op. cit.* at note 1, at p. 56.

51. Dawson, *op. cit.* at note 1, at p. 118.

52. *Ibid.*

53. Forsyth, *op. cit.* at note 4, at p. 96.

54. Beames, *op. cit.* at note 15, at p. 180; Forsyth, *op. cit.* at note 4, at p. 151.

55. Brunner, *op. cit.* at note 6, at p. 181.

56. Brunner, *op. cit.* at note 6, at pp. 182-83.

57. Beames, *op. cit.* at note 15, a footnote on pp. 40-41.

58. Brunner, *op. cit.* at note 6, at pp. 251, 348-49.

59. *The Mirror of Justices,* Andrew Horne, translated by William Hughes, 1646 (London, 1768), at p. 157-62.

60. Beames, *op. cit.* at note 15, at a footnote on pp. 40-41.

61. Beames, *op. cit.* at note 15, at p. 46.

62. *Ibid.*

63. Brunner, *op. cit.* at note 6, at p. 136.

V
Evolution of the Judgment Jury
1205-1400

In the law of English speaking people, the Magna Carta has loomed large since it was issued by King John on June 15, 1215. This charter has commonly been credited with guaranteeing trial by jury. Blackstone wrote in the 1760's that:

> The trial by jury, or the country, *per patriam*, is also that trial by the peers of every Englishman, which as the grand bulwark of his liberties, is secured to him by the great charter. . . .[1]

And, the Supreme Court of the United States said in 1898 that, "When Magna Carta declared no freeman should be deprived of life, etc., but by the judgment of his peers or by the law of the land, it referred to a trial by twelve jurors."[2]

The lawyers attending the American Bar Association meeting in London in July, 1971, pilgrimaged to Runnymede on Sunday, July 18, to relive a piece of history. The Chief Justice of the United States Supreme Court, Warren E. Burger, represented the American Bar Association and the Lord High Chancellor of Britain, Lord Hailsham, represented the English Bar. The Americans presented a piece of marble bearing the inscription,"18 July 1971, On this day, The American Bar Association again came here and pledged adherence to the Principle of the Great Charter." It will be recalled that the American Bar Association had made a similar pledge in 1957. Lord Hailsham commented upon the historical setting in which the charter was signed and noted its importance. He even displayed one of the four existing copies of the Magna Carta to those gathered for the occasion. Listening to these speeches and the conversation of the lawyers, both English and American, one gathered that the great charter was still widely revered among the legal profession for, among other things, guaranteeing jury trial.

However, in line with most modern authorities, Dawson does

47

not support the popular opinion that Article 39 of the Magna Carta guarantees jury trial. He said:

> As originally used it [Article 39] was clearly not intended either as a generalized guaranty of jury trial or as a buttress for more ancient modes of community judging [reference to compurgation]. But it was expressed as a restraint of royal action, and despite the narrow meanings that were originally intended, clause 39 of Magna Carta deserves an honorable place in the history of constitutionalism. It was not till much later that "peers" were connected with jury trial.[3]

Dawson did concede that Article 39 ". . . projected 'judgment by peers across the sky of history for all the world to see.'"[4]

This concession is not enough. It is no doubt true that "peers" did not necessarily mean "jurors", but the impression left by Dawson's comments is that the Magna Carta had little or nothing to do with trial by jury and that it was only later that it was mistakenly assumed that trial by jury was guaranteed by the great charter. While it is true that the main purpose of the charter was to make the king subject to law, several provisions of the charter nonetheless referred to the right to trial by jury. Some of the following articles are indicative of this.

> 18. Assizes of novel disseisin, and of mort d' ancestor, and of darrien presentment, shall not be taken but in their proper counties, and after this manner: We, or, if we should be out of the realm, our chief justiciar, shall send two justiciaries through every county four times a year, who, with four knights, chosen out of every shire by the people, shall hold the said assizes, in the county on the day and at the place appointed for holding the assizes in each county, so many of the knights and freeholders as have been at the assizes aforesaid, shall stay to decide them as is necessary according as there is more or less business.

> 36. From henceforth nothing shall be given or taken for a writ of inquisition upon life or limbs, but it shall be granted gratis, and shall not be denied.

39. No freeman shall be taken or imprisoned or dis-
seised, or outlawed, or banished, or any ways destroyed,
nor will we pass upon him, nor will we send upon him
unless by the lawful judgment of his peers, or by the law
of the land.

48. All evil customs concerning forests, warrens, fore-
sters and warreners, sheriffs and their officers, rivers and
their keepers, shall forthwith be inquired into each
county, by twelve knights of the same shire, chosen by
creditable persons of the same county; and with in forty
days after said inquest, be utterly abolished, so as never
to be restored: so as we are first acquainted therewith or
our justiciary, if we should not be in England.[5]

A reading of the Magna Carta indicates that Article 36 is the one
guaranteeing jury trial. If the word "inquisition" can be taken to
mean "jury", then the phrase in Article 36 stating that, ". . . it shall
be granted gratis, and shall not be denied" is particularly significant.
The charter even presupposes the existence of the criminal jury.

The charter itself was almost immediately revoked by King
John under the authority of the Pope, who held that it was void
by reason of coercion. (The Pope's authority in English affairs
resulted from the fact that King John had put his kingdom under
the Pope's protection, although John received it back shortly
before the barons forced him to sign the Magna Carta.) The relevant
documents are on display at the British Museum. The charter,
however, was reaffirmed by Henry III and is the first statute
in the collection of British laws in force from 1225 until the
present time.

Criminal juries existed prior to 1200,[6] but they were available
only for a price, as this was before the Magna Carta.[7] Sometimes the
money proved to have been wasted since there were convictions
even by juries who were "had for a fee".[8] An example of a case with a
happier result is the trial of one Randulph de Tottesworth who was
charged with assault and battery. He gave King John a mark of
silver for an inquisition of knights. The jury was granted, and
Tottesworth was acquitted.[9]

From the reign of Richard I (1189-99) until the time of Edward in

1272, in the majority of cases the jury that had returned the indictment was also responsible for returning a verdict of guilt or innocence.[10] Even under these circumstances, there were occasional acquittals, as in the case of Robert Fitz, who was accused of illegally amercing (fining) tenants. The accusing jury was the trial jury and rendered a verdict of not guilty.[11] Generally, however, trial by these early juries meant almost certain conviction.[12]

Trials of criminal charges were still not ordinarily tried by jury in the early thirteenth century, and the Magna Carta did little to improve matters. What was to eventually have great effect on the use of jury trial in criminal cases was the decision by Pope Innocent III, at the Fourth Lateran Council, in November, 1215, forbidding the clergy to assist in the ordeals of water and fire.[13] This ruling was not implemented in England until a writ of Henry III early in 1219. That writ reads:

> The King to his beloved and faithful . . . Justices Itinerant . . . greetings: Because it was in doubt and not definitely settled before the beginning of your eyre, with what trial those are to be judged who are accused of robbery, murder, arson, and similar crimes, since the trial by fire and water has been prohibited by the Roman Church, it has been provided by our council that, at present, in this eyre of yours, it shall be done thus with those accused of excesses of this kind; To wit, that those who are accused of the aforesaid greater crimes, and of whom suspicion is held that they are guilty of that whereof they are accused, by whom also, in case they were permitted to abjure the realm, still there would be suspicion that afterwards they would do evil, they shall be kept in our prison and safeguard, yet so that they do not incur danger of life or limb on our account. But those who are accused of medium crime, and to whom would be assigned the ordeal by fire or water, if it had not been prohibited, and of whom, if they should adjure the realm there would be no suspicion of their doing evil afterwards, they may abjure our realm. But those who are accused of lesser crimes, and of whom there would be no suspicion of evil, let them find safe and sure pledges of fidelity and

of keeping our peace, and then they may be released in our land. . . . We have left to your discretion the observance of this aforesaid order . . . according to your own discretion and conscience. (dated Jan. 26, 1219).[14]

This writ does not spell out the mode of trial, no doubt leaving it, in some measure, to the discretion of the judges. The king's writ, however, and the Constitution of Clarendon made the jury an obvious alternative by process of elimination.[15] In 1226, an old woman was charged with a serious crime. Trial by battle was therefore impossible due to her physical condition, in addition to the fact that trial by battle itself was no longer in favor. She was thus tried by jury.[16]

It was uncertain at the time of the king's writ whether or not the defendant could be tried by a jury without his consent. A number of persons had been tried by juries, convicted and hung during the years 1220-22 who had never consented to a jury trial. Actually, the demandant had never been required to consent to a jury in the Grand Assize.[17] In addition, Wells gives examples for the years 1220, 1222, and 1235 of defendants being tried by juries without their consent.

One judge solved the dilemma by dispensing with trial altogether and hanging those accused, even though they had not confessed and had not been caught in the act. He was fined for this practice.[18] In 1284, a statute applicable to Wales solved the problem in a limited way by declaring as guilty any person accused of personal trepass when damage was less than 40 shillings and the defendant refused to submit to trial by jury.[19] This simple solution did not prevail, and by 1268 it was firmly established that the defendant must consent to trial by jury.[20] So it was that the judges, in their comments to the jury, came to say, ". . . and by this plea he hath put himself upon God and the country which country ye are."[21]

Obviously, the peace and order of society required that the guilt or innocence of those accused of crime be determined by some mode of trial. Criminals could not be allowed to escape punishment by the expedient of refusing to consent to jury trial. A statute was enacted in 1275 that helped solve the problem. It reads:

Notorious felons, openly of ill fame, who will not put
themselves on inquests for felonies with which they are
charged before the justices at the king's suit, shall be put
in strong and hard imprisonment as refusing the common
law of the land. But this is not to be understood of persons
who are taken on light suspicion.[22]

This statute became known as *prison forte et dure*. Wells suggests
that the origin of this solution dates back to King Henry III's statute
of 1219, quoted earlier in the chapter, which required the accused to
be held in prison.[23] It is not surprising that most defendants did
come to consent to trial be jury. Andrew Horne, the author of the
Mirror of Justices, complained that persons were being compelled to
be tried by their country, although they were willing to defend
themselves against the charges by battle.[24]

Even this incentive to elect the jury was not deemed sufficient,
and by 1291-92 additional provisions had been added to *prison forte
et dure*. Thayer quotes Britton as to the fate of prisoners who refused
to put themselves on their country at that time:

> . . . barefooted, ungirt and bearheaded, in the worst
> place in the prison, upon the bare ground continually
> night and day, that they eat only bread made of barley or
> bran, and that they drink not, the day they eat, nor eat,
> the day they drink, nor drink anything but water and that
> they may be put in irons.[25]

The misfortunes of the recalcitrant prisoner escalated, and by
1302 the defendant was put in

> . . . a house on the ground in his shirt, laden with as much
> iron as he could bear, and that he should have nothing to
> drink on the day when he had anything to eat, and that he
> should drink water which came neither from fountain nor
> river.[26]

In keeping with these changes, the treatment was to be known from
this time forward as *peine forte et dure*, or, "pain, hard and long." The
specifics of this punishment varied, although invariably strong
measures were believed to be necessary. Two defendants in 1406
were to ". . . have iron as much and more than they could

bear . . . ," and their water was to be ". . . standing water from place nearest jail . . ."[27]. A case in 1464 was similar except the prisoner was pressed with stones as well as with iron. One woman managed to live 40 days under this treatment in the middle of the fourteenth century.[28]

Such punishment as this before conviction makes one curious as to what happened to those who were convicted. About 1290, capital punishments included beheadings, drawing, hanging, burning alive, burying alive, falling from a dangerous place, and so on. Corporal punishments could have included the loss of an extremity; for example, a hand could be taken as punishment for stealing or the tongue for perjury, as well as beating and imprisonment. Punishments also included forfeiture of possessions (moveable and otherwise), exile and excommunication.[29] Not all punishments were so drastic. It was possible that the sentence could include labor on roads, pillory, stocks, imprisonment or a simple pecuniary fine.[30] The possibilities open to a judge of those days gave great room for the exercise of judicial discretion and imagination.

As has been noted in this chapter, the older accusatory jury in many cases during the thirteenth century also assumed the function of a trial jury. Thus, by the end of Henry III's reign in 1272, it was common for criminal cases to be submitted to the presenting jury, the jury of another hundred, and to four townships. These combined juries tried the case as a single body, and a unanimous verdict was necessary. The number of these enlarged juries ordinarily ranged from 24 to 84 members.

In the last years of the reign of Henry III and the early years of the reign of Edward I, a new method was used to appoint the trial panel once the accusing court had returned an indictment. The practice involved taking one member of the accusing jury to serve on the trial panel, along with members from other juries to make 12 jurors (the customary number in an accusing jury). Examples of this process in 1293 vary, however, with 2, 3, and 9 members having been selected from the accusing jury. In occasional cases, members from the accusing jury were not always chosen although in unusual situations as many as 14 jurors were chosen.[31] These jurors were usually knights,[32] and no oath was necessary, as the members had previously taken an oath as members of the accusing juries.

As late as 1340, it was thought to bode ill for the king if members of the accusing jury were not on the trial panel.[33] By a statute in the twenty-fifth year of the reign of Edward III, indictors were not permitted to remain on the trial jury if there was objection by the defendant.[34] Even after this it was the agents of the crown who picked the panel from which the jury was selected.[35]

At common law, where death was a possible penalty, the defendant was permitted to challenge 35 jurors, although the crown had no limit in the number of challenges. By a statute passed about the year 1305, the king's right to challenge was removed. This advantage to the defendant was nullified due to the fact that the crown was permitted to ask jurors to stand by until the panel was exhausted. There was no limit to the number that could be asked to stand by, and only if the panel was exhausted did the crown have to show cause.[36]

Wells summed up the development of criminal juries in four steps: (1) The accusing jury decided the mode of proof by which the defendant would clear himself; i.e., what kind of ordeal he must pass; (2) The accusing jury helped comprise the trial jury; (3) The accusing jury in addition to other jurors became the trial jury; and (4) A jury with new members, generally 12, was the trial jury.[37]

A verdict was accepted by the majority of the jurors as late as 1346,[38] but it was decided in 1367 that the verdict must be unanimous. The 1346 verdict involved a case in which a juror had refused to agree with the other 11 members of the court; he was sent to jail and the verdict of the other 11 was accepted.[39] Other restrictions were also placed on the jury; for example, during the reign of Edward I (1272-1307), the jury was not permitted to eat and drink until their verdict had been received.[40] The privy verdict was in use by 1401 and could be returned by the jury after court had been adjourned for the day. After having delivered the verdict to the judge, the jurors could eat but had to verify the verdict in court the next day.[41]

A decision was made to cut off inquiry into the source of jury knowledge by 1300. Earlier, in 1224, a Jew named Bonamy Botun and his wife were accused of the murder of a Christian servant. Two juries were impanelled, one consisting of 12 Jews and the other of 18

Christians. The Jewish jury found him innocent and the Christian jury, on interrogation by the judge, also thought he was innocent, suspecting his family only. Dawson says, rightly, that if this type of interrogation had been permitted to develop it would have led to a canonist-civil law type of procedure.[42]

Forsyth claimed in 1852 that the criminal trial jury in the reign of Edward III (1327-1377) was ". . . nearly if not quite the same as at the present day."[43] This was not necessarily true, particularly with regard to criminal trial juries. For example, the defendant could not call witnesses although the crown could,[44] and the defendant was not permitted counsel.[45] In addition, a jury could be fined and imprisoned for a verdict in favor of the defendant,[46] although the reverse did not hold true.[47] It therefore seems impossible to agree with Forsyth's assessment after considering these major exceptions to his thesis.

Most of the preceding material in this chapter has concerned the criminal jury only. The procedure in civil trials came nearer to putting the plaintiff and defendant on an equal footing. Parties were permitted to be represented by counsel who were given a great deal of leeway. Counsel could make statements of fact to the jury, not necessarily based upon the evidence, and could exhibit unsealed writings to the jurors, while sealed writings could be taken into the jury room when the jury withdrew for deliberations.[48] By 1292 the judges were charging the jury much as in modern times.[49] In 1221 it was proper for the parties to talk to the jury after they had retired.[50] By a statute of Edward I in 1285, juries were permitted to return a special verdict if they desired, whereupon the judge would determine the legal effect of the facts found.[51]

Juries are often popular in the abstract but individuals are seldom enthusiastic about jury duty. This was as true in the thirteenth century as it is in the twentieth. In 1258 there were so many exemptions from jury service that some counties had trouble finding enough knights to make up the number needed for the Grand Assize.[52] Still, Edward I relieved freeholders whose land was not worth 20 shillings a year from jury duty.[53] Also, it was held in the fourteenth century that persons under the age of 21 could be witnesses but not jurors.[54]

A feature distinguishing the civil jury system from the criminal was that a civil jury was subject to attaint, or punishment for a false verdict, while a criminal jury was not. It was said that the procedure in criminal cases was so favorable to the crown that it did not need attaint.[55] We have noted in Chapter IV that jurors were punished for this conduct as early as the time of Glanville (1181). The first judicial notice of such punishment was in 1202, and legislation concerning attaint has been extant since 1268.[56] The scope of attaint expanded to include actions relating to real estate in 1275,[57] but about 1290 Andrew Horne complained that it was still not as widely and easily available as it ought to be.[58] It was expanded again in 1327 to include trespass, and by 1360 the jurors were subject to attaint in all civil actions, both real and personal.[59]

If the 24 jurors of the attaint jury could not agree concerning the accusation of a false verdict against the original trial jury, they were afforced; i.e., members were added until there were 24 who could agree. If the attaint verdict went against the first 12, they were punished much as in the time of Glanville, but with a few differences. All their land and personal property was either destroyed or relinquished to the king, with their wives and children left homeless, and they were thus declared "infamous" by the community, and held not "oathworthy" for future trials.[60]

The process by which the "modern" jury evolved, where jurors ceased to be witnesses and became judges of fact, began in the early thirteenth century and was largely, although not absolutely, completed by the end of the fourteenth century. The beginning of the change could be seen in a case in 1219 where a party "put himself on the jury and document witnesses."[61] These witnesses served as a constituent part of the trial jury, bridging the gap until the time when they would testify to the jury and not be a part of it. The witness nature of the jurors was emphasized when a writ to a sheriff ordered him to summon those persons present at a partition of property.[62] Generally in the thirteenth century, witnesses to deeds were summoned and deliberated with the jurors.[63] Also, persons who had expert knowledge were summoned as jurors, once again highlighting the jurors' character as witnesses. In 1280, Florentines in London were summoned as jurors when the fact in issue had been done in Florence. In 1351 experts were summoned from particular trades when their special knowledge was useful in understanding a factual dispute. When a certificate was to be contradicted in 1363 merchants who best knew about it were summoned to serve on the jury.[64]

Process was issued for witnesses along with the jurors in 1218,[65] but the witnesses were so unessential that the taking of the inquest was not delayed or postponed for them.[66] And, in 1223, deed witnesses were still sitting with the jurors.[67] However, the distinction between the role of a witness as distinguished from the role of a juror was beginning to be recognized at this time. In 1338 witnesses could not be challenged. In 1349 the jury was charged to tell the turth to the best of its knowledge, while the witnesses were charged to tell the truth and to loyally inform the inquest.[68] The rule, effective by 1361, that deeds and documents had to be delivered in open court also aided in the evolution of the modern jury.[69] The first example of witness testimony being presented to the trial jury dates from 1371-75.[70] By the end of the fourteenth century the character of the jurors as judges of the facts predominated over their role as witnesses.[71] This process had begun by separating the document witnesses from the jury, and this subsequently led the way to separating other witnesses. The process was complete for most purposes by 1460.[72]

During the thirteenth century there were a number of curious juries and trials. First of all, there continued to be trials in the original sense of the Frankish *inquisitio*. In 1248 the king directed a writ to the Mayor and citizens of London ordering them

> . . . to elect twelve of the more discreet and lawful men of our city of London and join with them twelve good goldsmiths of the same city, making twenty-four discreet men in all, who shall go before the Barons of our Exchequer at Westminster and examine, upon oath, together with the barons, both the old and the new money of our land, and make provision how it may be bettered; and that it be made of good silver, and that it be lawful and for the good of the realm.[73]

This was the first form and instance of what was to become known as the trial of the Pyx, which we will return to in a later chapter.

Trial juries were almost uniformly coming to consist of 12 members, but juries that were in the nature of a public inquest did not necessarily conform to that number. The earliest statute enacted with regard to a coroner's inquest became effective in 1276. It directed that coroners, when required by a bailiff, the king, or "honest men" of the county, to summon five or six citizens and require them on oath to inquire into matters of violent death, treasure trove (concerning the property of the Crown), and housebreaking.[74]

In 1302 a knight objected to a jury picked to try him because the members were not knights, i.e., his peers. His objection was upheld, and when the knights were called, he was also permitted to object to the individual members.[75]

The jury De Medietatem Linguae was an extraordinary institution. It provided, by a charter granted by Edward I in 1303, that foreign merchants living within the kingdom should, in all cases in which they were involved except capital cases, be entitled to a jury trial which consisted of six foreign merchants resident in the city or town and six other good and lawful men of the place where the trial was to be held. If six foreign merchants could not be found, domestic merchants would serve in their place. There is a record of a foreign merchant in 1320 praying for a jury of 12 native and 12 foreign persons. The statute of 1303 was reaffirmed in 1353 with the additional provision that when both merchants were foreign the jury would be entirely foreign. This type of jury, with variations, was to be found in English law until the middle of the nineteenth century or later.[76] A similar principle was embodied in a statute of 1308 which directed a trial of ejectment in Shropshire to be tried by juries composed of half English and half Welsh.[77]

A case that occurred in 1356 would no doubt be a frightening prospect to modern citizens and lawyers alike. It consisted of a jury composed entirely of lawyers. A judge of the Common Pleas Bench had complained in the Court of the Exchequer that a woman had called him a ". . . traitor, felon and robber." The case was tried to a jury consisting of lawyers who practiced before the Court of Common Pleas.[78]

In 1219 we find a plaintiff proving his age by selecting 12 legal men, one of whom swore the plaintiff was of age. The other 11 persons selected swore that the oath of the first juror was true. This, of course, was a variation of compurgation. However, in 1397, there is an example of age being proved by a jury whose members were all 42 or older. The reason for requiring this age of the jurors was that they would all have been approximately 21 when the person whose age was in question was supposed to have been born.[79] This is reminiscent of the time when jurors functioned as witnesses as opposed to judges.

As to courts generally in the thirteenth century, the sheriff continued to hold court twice a year and preside at the county court once a month. A bailiff continued to preside over the court of the hundred every third week, and it functioned much like a county court.[80] Other courts of limited jurisdiction emerged more clearly in this century. There are clear records of the manor courts from 1237. They are very numerous toward the end of the thirteenth century and abundant in the fourteenth century.[81] Leet court was a local court similar to Baron's Court, with the distinction that the Leet court was interested in the community, as opposed to the business connected with a Baron's estate.[82] Leet juries and "homage" juries (form of jury in "Court Baron") sometimes served as local councils.[83] Justices of the peace were made custodians of the peace and were appointed by the king. They became stabilized by the fourteenth century, handling minor criminal matters. The local gentry got the appointments.[84] The private courts were somewhat hampered in adopting the jury system because of a statute of 1267 forbidding them to coerce freeholders to serve on juries against their will.[85] But local courts were eventually allowed to borrow the jury procedure for trial as well as for presentment.[86] Even justices of the peace were permitted to empanel juries to try the more serious cases.[87] Local courts (including the court of hundreds) were limited by a statute of 1278 to actions where the amount in controversy did not exceed 40 shillings.[88]

By 1300 the Court of Common Pleas had completed its separation from the Curia Regis and was stationary at Westminster.[89] In the thirteenth century the Court of Common Pleas had seven or eight judges, while the King's Bench had three. The fact-finding part of the court's work consisted of dispatching commissions to local gentry who were required to preside, receive verdicts, and render judgments. These commissions came to be known in the thirteenth century as commissions of "over" and "terminer" (to hear and determine). In 1273 there were 2,000 commissions of assize. A royal judge was not always a member of the commission, but it was common for one royal judge to preside with other members of the commission including local nobles, clergy, and the like. The circuit court became similar to, but more important than, the county courts.[90]

During these two centuries trial by jury had become the dominant mode of trial. This did not mean that the older modes of trial had died altogether. For example, an interesting type of compurgation took place in the thirteenth century. In an action for a debt the person who had the burden of proof brought 10 witnesses to the trial with him. Five were lined up on one side and five on the other. A knife was thrown into the ground between the two lines. A man was selected from the five on the side toward which the handle of the knife inclined. One of the five selected was removed and the other four took an oath as compurgators.[91] In an action for trespass in 1304 a party offered combat and the opposite party accepted it but the court refused to permit it.

The thirteenth and fourteenth centuries saw many significant developments in the jury procedures. The next four centuries were to see the most significant development of all. The jury would be transformed into a just mode of trial.

Chapter V Footnotes

1. *Commentaries On the Laws of England,* William Blackstone, Esq. (4 Vols, 7th Ed., Oxford, 1775, 1st Ed. 1765), IV-349.

2. *Thompson v. Utah,* 170 U.S. 343 (1898).

3. *A History of Lay Judges,* John P. Dawson (Harvard Univ. Press, Cambridge, Mass., 1960), pp. 289-90.

4. *Id.* at p. 289.

5. *Federal Code Annotated* (Bobbs-Merrill Co., 1950), Constitution Vol., pp. 3-4.

6. *History of Trial by Jury,* William Forsyth (London, 1852), pp. 200-01.

7. *The Origin of Juries,* Heinrich Brunner (Berlin, 1872), p. 472.

8. "Early Opposition to Petty Juries in Criminal Cases," Charles L. Wells, 30 Law Q. Rev. 97 (1914) at p. 102.

9. Forsyth, *op. cit.* at note 6, at p. 201.

10. "The Origin of the Petty Jury," Charles L. Wells, 27 Law Q. Rev. 347 (1911), at p. 350.

11. Forsyth, *op. cit.* at note 6, at p. 200.

12. *The Proof of Guilt*, Glanville Williams (Stevens and Sons, London, 1963), pp. 4-5; and Wells, *op. cit.* at note 8, at p. 101.

13. Wells, *op. cit.* at note 8, at p. 98.

14. Wells, *op. cit.* at note 10, at p. 352.

15. *A History of Lay Judges*, John P. Dawson (Harvard Univ. Press, Cambridge, Mass. 1960), p. 293.

16. *A Preliminary Treatise on Evidence*, James Bradley Thayer (Sweet and Maxwell, London, 1898), pp. 70-71.

17. *Id.* at p. 70.

18. Thayer, *op. cit.* at note 16, at p. 72.

19. Thayer, *op. cit.* at note 16, at p. 78.

20. Wells, *op. cit.* at note 8, at p. 104.

21. *Trial By Jury*, Sir Patrick Devlin (Stevens and Sons, London, 3rd ed. 1966, 1st ed. 1956), p. 16.

22. Thayer, *op. cit.* at note 16, at p. 74.

23. Wells, *op. cit.* at note 10, at p. 352.

24. *The Mirror of Justices,* Andrew Horne, translated by William Hughes 1646, (London, 1768), p. 227.

25. Thayer, *op. cit.* at note 16, at pp. 74-75.

26. Thayer, *op. cit.* at note 16, at p. 75.

27. Thayer, *op. cit.* at note 16, p. 75.

28. Thayer, *op. cit.* at note 16, at pp. 75-76.

29. Horne, *op. cit.* at note 24, at pp. 190-91, 193-94.

30. Horne, *op. cit.* at note 24, at p. 206.

31. Wells, *op. cit.* at note 10, at pp. 354-58.

32. Thayer, *op. cit.* at note 16, at p. 71.

33. Thayer, *op. cit.* at note 16, at p. 83.

34. Wells, *op. cit.* at note 10, at p. 361.

35. *A History of English Law,* Sir William Holdsworth (Sweet and Maxwell, London, 7th Ed. 1956, 1st Ed. 1903), I-325-26.

36. Forsyth, *op. cit.* at note 6, at pp. 231-33.

37. Wells, *op. cit.* at note 10, at p. 359.

38. Holdsworth, *op. cit.* at note 35, I-318.

39. Devlin, *op. cit.* at note 21, at p. 48.

40. Forsyth, *op. cit.* at note 6, at p. 243.

41. Holdsworth, *op. cit.* at note 35, I-319.

42. Dawson, *op. cit.* at note 15, at pp. 124, 126.

43. Forsyth, *op. cit.* at note 6, at p. 207.

44. Williams, *op. cit.* at note 12, at p. 5.

45 *The Jury,* W.R. Cornish (Penguin Press, London, 1968), p. 72.

46. Holdsworth, *op. cit.* at note 35, at I-326.

47. Thayer, *op. cit* at note 16, at p. 112.

48. Thayer, *op. cit.* at note 16, at pp. 103, 107-08.

49. Thayer, *op. cit.* at note 16, at p. 112.

50. Thayer, *op. cit.* at note 16, at p. 110.

51. Forsyth, *op. cit.* at note 6, at p. 260.

52. *The History of English Law,* Sir Frederick Pollock and Frederic Maitland (Cambridge Univ. Press, 1898), II-631.

53. *Id.* at II-631-2.

54. Holdsworth, *op. cit.* at note 35, I-336.

55. *Id.* at I-341.

56. Thayer, *op. cit.* at note 16, at p. 141.

57. Holdsworth, *op. cit.* at note 35, at I-339-40.

58. Horne, *op. cit.* at note 24, at pp. 235-36.

59. Holdsworth, *op. cit.* at note 35, at I-339-40.

60. Forsyth, *op. cit.* at note 6, at pp. 181-83.

61. Thayer, *op. cit.* at note 16, at p. 95.

62. Thayer, *op. cit.* at note 16, at p. 102.

63. Holdsworth, *op. cit.* at note 35, at I-334.

64. Thayer, *op. cit.* at note 16, at p. 94.

65. Holdsworth, *op. cit.* at note 35, at I-334.

66. Thayer, *op. cit.* at note 16, at p. 101.

67. Thayer, *op. cit.* at note 16, at p. 103.

68. Thayer, *op. cit.* at note 16, at p. 100.

69. Holdsworth, *op. cit.* at note 35, at I-334.

70. Thayer, *op. cit.* at note 16, at p. 123.

71. Holdsworth, *op. cit.* at note 35, at I-319.

72. Brunner, *op. cit.* at note 7, at p. 436.

73. "Royal Mint Annual Report for 1963," Royal Mint (London 1963), p. 5.

74. Forsyth, *op. cit.* at note 6, at p. 226.

75. Holdsworth, *op. cit.* at note 35, at I-324.

76. Forsyth, *op. cit.* at note 6, at pp. 228-30.

77. Forsyth, *op. cit.* at note 6, at p. 230.

78. Thayer, *op. cit.* at note 16, at p. 93.

79. Thayer, *op. cit.* at note 16, at p. 19.

80. Dawson, *op. cit.* at note 3, at pp. 182, 133, 178.

81. Dawson, *op. cit.* at note 3, at pp. 192, 198.

82. Dawson, *op. cit.* at note 3, at pp. 200, 221.

83. Dawson, *op. cit.* at note 3, at p. 244.

84. Dawson, *op. cit.* at note 3, at p. 136.

85. Dawson, *op. cit.* at note 3, at pp. 185-86.

86. Dawson, *op. cit.* at note 3, at p. 296.

87. Dawson, *op. cit.* at note 3, at p. 139.

88. Dawson, *op. cit.* at note 3, at p. 180.

89. Forsyth, *op. cit.* at note 6, at p. 168.

90. Dawson, *op. cit.* at note 3, at pp. 129-32.

91. Thayer, *op. cit.* at note 16, at p. 26.

VI
Tudor Oppression: Georgian Justice 1400-1790

During this period a criminal defendant could answer an indictment either by demurrer or by a plea of "not guilty."[1] Although specific evidence was not always consistent with the charge as contained in the indictment, the jury could convict on contradictory evidence as long as it was received at least one day before the action was commenced.[2]

It was still difficult for the defendant to refuse to accept a trial by jury. *Peine forte et dure* was still an effective remedy for recalcitrancy. Two who were charged with robbery in 1406 were said to be "Mute of malice [to] delay their death." It was ordered that they undergo *peine forte et dure* "so to the death."[3] At Newgate Prison in London, 1662, George Harley was indicted for robbery and refused to plead. His thumbs were tied together with whipcord so the pain could compel him to submit to a jury.[4] Burnwater was accused of murder in 1728 and refused to plead. He was pressed for one and three-fourths hours under 400 pounds of iron. He changed his mind, pleaded not guilty, was tried by a jury, convicted and hung.[5] Tying the thumbs with whipcord continued at Newgate until at least 1734. This prison also added the refinement to *peine forte et dure* by placing either a stake or sharp stone under the prisoner's neck.[6]

The year 1772 was to see the end of *peine forte et dure*, as it was abolished by statute. After that time the accused either stood as convicted by his refusal to plead,[7] or his refusal to plead was taken as a plea of not guilty.[8] For example, on a charge of treason a refusal to plead was equivalent to conviction except when insanity was suspected. In such a case it was left to a jury to decide whether the defendant remained silent to avoid punishment, or whether he did so rightfully by "the providence of God."[9]

When the defendant's plea was entered and a writ of *venire facias* (order for the jury panel to be summoned) had been issued, it was up to the sheriff to return the jurors. If he excused anyone under the age of 70 he was subject to a fine of 20 pounds to be recovered by the person bringing the charge.[10] If the sheriff was not impartial the panel was returned by the coroner. If the coroner in turn was not impartial the judges nominated two persons to direct the process.[11]

The requirements as to the composition of the jury varied from time to time. In 1543-44 a statute set forth that only six members of the panel need be from the hundred. This was reduced to two in 1584-85,[12] and, in 1705, it was sufficient that the jurors be from the county.[13] The general requirements for the selection of jurors were that they be peers or equals, and 21 to 70 years of age, not outlawed, attainted or convicted of treason, a felony, perjury, conspiracy or adjudged to the pillory, and not an alien (unless an alien was being tried). In general the most highly respected members of the community were selected.[14] At common law there was no requirement that the freehold of a juror be of a certain value, and jurors in cities and towns were not required to have a freehold at all, although there would be a monetary requirement; e.g., 100 marks in London (a mark is equal to 12 shillings and four pence).[15] In the English Bill of Rights (1688) it was complained that jurors had been chosen in cases for high treason who were not freeholders.[16] If the case involved a capital offense a juror was required to have a freehold in the county worth 40 shillings a year.[17] A statute of 1751 eliminated the requirements that there be a knight on the panel.[18]

In some cases qualified jurors might be exempt from serving on juries. Jurors were exempt if they had served on a jury within the previous year in the same jursidiction, or within the previous four years in the county of York.[19] A member of any holy order, a sailor, or an apothecary living in London or within seven miles of the city were exempt from jury service. By a statute of 1696 no Quaker could serve on a jury because his religion prevented him from taking the oath.[20]

A party could challenge both the array (entire panel returned by the sheriff) or the polls (individual jurors).[21] At common law, in cases of high treason or felony, the defendant had 35 challenges. This was reduced in 1531 to only 20. If a party challenged a greater number than allowed, he was "put on his penance"; i.e. the *peinte forte et dure.*[22] The king had no peremptory challenges,[23] although both sides could challenge for cause. The following reasons were judged to be sufficient causes to challenge a juror: (1) the juror had been on the grand jury which had indicted the defendant (criminal case); (2) the juror was a serf or servant; (3) the juror had been convicted of certain crimes; (4) he was related to one of the parties or to the sheriff[24] (a degree of relationship could be objectionable to the ninth degree);[25] (5) the juror had an action pending against a party; (6) the juror would benefit by the judgment to be rendered; and (7) the juror had served as an arbitrator in the matter, or had declared his opinion on the question to be submitted.[26]

In the case of challenge to the array two individuals (perhaps two attorneys or two coroners) were appointed by the judge to hear the case. In a challenge to polls the judge again selected two persons to hear the case, and the polls were tried two at a time until all challenges were settled.[27] As had been discussed, although the king had no peremptory challenges, he could ask an unlimited number of jurors to stand aside. The king did not have to show cause unless the panel was exhausted. After a juror was sworn, he could not be challenged except for cause occurring after he was sworn.[28] In the sixteenth century the various parties were often able to interview individual jurors to determine their fitness to hear the case. A list of prospective jurors could be obtained from the sheriff,[29] and ordinarily jurors were selected from the panel by lot.[30]

After the jurors or a portion of them were selected, a view of the scene by the jurors could be had in most actions involving real property. When it was decided to have a view, at least six jurors were selected either by the consent of the parties involved or chosen by the judge. Upon completion of the view and by the day set for trial, enough other jurors were added to make 12.[31]

In the fifteenth and sixteenth centuries, the parties had a right not only to question the jurors for the purpose of obtaining information on which to base challenges, but they also had a right to inform the jurors of their position before the day of trial.[32] This right was incorporated in a statute of 1427 which provided that, upon request, the parties would be given a list of the jurors six days before the trial so as to "...inform them of their right and title before the day of the session".[33] In a letter to Sir Richard Plumpton

in 1498-99 the writer recited that he had previously sent a copy of
the panel of jurors to Sir Plumpton and continued,

> Therefore, Sir, between you and my lady ye must cause
> special labor to be made, so it be downe prevely, to such of
> the Jurrours, as ye trust wilbe made frindly in the cause.[34]

In another letter, Sir Richard was urged,

> ...to make labor to them that they appeare not, or else to
> be favorable to you according to right, and enform them
> of the matter as well as ye can for their consciences.[35]

But in 1682 it was punishable to use this technique in order to
influence the jury's verdict.[36]

If insufficient jurors were left after challenges to make up 12, it
was permissible to appoint tales; i.e., persons on the spot at the
courthouse who were pressed into service. They are first mentioned
in the year 1544.[37] In the past the parties could even challenge
a judge, but this ceased to be permitted under Justice Coke
(1552-1634).[38] Perhaps the right to challenge the judge was not as
necessary after 1700 when judges no longer served at the pleasure
of the crown, but for life or good behavior.[39]

The prohibition against jurors eating and drinking continued
in force. A statute of Henry VIII, issued in 1535 without the sanction
of Parliament, directed the officer in charge of the jurors to keep
them from eating, drinking, and talking with others.[40] It was especially undesirable if the jurors had their nourishment at the
expense of one of the parties, and the jurors could be challenged for
this.[41] In one case in 1588 jurors were searched for food by the
officer in charge. Two were found to have some figs, having eaten
some, while three jurors were found with apples but had not eaten
any. Those with the figs were fined five pounds each, and those
with the apples were fined 40 shillings each. The verdict which they
had returned, however, was found to be good.[42] The reign of Elizabeth I seems to have been less severe than that of her father's reign
(Henry VIII). During his reign jurors who ate apples were not only
fined five pounds each but were committed to the fleet.[43]

The jury could eat and drink after delivering a privy verdict to
the judge after he had retired for the day, but they had to affirm their

verdict in open court the next day.[44] In one case an enterprising solicitor (lawyer) paid the bill for wine which a jury, while deliberating in a tavern, had ordered before returning a privy verdict. After the privy verdict in his client's favor was given to the judge, the solicitor again treated the jury at the tavern. The bill for both the wine and the rest of the celebration was not paid until after the verdict was given to the judge. (The verdict was good.)[45] With the permission of the justices the jurors were permitted to eat, even at the cost of the parties, if they agreed. After the conclusion of a trial at Old Bailey in London, England, in October and November, 1971, the victorious defendants (the "Notting Hill Gate eight") and jurors had refreshments at a nearby public house. A month later, one of the defendants treated the jury and others to a party at a restaurant which he owned.

Criminal defendants were not generally permitted the assistance of counsel during this time, even though the crown might have as many as four lawyers.[46] Counsel were permitted for the purpose of arguing law to the court by 1681. In fact it was suggested at that time that the court ought to appoint counsel for that purpose if necessary and the defendant desired it.[47] The author to *A Guide to English Juries* gives us the reason for not permitting defendants charged with crime to be represented by counsel. Quoting from a trial, he says:

> The only Reason . . . why a prisoner is allowed no councel in matter of Fact or in any thing but matter in law, when life or member is concerned, is only this, the Evidence whereby he shall be condemned, ought to be plain and evident, that all the councel in the world may be presumed able to say nothing against it or in his defense.[48]

As late as 1752, defendants in criminal cases, for the most part, were not permitted counsel to assist in their defense. Treason and misprision, however, had been excepted from this practice by statute since 1696. The reason for this practice was that it was felt that the judge ought to be the prisoner's counsel.[49] By the eighteenth century defense counsel were permitted to cross-examine witnesses.[50]

Among other obstacles facing the criminal defendant, he was not permitted to testify in his own behalf.[51] His wife was also not permitted to testify except as to certain offenses such as offenses against his children or his wife.[52] Ordinarily, however, the wife could not be a witness against her husband.[53] It was not until the seventeenth century that the defendant was permitted to call witnesses.[54] A statute in 1606 gave the accused the right to have witnesses under oath in certain felony cases.[55] Apart from statute, several witnesses in one case testified for a defendant in 1632, but they were not sworn.[56] It became the usual practice for the defendant to call witnesses after 1640, although they were still not permitted to be sworn.[57] Chief Justic Coke followed this practice in 1679.[58] Even crown witnesses were not always sworn by the mid-seventeenth century.[59] By the late 1600's, however, the judges had come to the view that unsworn testimony was no evidence at all, [60] and by the eighteenth century the defendant's witnesses were finally allowed to be sworn.[61] Another problem in court procedure was that ordinarily court papers were in Latin, although during Cromwell's time English was used.[62] When necessary, the papers were read to the jurors in English.[63]

In addition to other problems, a witness had to contend with the threat of physical violence from the party opposed to his testimony.[64] He could be compelled to attend court from as early as the mid-sixteenth century.[65] If the witness volunteered his testimony without process, he was subject to a charge of maintenance, a crime dating back to as early as 1433.[66] The Star Chamber decided in 1562-63 that a witness could be punished for perjury, but excepted those cases where there had been a conviction for a felony or murder. This court did not want to deter witnesses for the king from coming forth.[67]

The courts established elaborate rules of evidence to control what the jury would hear. The most familiar of these rules is that excluding hearsay evidence, which was invented about 1700.[68] Before the judge summed up, it invalidated the verdict if the jury separated and the jury could be punished for violation of this rule.[69] Judges had charged the jury long before 1400, and were allowed to give their opinions on the case.[70] In a case in 1597 a judge ruled, as a matter of law, that certain articles of clothing could not be necessities for an infant.[71] If the jury was unable to reach a verdict before the court had to continue on its circuit to the next town, the court would have the jurors put in a cart and carried around the circuit with the judge until they reached a decision.[72] Instead of returning a general verdict, the jury could return a special verdict; i.e., specially finding the fact in dispute and leaving it for the judge to apply the law.[73]

The King's Bench began ordering special venires (panels of jurors) of high or special standing in the late seventeenth century.[74] The procedure for selecting a special jury was for the sheriff, the parties and an officer of the court to choose 48 freeholders. Each side struck 12 alternately, one at a time, the plaintiff beginning. If a party did not appear, 12 were stricken for him. There were no special juries in capital cases because the defendant would have been deprived of his peremptory challenges.[75] One of the early special juries was convened in 1645-46 in the King's Bench. This jury consisted of merchants who were to try an issue between two other merchants concerning their business affairs.[76] An inquiry held in 1730 disclosed that special juries had been ordered in cases presenting difficult issues without the consent of the parties, but only prior to 1700.[77] A statute of 1730, amended in 1751, provided that any person who applied for a special jury could have it upon payment of the expense for striking it, and all additional expense occasioned thereby. No allowance was to be made in the costs for this expense unless the judge ruled the case a proper one to be tried to a special jury. The statute provided that the special jurors were to be paid a reasonable sum not to exceed one pound and one shilling (a guinea, hence the name "guinea men"), unless a view was necessary.[78]

Quite apart from attaint, jurors were subject to punishment by the contempt power of the court. For example, jurors could be punished for receiving a paper from a party after retiring for deliberation. In 1410 a verdict was set aside for this specific reason.[79] In 1585 a verdict was set aside when it was discovered that the jury had examined a witness in private after retiring, although in another case the verdict was held good after both parties had delivered a paper to the jury by mutual consent.[80] Verdicts were set aside in 1675, 1677, and 1722 because the jurors had cast lots to arrive at verdicts. In the 1677 case the offense was proved by the affidavit of a juror.[81]

The law courts copied the Star Chamber in fining and imprisoning jurors who refused to convict.[82] A rare exception to the contrary was a case in 1500 in which a judge was fined for imprisoning a jury that had refused to convict.[83] A statute of 1534, applicable to Wales and the marches only, authorized the fining and imprisoning of jurors.[84] A similar statute applicable to England was issued without authority of Parliament by King Henry VIII in 1535. It provided that if the jurors acquitted felons contrary to the weight of the evidence or otherwise "misbehaved", they could be fined and imprisoned at the discretion of the court. This act was soon declared illegal,[85] although the practice continued. Cases are recorded in 1535 and 1554 of juries being fined on failure to convict,[86] and from 1571 to 1597 jurors were frequently fined for finding contrary to the direction of the court.[87] During the years 1664-65 jurors insisted on acquitting Quakers of various charges and were fined for their actions. The judges of the Common Bench generally agreed that this pratice of fining was unlawful, although it nonetheless continued, and more jurors continued to be punished in 1666 and 1667.[88]

A resolution of the Commons dated December 13, 1667, declared, "That the precedents and practice of fining or imprisoning jurors, for verdicts is illegal."[89] Not surprisingly, there is no record, according to Williams, of punishing jurors for conviction.[90] At long last the practice came to a permanent halt with Bushell's case in 1670.[91] After that, jurors could be punished for ministerial acts only.[92] The jury did have some protection under the law, however. An irate party, having lost his case, assaulted a juror and was sentenced to life imprisonment.[93]

The Star Chamber, a criminal court which had extraordinary powers, was composed of members of the king's privy council. It did not use a jury.[94] The Star Chamber and its powers are described in a work written in 1764:

> . . . Henry the 7th, one of the worst Princes this nation
> ever knew, procured an act of Parliament which, after
> reciting many defects and abuses in trials by Jury, and

pretending a remedy for the same, gives a summary jurisdiction to certain great officers of state, taking to their aid a bishop, to summon, try and punish of their own mere discretion and authority, any persons who shall be accused of the offenses therein very generally named and described. In short, the court of the Star Chamber is, by this act, so enlarged in its jurisdiction, that it may be said to be erected, and both grand and petit Juries in crown matters are in great measure laid aside . . .[95]

The Star Chamber used torture to extract confessions,[96] and it was apt to treat as corrupt any verdict of acquittal which it considered as against the weight of the evidence. There are many examples of this court punishing jurors with fines and imprisonment for verdicts of acquittal during the reigns of Henry VIII, Mary and Elizabeth I.[97] There are even rare fines imposed for verdicts of conviction,[98] and in all cases the penalties could be heavy. The foreman and another juror from the jury acquitting Throctmorton in 1554 were fined 2,000 pounds each and committed to prison. Six of the jurors were fined 1,000 marks each and sent to prison, while four members of this jury admitted they had been in the wrong and were released.[99] Edmund Bruke insisted that although the Star Chamber was abolished in 1635, its maxims continued to persist.[100]

Although testimony by witnesses appearing before the jury was to be the chief source of evidence, the jurors themselves, to a lesser degree, were also permitted to testify. In 1472 a statute of Edward IV provided that process for witnesses was not to issue unless it was requested.[101] Considering that witnesses were subject to fine for volunteering, this probably meant that if no process was issued, there would be no evidence other than the private knowledge of the jurors. The last record of deed witnesses being summoned with the jury is in 1489.[102] Justice Vavaseur, in 1499, decided that the jury could bring in a verdict even if no evidence was offered.[103] It was held in 1598 that a juror could communicate his private knowledge to the other jurors.[104] Even though it was discovered in 1599 that a juror had taken a paper into deliberation with him and had shown it to the other jurors, the verdict was held to be good.[105] The court said, during the trial of Nathaniel Reading in 1679, that jurors were not strangers to the facts, but if they had evidence to offer, they ought to be sworn as witnesses.[106] This was similar to a case of 1650, the only difference being that, in the earlier case, the juror was not required to take an oath as a witness in addition to his oath as a juror.[107]

However, Brunner makes reference to a statute of 1650 which further differentiates between the roles of witnesses and jurors.[108] It was held to be improper for a jury to approve a deed that had not been pleaded or given in evidence.[109] These authorities notwithstanding, Blackstone declared in 1765 that there were two kinds of evidence—that given in proof and the private knowledge of the jurors.[110]

The practice of granting new trials in civil cases was claimed by one justice to have been an ancient tradition, while another claimed that the practice originated in 1652.[111] Perhaps this passage from the *Plumpton Correspondence,* written before 1523, is evidence of an early new trial:

> . . . in which drytinge is conteyned how the Justices of the Common Place awarded a new *venire facias* betwyxt my master your son and William Babthorpp . . .[112]

This second panel could have been ordered because of some defect in procedure before the completion of the first trial. Most authorities, however, agree that the first instance of calling a new trial in a civil case was ordered in 1655 in the case of *Wood v Gunston.* The action was libel, and the ground for the new trial was excessive damages of 1,500 pounds.[113] In any event it became common in the last of the seventeenth century to set aside the initial civil verdict and to call a new trial on various grounds,[114] such as: lack of notice, variance, want of a proper jury, misbehavior of a party, new evidence, surprise testimony, absence of a witness or attorney, subsequent conviction of a witness for perjury, misdirection of the jury by the judge, verdict not supported by evidence, misbehavior of jurors, and excessive damages.[115]

As to criminal trials, in two cases in 1660 new trials were ordered in favor of the king after verdicts of acquittal.[116] New trials were ordered in favor of the defendants in cases in 1673 and 1681 after a charge of perjury had been brought and proved concerning the original trials.[117] Justice Hawkins said, in 1621, that a verdict against the crown could not be set aside, although one against the defendant could.[118] The defendant, however, could not get a new trial after conviction of a capital crime, the only known exception to this taking place in 1851.[119] In 1752 it was uncertain whether the crown, at the close of the evidence, could withdraw a juror and have the cause retried. The anonymous author of *The Complete Juryman* concluded that it could not be done in capital cases and was permissible in other cases only with the consent of both parties.[120]

The procedure of a civil trial as it might have taken place in 1752 is briefly described in *The Complete Juryman*.[121] The names of the jurors were first drawn and they were sworn to this oath, "You shall well and truly try this Issue between the parties, and a true Verdict give, according to the Evidence. So help you God." When 12 were selected, the plaintiff opened with his witnesses (assuming he had the burden of proof) and the defense was permitted to cross-examine them. Then the defendant produced his witnesses after which the plaintiff was permitted to reply. After the judge summed up, the jury retired and returned with the verdict. The judge rendered judgment accordingly. Attorneys of today would not find this procedure unfamiliar.

On a charge of high treason the procedure was somewhat different.[122] The jurors were called, challenged, and sworn. The bailiff called for anyone who could inform on the charge, and the king's counsel thus opened his case. All witnesses endorsed on the back of the indictment were sworn by the clerk. This was the oath:

> The Evidence which you and every of you shall give to the court and Jury not sworn, for our Sovereign Lord the King, against the Prisoner at the Bar, shall be the Truth, the whole Truth, and nothing but the Truth. So help you God.

The defendant was permitted to cross-examine the king's witnesses and, in his turn, to question his own witnesses. The king had the right to present rebuttal. Both the prisoner and counsel for the king presented arguments and the Chairman (presiding judge) summed up the case. Then the clerk had the crier swear the bailiff:

> You shall well and truly keep this Jury without meat,

drink, Fire or Candle (if it be in the night-time, the word candle is to be omitted): You shall not suffer any person to speak unto them nor you yourself, unless to ask them, whether they are agreed of their Verdict, until they shall be agreed of their verdict. So help you God.

The jurors were then taken to a private and convenient room. They were not permitted to give a privy verdict in a case of treason. When they returned, the judge addressed them, "You of the Jury look upon the prisoner; how say you, is A.D. guilty of the High Treason of which he stands indicted, or not guilty."

If the verdict was "guilty" and the defendant was a woman, she was asked what she could say to stay execution. If she claimed to be pregnant, a panel of matrons, "12 good and motherly women," was selected" . . . to handle and inspect her Body and secret Parts." They were sworn to ". . . enquire, search and try whether the prisoner be quick with child." The oath was again given to the bailiff with the difference that it provided for the prisoner retiring with the matrons.[123] This seems to be the only jury of women in the history of the English jury, at least before the twentieth century.

In the years previous to the middle of the nineteenth century, executions were a public affair. A passage from the *Plumpton Correspondence* gives some idea of what was involved in this ceremony. The following is a reference to persons recently convicted of treason:

> . . . they should be drawn on hirdiles from the Tower, throwout London, to the Tyburne, and there to be hanged, and cut down quicke, and ther bowels to be taken out and burned; their heads to be strike of, and quartered, their head and quarters to be disposed at the Kyngs pleasure.[124]

It is to be assumed that the King would have had the heads and quarters displayed from gibbets, or stakes, along the public highways to discourage future evil conduct.

Attaint, or the punishment of jurors for rendering a false verdict, continued to be used during this period. Although knights were no longer required on ordinary juries, it remained the practice to have a knight among the 24 members of the attaint jury.[125] The early punishment heaped upon the convicted jurors (namely, forfeiture of goods, "chattels," lands, and tenements to the king; wife and children thrust out of doors; houses razed and thrown down; meadows plowed and bodies thrust into prison) was somewhat ameliorated by a statute of 1490 which provided for a 20 pound fine to be divided between the king and the prosecuting party, plus a ransom and fine at the discretion of the judge. In addition, the attainted party could never be a witness in court, and the party damaged by the first verdict was restored to what he had lost. If the matter had involved less than 40 pounds, the fine was to be five pounds only. But it seems that a party could elect to bring the attaint action under either the common law procedure or this statute.[126] A provision restricted to London and dating from 1495 limited the punishment for attaint to a 20 pound fine or more and imprisonment for six months or less, in addition to being forever forbidden to be a witness in court.

In 1542 it was held that the only evidence which could be presented to the attaint jury was that which had been submitted to the original jury.[127] If, however, the original jurors chose, they could give evidence of private knowledge which they had had at the time they gave the original verdict. If they chose to submit such evidence the party bringing the attaint could offer evidence in rebuttal[128]. This practice was more frequently used when the roles of juror and witness were more closely intertwined; after the middle of the sixteenth century, attaint was seldom used.[129]

As has been noted in an earlier chapter, the form of the early inquests left the members little room to decide questions of law. When inquests or juries began to be used more extensively in criminal cases to judge guilt or innocence, they had the power, if not the right, to decide questions of law as well as fact. This is still true today. This situation was not quite the same with respect to civil trials. In those cases, the judge had a much greater control over the result by means of such devices as the demurrer, summary judgment, directed verdict, judgment notwithstanding the verdict, new trials, remittiturs, addittiturs, and much more.

It is probable in England that the juries were far too intimidated until the last third of the seventeenth century to presume to judge anything except that which the justices told them to judge, and we can be reasonably sure the justices kept the jurors to the facts alone. At that time, however, there was great dissatisfaction with the quality of royal justice, and the jury's power to decide law as well as facts was scrutinized. In *The Security of Englishmen's Lives*, Lord Somers, Lord High Chancellor of England under King William, said in 1681:

> As it hath been the law, so it hath always been the custom, and practice of these juries, upon all general issues, pleaded in cases civil as well as criminal, to judge both of the law and fact.[130]

Sir John Hawles in 1771 stated his opinion that law should be the prerogative of the judge and facts should be left to the jury, although the jury resolves law and fact in a general verdict.[131] Part of the judge's job, according to Hawles, was to sum up fact and law, but without binding the jury.[132] Justice Holt said, in 1697:

> . . . that in all cases and in all actions the jury may give a general or special verdict, as well in causes criminal as civil, and the court ought to receive it, if it is pertinent to the issue, for if the jury doubt they may refer themselves to the court, but are not bound so to do. . . .[133]

Thus, in 1704, Justice Holt submitted not only the fact of publication of a libel and the identity of the persons in question to the jury, but the issue of criminality as well.[134]

In spite of these opinions in favor of the jury's right as well as its power to decide law, the following could be thought of as an accurate description of the state of English law in 1752:

> A question of law is not capable of being decided by any, but by those, who are learned in the Law: and therefore it is always to be determined by the Judges; but a Question of fact is for the most part to be tried by a Jury of twelve men. . . .[135]

In addition,

> If the Jury will take upon themselves the knowledge of the law, they may give a general verdict, but it is dangerous for them so to do; for if they mistake the law they run into the danger of an attaint; therefore, where

the case is doubtful, it is safest for them to find the special matter.[136]

Under this view if the jurors decided law, they were exercising a power, not a right. They would therefore be subject to punishment for attaint, which would not be true if they were exercising a right.

Contrary to this, Pettingal, writing in 1769, said that juries should have "power of Judgment in themselves."[137] Although Pettingal may in some instances be considered a "romantic," Lord Camden agreed, and was a strong advocate of this position throughout his career as defense attorney, attorney general, and upon the bench. In a speech in the House of Lords in 1770 he took exception to an opinion of Lord Mansfield's doctrine that denied the jury the right to decide the law in cases of libel. In his last speech in the House of Lords in 1792 in the debate on Fox's libel bill, he said:

> ...the jury had an undoubted right to form their verdict themselves according to their consciences applying the law to the fact; and if it were otherwise, the first principle of the law of England would be defeated and over-thrown.[138]

Burke, during debate in the House of Commons on recent decisions holding that juries had no right to decide the criminality of a libel, said, "Juries ought to take their law from the bench only; but it is our business that they should hear nothing from the bench but what is agreeable to the principles of the constitution."[139] It should be added that Burke thought juries ought to have the right to decide the criminality of the libel, and he was in favor of Parliament insuring this right.[140] This was different from saying that juries had the right to make law. He considered making law the job of Parliament.

So it is clear that, although the jury did have the right to decide matters of law in the years following the Glorious Revolution of 1688, the right eroded, and thus by the time of the American Revolution the jury in England no longer held this privilege.[141] It would have died altogether except for the agitation which was stirred up in England on the subject of libel. This debate on the right of the jury to decide law, as we will see, spilled into the colonies where it was seldom understood in terms of the origin of the controversy.

The history of the grand jury during this period was not extraordinary, as it suffered, along with the petit jury, from the existence of the Star Chamber. A statute of 1520, during the reign of Henry VIII, provided for a certificate of justice to be substituted for an indictment in a grand jury action.[142] In the eighteenth century it was the practice for the grand jury to consist of an odd number of jurors, usually more than 12. The judge would swear the foreman, and the rest of the jurors swore to abide by that oath insofar as it applied to them. It was punishable for the jurors to disclose the names of those indicted.[143] A peer would not have another trial on oath aside from a grand jury, since he would be tried in the House of Lords where no special oath would be given. In addition he would not necessarily be tried by his neighbors, but by his peers in the House. In this way it was hoped that the grand jury would have protection from having groundless charges brought against them.[144]

Several special procedures of interest have not yet been mentioned. In 1752, a jury of 12 members could be summoned in cases where only the amount of damages was contested.[145] Another hearing, apparently without the presence of a judge, was established for the County of Middlesex for causes not exceeding 40 shillings. Twelve freeholders were summoned to the court, and with the clerk decided the causes in a summary way by majority vote.[146] In an action De Aetate Prolanda in 1515 (action by a minor to establish his minority to avoid debt), the age was proved by a jury of 12. The jurors were required to give the reasons for their decisions; e.g., they had children of their own about the same age.[147] These jurors were to be at least 42 years old. The procedure was still in use in 1752.[148] Age was not, however, always proved in this way. If the cause was an action to recover a fine by reason of the fact that it had been wrongfully levied on a minor, the question of age was tried by the judges by inspection.[149]

The trial Per Medietatem Linguae was of ancient origin. In 1586, during the reign of Elizabeth, it had this form:

All manner of Inquests and Proofs, which be to be taken or made amongst Aliens and Denizens, be they Merchants or other, as well before the Mayor of the Staple as

before any other Justices or Ministers, although the King
be party, the one half of the Inquest or Proof shall be of
Denizens, and the other Half of Aliens, if so many Aliens
and Foreigners be in Town or Place where such Inquest
or Proof is to be taken, that be not Parties, nor with the
Parties in Contracts, Pleas or other Quarrels, where of
such Inquests or Proofs ought to be taken; and if there be
not so many Aliens, then shall be put in such Inquests or
Proofs as many Aliens as shall be found in the same
Towns or Places, which the Parties as afore is said, and
the Remnant of Denizens, which be good men and not
suspicious to the one Party nor to the other.[150]

This statute was repealed in the case of treason in 1554. A party
entitled to the benefit of the statute had to claim it on the award of
the writ of *venire facias* which directed the sheriff to summon the
jury. Denizens and aliens were sworn alternately. Denizens,
neither aliens nor naturalized citizens, could not be challenged
because of the lack of a freehold.[151]

Older modes of trial continued to have some validity. Trial by
compurgation was used in the court of the Hundred of Winchester
in Sussex in 1440-41,[152] and another example is found in 1699.[153]
In 1752 a person could still defend himself against the claim for a
debt not evidenced by any writing by swearing that he did not
owe the debt and finding 11 of his neighbors who would swear
to his honesty.[154] By this time, however, compurgation was
seldom used.[155]

Trial by battle continued to be at least a strict legal possibility.
In one example the parties went through the usual preliminaries in
1422. The action concerned a Writ of Right, or an action to recover
real estate in which the tenant (defendant) could either elect to put
himself upon the Grand Assize, or appeal to battle and the judgment of God. In this example the tenant chose battle and named
his champion. The demandant did likewise. Both champions were
commanded to put a penny in each finger stall of their gauntlets.
They both appeared in court on the day named, one on either side,
bare-headed and kneeling. They then went to separate churches to
pray that the outcome of the battle would be just. It is recorded that

one went to St. Paul's and the other to Westminster. The battle itself did not occur because the tenant defaulted, as his champion did not appear.[156] There were similar examples in 1571 and 1638.[157]

In 1752 *The Complete Juryman,* in addition to trial by jury, compurgation and battle, also lists trials by record (this includes former judgments, legality of marriage, bastardy, excommunication and the like by certificate of the bishop of the diocese); customs of London by word of mouth of the recorder of London; and dower by a justice.[158]

In addition to the Court of Common Pleas and the King's Bench, there were several other courts during these centuries. The Court of Equity, for example, became a distinct court in the fifteenth century.[159] The Admiralty was reorganized under Henry VII, and even held jury trials in criminal cases. The use of juries by this court disappeared when that jurisdiction was transferred to the common law courts.[160] There were also the ecclesiastical courts, the Court of the Exchequer (a branch of the Privy Council), the courts of the hundreds, and private courts.[161] A Court of High Commissioners existed only under the Tudor monarchs.[162] Justices of the Peace continued to gain in prestige and importance and, in the 1660's, were the county officials of most importance.[163]

A description of the trial of Alice Lisle for high treason in 1685 gives some idea of why there was dissatisfaction with the brand of royal justice to be had under the Restoration monarchy. The treason Alice Lisle was alleged to have committed was giving shelter to a man named Hicks after he had been engaged in rebellion against the king. The entire question depended on whether the defendant knew that Hicks had been in the rebel army when she had him in her home.

After some deliberation, this dialogue was held between the foreman of the jury and George Jefferies, Lord Chief Justice of the King's Bench:

> Foreman: My Lord, we have one thing to beg of your lordship, some directions in, before we can give our verdict in this case; We have some doubt upon us, whether there be sufficient proof that she knew Hicks to have been in the army.

L.C.J. Jefferies: There is as full as proof as proof can be, but you are judges of the proof, for my part I thought there was no difficulty in it.

Alice Lisle was convicted, attainted, and executed.

An Act of Parliament in 1689 declared:

> Whereas Alicia Lisle . . . by an irregular and undue prosecution was indicted for entertaining, concealing and comforting John Hicks, clerk, a false traitor, knowing him to be such, though, the said Hicks was not at the trial of the said Alicia Lisle, attainted or convicted of any such crime: and by a verdict injuriously exhorted and procured by the menaces and violences and other illegal practices of George Lord Jefferies, baron of Wren, the Lord Chief Justice of the King's Bench . . . that it be declared by the authority of Parliament . . . that the said conviction, judgment and attainter of the said Alicia be and are hereby repealed. . . .[164]

In the history of the jury two cases of the greatest importance were the trial of William Penn and William Mead before a jury at Old Bailey in 1670, and the sequel to the case, the Habeas Corpus action on behalf of Edward Bushell, one of the jurors at the Penn and Mead trial. The trial took place on September 1, 3, 4, and 5, 1670.[165] The case charged that Penn and Mead, with about 300 others, on the 10th of August at 11:00 o'clock in the Parish of St. Bennet Grace-Church,

> . . . unlawfully and tumultously did assemble and congregate themselves together, to the disturbance of the peace of the said lord the king . . . William Penn . . . did take upon himself to preach and speak . . . unto the . . . persons there assembled . . .

causing, it was alleged, great terror and disturbance to the people. Mead was charged with conspiring with Penn to cause the disturbance.

As the trial commenced, Penn desired a copy of the indictment to read before making his plea. He was told that he could have it afterwards. Penn and Mead were both fined 40 marks for not having their hats on, although one of the court attachés had told them to uncover their heads. Bushell, one of the jurors, had to be sworn again, as it was claimed he had not kissed the book. During the evidence, which apparently consisted only of crown witnesses, Penn conducted an intelligent and spirited cross-examination. Mead refused to answer a question of the recorder (judge) on the ground "that no man is bound to accuse himself."

The jury had been retired for an hour and a half when it returned with eight in agreement. At this point, J. Robinson, a member of the bench in the case, had this exchange with Bushell:

> J. Robinson: Mr. Bushell, I have known you near this 14 years; you have thrust yourself upon this jury because you think there is some service for you: I tell you, you deserve to be indicted more than any man that hath been brought to bar this day;

> Bushell: No, Sir John, there were threescore before me, and I would willingly have got off, but could not.

The jury retired for the second time and returned with this verdict, "Guilty of speaking Grace-Church Street." This did not satisfy the court who wanted the words "unlawful assembly" to be included in the verdict. The Recorder said:

> The law of England will not allow you to part till you have given in your verdict.

> Jury: We have given in our verdict and we can give in no other.

The jury asked for and was given pen and ink whereupon they retired again. They soon returned with this written verdict:

> William Penn to be Guilty of speaking or preaching to an assembly, met together in Grace-Church Street, the 14 of August last 1670. And that William Mead is Not Guilty of the said Indictment.

Foreman Thomas Veer and the names of the others were on the verdict, the second being Bushell. The Recorder's reply was,

> Gentlemen, you shall not be dismissed till we have a verdict that the court will accept: and you shall be locked

up, without meat, drink, fire, and tobacco; we shall have
a verdict, by the help of God, or you shall starve for it.

Penn then addressed the jurors, telling them that he and Mead
had used no force of arms but had met outdoors because soldiers
had kept them out of their houses. He also said,

You are Englishmen, mind your privilege, give not away
your right.

Bushell and others: Nor will we ever do it.

One juror now claimed to be indisposed and desired to be
dismissed. The mayor, also a part of the bench, said, "You are as
strong as any of them; starve them; and hold your principles."

This was on the third of September. It being time for court to
close for the day, an observer (probably Penn) described the
proceeding:

The court swore several persons to keep the Jury all night
without meat, drink, fire or any other accommodation;
they had not so much as a chamberpot, though desired.

The next day the jury returned a verdict finding Mead not
guilty and Penn guilty of speaking in Grace-Church Street. The
Recorder said he could not receive the verdict because the charge
included conspiracy and the verdicts were inconsistent. Whereupon, Penn said:

If Not Guilty be not a verdict, then you make the jury and
Magna Carta but a mere nose of wax.

The jury retired again and returned with the same verdict. This was
once more turned down by the bench. On their part the jury
refused the suggestion that they return a special verdict. They were
remanded to Newgate for the night. The following day, the fifth, the
jury returned a verdict of not guilty as to both parties. It appears
that the jury had been without food and drink in excess of two days.

The Recorder fined the jury 40 marks each (a little over 26
pounds) and sent them to jail until it was paid. Penn was fined for
contempt. He protested, citing passages of the Magna Carta. Penn
also had the last word, saying later, "Magna Charta is Magna f____

with the Recorder of London; and to demand right an affront to the court."

Bushell, on his part, did not take the fine lying down. He obtained a writ of Habeas Corpus.[166] The opinion was written on November 20th of the same year by Chief Justice Vaughan, and never after were juries to be punished for not finding in accordance with the court's instructions. The moment is marked for posterity by a plaque hanging in Old Bailey and inscribed as follows:

Near this Site
WILLIAM PENN and WILLIAM MEAD
were tried in 1670
for preaching to an unlawful assembly
in Grace-Church Street
This tablet Commemorates

The courage and endurance of the Jury Thos Vere, Edward Bushell and ten others who refused to give a Verdict against them, although locked up without food for two nights and were fined for their final Verdict of Not Guilty.

The case of these Jurymen was reviewed on a Writ of Habeas Corpus and Chief Justice Vaughan delivered the opinion of the Court which established 'The Right of Juries' to give their Verdict according to their Convictions.

Another famous and important jury trial in England in the late seventeenth century was the "The Trial of Seven Bishops."[167] The seven bishops, including Dr. William Sancroft, the Archbishop of Canterbury, were arrested on June 15, 1688. They were charged with publishing a seditious libel against his Majesty King James II and his government.

The King had issued a paper entitled Declaration of Indulgence (the second such paper) in April of 1688. He ordered that this Declaration be read in all churches. On May 18 the seven Bishops, headed by Dr. Sancroft, objected to this order and drafted a petition of protest which was sent to the King. The Bishops were released on their own recognizance, and the trial was scheduled to commence on June 29, 1688. In the meantime the Bishops, never particularly popular, were greeted with enthusiasm by large crowds in London.[168]

The Lord Chief Justice, Sir Robert Wright, summed up the case for the jury. He told the jury that they had two questions to decide, namely, was there a libel and was it published. He gave it as his opinion that the answers to these questions were that there was a libel and that it was published. There were three other justices. Of these, Justices Holloway and Powell summed up favorably to the defendants, and Justice Allybond summed up favorably to the crown.

The Lord Chief Justice asked the jury if they wanted a drink before retiring. After the jury retired, at their request, they were furnished with certain items of evidence and the charges against the Bishops. The jury stayed in session all night without fire or candle. They were unanimous in returning a not guilty verdict. Shouts of joy went up in Westminster Hall. This series of events helped trigger The Glorious Revolution of 1688 which saw James II deposed and William of Orange enthroned as King of England.

Because of the jurors in the Penn and Mead case and the jurors in the Trial of the Seven Bishops, the jury deserved the high position it held in the esteem of Englishmen. In time to come the jury was to lose much of its vitality in the country that had nurtured it. The Englishmen, however, who were at the very time settling the American colonies, carried with them from the earliest times the jury as a guarantee of liberty. In North America the jury was to gain new life and new meaning.

Chapter VI Footnotes

1. *The Security of Englishmen's Lives,* Lord Somers (London, 1766 Ed., reprint of 1681), p. 102.

2. *History of Trial By Jury,* William Forsyth (John W. Parker and Son, London, 1852), pp. 96-97.

3. *A Preliminary Treatise on Evidence,* James Bradley Thayer (Sweet and Maxwell, London, 1898), p. 75.

4. *Id.* at p. 76.

5. "Early Opposition to the Petty Jury In Criminal Cases," Charles L. Wells, 30 Law Q. Rev. 97, at 104.

6. Thayer, *op. cit.* at note 3, at p. 76.

7. Wells, *op. cit.* at note 5, p. 104.

8. *The Proof of Guilt,* Glanville Williams (Stevens and Sons, London, 1963 ed., 1st printed 1955), p. 13.

9. *The Complete Juryman,* anonymous (London, 1752), pp. 162-63.

10. *Id.* at p. 35.

11. *The Complete Juryman, op. cit.* at note 9, at p. 36.

12. *A History of English Law,* Sir William Holdsworth (Sweet and Maxwell Ltd., London, 7th Ed. 1956, 1st Ed. 1903), I-332.

13. Thayer, *op. cit.* at note 3, at p. 91.

14. *A Guide To English Juries,* By a Person of Quality (Attr. by Forsyth to Lord Somers) (London, 1682), p. 5.

15. *The Complete Juryman, op. cit.* at note 9, at pp. 26, 27.

16. *The Statutes at Large,* I William and Mary, Sess. 2.C2. 1698 (Cambridge, 1762), Vol. I.

17. *The Complete Juryman, op. cit.* at note 9, at p. 11.

18. *The Complete Juryman, op. cit.* at note 9, at p. 5 of preface.

19. *The Complete Juryman, op. cit.* at note 9, at p. 79.

20. *The Complete Juryman, op. cit.* at note 9, at pp. 37-40.

21. *A Guide To English Juries, op. cit.* at note 14, at p. 7.

22. *The Complete Juryman, op. cit.* at note 9, at pp. 107-10.

23. *The Complete Juryman, op. cit.* at note 9, at pp. 128-30.

24. Holdsworth, *op. cit.* at note 12, at I-336.

25. *The Complete Juryman, op. cit.* at note 9, at p. 114.

26. *The Complete Juryman, op. cit.* at note 9, at pp. 31-33.

27. *The Complete Juryman, op. cit.* at note 9, at pp. 135-38.

28. *The Complete Juryman, op. cit.* at note 9, at pp. 128-30, 133.

29. *Plumpton Correspondence,* Thomas Stapleton, editor (John Bowyer Nichols and Son, London, 1839), p. 134.

30. *The Complete Juryman, op. cit.* at note 9, at p. 151.

31. *The Complete Juryman, op. cit.* at note 9, at pp. 73-75.

32. Thayer, *op. cit.* at note 3, at p. 92.

33. *Id.*

34. *Plumpton Correspondence, op. cit.* at note 29, at p. 159.

35. *Plumpton Correspondence, op. cit.* at note 29, at p. 134.

36. *A Guide To English Juries, op. cit.* at note 14, at p. 202.

37. *History of Trial By Jury,* William Forsyth (John Parker and Son, London, 1852), p. 172.

38. *Id.* at p. 176.

39. "Trial By Juror and the Reform of Civil Procedure," Austin Wakeman, 31 Harv. L. Rev. 669 (1918), at p. 677.

40. *History of the English Law,* John Reeves (Reed and Hunter, London, 1814), IV-195.

41. *The Complete Juryman, op. cit.* at note 9, at p. 122.

42. *The Complete Juryman, op. cit.* at note 9, at p. 171.

43. *The Complete Juryman, op. cit.* at note 9, at p. 170.

44. *The Complete Juryman, op. cit.* at note 9, at p. 171.

45. *Ibid.,* and *Trial by Jury,* Sir Patrick Devlin (Stevens and Sons, London, 3rd Ed. 1966, 1st printed 1956), p. 50.

46. Williams, *op. cit.* at note 8, at p. 6.

47. Somers, *op. cit.* at note 1, at p. 103.

48. *A Guide to English Juries, op. cit.* at note 14, at p. 103.

49. *The Complete Juryman, op. cit.* at note 9, at p. 4.

50. *The Jury,* W.R. Cornish (Penguin Press, London, 1968), p. 70.

51. Williams, *op. cit.* at note 8, at p. 11.

52. Williams, *op. cit.* at note 8, at p. 73.

53. *The Complete Juryman, op. cit.* at note 9, at p. 206.

54. Williams, *op. cit.* at note 8, at p. 70.

55. Wells, *op. cit.* at note 5, at p. 108.

56. *Ibid.*

57. Williams, *op. cit.* at note 8, at p. 6.

58. Wells, *op. cit.* at note 5, at p. 108.

59. Cornish, *op. cit.* at note 50, at p. 72; Wells, *op. cit.* at note 5, at p. 108, citing cases in 1565 and 1590 where only crown witnesses were presented.

60. Williams, *op. cit.* at note 8, at p. 70.

61. Holdsworth, *op. cit.* at note 12, at I-325-26.

62. *State Trials,* T.B. Howell, editor (T.C. Hansard, London, 1816), Vol. I, p. xxix of the preface.

63. Forsyth, *op. cit.* at note 37, at p. 161.

64. Holdsworth, *op. cit.* at note 12, at I-335.

65. *Ibid.*

66. Thayer, *op. cit.* at note 3, at p. 125.

67. Holdsworth, *op. cit.* at note 12, at I-335.

68. Williams, *op cit.* at note 8, at p. 206.

69. Holdsworth, *op. cit.* at note 12, at I-319, 343.

70. Wakeman, *op. cit.* at note 39, at p. 680.

71. Thayer, *op. cit.* at note 3, at p. 211.

72. *A Guide to English Juries, op. cit.* at note 14, at p. 38.

73. *Id.* at p. 125.

74. Cornish, *op. cit.* at note 56, at p. 32-33.

75. *The Complete Juryman, op. cit.* at note 9, at pp. 66, 68.

76. Thayer, *op. cit.* at note 3, at p. 94.

77. Thayer, *op. cit.* at note 3, at p. 96.

78. *The Complete Juryman, op. cit.* at note 9, at p. 5 of preface and p. 66.

79. *The Complete Juryman, op. cit.* at note 9, at p. 175.

80. *The Complete Juryman, op. cit.* at note 9, at p. 176.

81. *The Complete Juryman, op. cit.* at note 9, at pp. 174, 194.

82. Forsyth, *op. cit.* at note 37, at p. 185.

83. Thayer, *op. cit.* at note 3, at p. 162.

84. *Ibid.*

85. Reeves, *op. cit.* at note 40, IV-195.

86. Cornish, *op. cit.* at note 50, at p. 128.

87. Thayer, *op. cit.* at note 3, at p. 164.

88. Thayer, *op. cit.* at note 3, at pp. 164-66.

89. *State Trials, op. cit.* at note 62, at VI-995.

90. Williams, *op. cit.* at note 8, at p. 257.

91. Holdsworth, *op. cit.* at note 12, at I-343-44.

92. *The Englishman's Right,* Sir John Hawles (6th ed., London, 1771, reprint of 1680 ed.), p. 31.

93. *The Complete Juryman, op. cit.* at note 9, at p. 205.

94. *The History of Lay Judges,* John P. Dawson (Harvard Univ. Press, Cambridge, Mass., 1960), p. 172.

95. *An Enquiry Into the Doctrine Lately Propagated Concerning Libels, Warrants and the Seizure of Papers,* Father of Candor (Burlington House, London, 1764), p. 5.

96. Williams, *op. cit.* at note 8, at p. 402.

97. Holdsworth, *op. cit.* at note 12, at pp. I-343-44.

98. Forsyth, *op. cit.* at note 37, at p. 185.

99. Thayer, *op. cit.* at note 3, at pp. 162-63.

100. *The Works and Correspondence of Edmund Burke,* Charles William, editor (Francis and John Rivington, London, 1852 ed., 1st ed. 1844), IV-40.

101. Thayer, *op. cit.* at note 3, at p. 101.

102. Thayer, *op. cit.* at note 3, at p. 102.

103. Devlin, *op. cit.* at note 45, at pp. 69, 70.

104. Thayer, *op. cit.* at note 3, at pp. 111, 174.

105. *The Complete Juryman, op. cit.* at note 9, at p. 177.

106. *State Trials, op. cit.* at note 62, at VII-259.

107. Thayer, *op. cit.* at note 3, at p. 174.

108. *The Origin of Juries,* Heinrich Brunner (Berlin, 1872), p. 437.

109. Thayer, *op. cit.* at note 3, at p. 104.

110. *Commentaries on the Laws of England,* William Blackstone (7th Ed., Oxford, 1775, 1st ed. 1665), III-367.

111. *The Complete Juryman, op. cit.* at note 9, at p. 262.

112. *Plumpton Correspondence, op. cit.* at note 29, at p. 141.

113. Wakeman, *op. cit.* at note 39, at p. 681; Forsyth, *op. cit.* at note 37, at p. 161; Thayer, *op. cit.* at note 3, at p. 170.

114. Thayer, *op. cit.* at note 3, at p. 172.

115. Forsyth, *op. cit.* at note 37, at pp. 188-91.

116. Thayer, *op. cit.* at note 3, at p. 175.

117. Thayer, *op. cit.* at note 3, at p. 177.

118. *Ibid.*

119. Thayer, *op. cit.* at note 3, at p. 178.

120. *The Complete Juryman, op. cit.* at note 9, at p. 166.

121. *The Complete Juryman, op. cit.* at note 9, at p. 164.

122. *The Complete Juryman, op. cit.* at note 9, at pp. 154-59.

123. *The Complete Juryman, op. cit.* at note 9, at pp. 159-61.

124. *Plumpton Correspondence, op. cit.* at note 29, at p. 141.

125. *The Complete Juryman, op. cit.* at note 9, at p. 23.

126. Thayer, *op. cit.* at note 3, at pp. 151-52.

127. Thayer, *op. cit.* at note 3, at p. 154.

128. *A Guide to English Juries, op. cit.* at note 14, at pp. 29-30.

129. Holdsworth, *op. cit.* at note 12, at I-342.

130. Somers, *op. cit.* at note 1, at p. 11.

131. Hawles, *op. cit.* at note 92, at p. 14.

132. Hawles, *op. cit.* at note 92, at p. 11.

133. *Reports of Cases Argued and Adjudged in the Superior Court of Judicature of the Province of Massachusetts Bay Between 1761-1772,* Josiah Quincy, Jr., editor (Little, Brown, and Company, Boston, 1865), p. 561.

134. *Ibid.*

135. *The Complete Juryman, op. cit.* at note 9, at p. 2.

136. *The Complete Juryman, op. cit.* at note 9, at p. 246.

137. *An Enquiry into the Use and Practice of Juries Among the Greeks and Romans,* John Pettingal (London, 1769), pp. 121-22.

138. Quincy, *op. cit.* at note 133, at p. 562.

139. Williams, *op. cit.* at note 100, at IV-145.

140. Williams, *op. cit.* at note 100, at IV-138-46.

141. Quincy, *op. cit.* at note 133, at p. 562; Wakeman, *op. cit.* at note 39, at p. 677.

142. Pettingal, *op. cit.* at note 137, at p. 35.

143. *The Complete Juryman, op. cit.* at note 9, at pp. 12, 18.

144. *A Guide to English Juries, op. cit.* at note 14, at p. 60.

145. *The Complete Juryman, op. cit.* at note 9, at p. 3.

146. *Capital Traction v. Hof,* 174 U.S. 1 (1898), at p. 17.

147. Thayer, *op. cit.* at note 3, at p. 20.

148. *The Complete Juryman, op. cit.* at note 9, at p. 36.

149. *The Complete Juryman, op. cit.* at note 9, at p. 278.

150. *The Complete Juryman, op. cit.* at note 9, at p. 146.

151. *The Complete Juryman, op. cit.* at note 9, at pp. 23, 148, 165.

152. Thayer, *op. cit.* at note 3, at p. 26.

153. Thayer, *op. cit.* at note 3, at p. 31.

154. *The Complete Juryman, op. cit.* at note 9, at p. 281.

155. Thayer, *op. cit.* at note 3, at p. 32.

156. *The Complete Juryman, op. cit.* at note 9, at pp. 283-84.

157. Thayer, *op. cit.* at note 3, at p. 43.

158. *The Complete Juryman, op. cit.* at note 9, at pp. 278-82.

159. Dawson, *op. cit.* at note 94, at p. 149.

160. Dawson, *op. cit.* at note 94, at p. 174.

161. Dawson, *op. cit.* at note 94, at pp. 174, 182.

162. Dawson, *op. cit.* at note 94, at p. 174.

163. Dawson, *op. cit.* at note 94, at p. 297.

164. *State Trials, op. cit.* at note 62, at VI-298-307.

165. *State Trials, op. cit.* at note 62, at VI-951-969.

166. *State Trials, op. cit.* at note 62, at VI-999-1111.

167. *State Trials, op. cit.* at note 62, at XII-183-431.

168. *A History of the English-Speaking Peoples, The New World,* Vol. 2, p. 402, Winston S. Churchill, Dodd, Mead & Company, New York, 1966.

VII
The Jury in America to 1791

When Englishmen first came to North America, they brought trial by jury with them. The First Charter of Virginia (1606) provided that all subjects in the colonies should,

> ... have and enjoy all Liberties, Franchises, and Immunities within any of our Dominions, to all Intents and Purposes, as if they had been abidding and born, within this our realm of England, or any other of our said Dominions.[1]

The right to trial by jury was specifically mentioned in King James I's Instructions for the Government of the Colony of Virginia, on November 20, 1606. Minor offenses such as drunkenness and idleness were not tried by a jury. All capital crimes, which included major disturbances, rebellion, conspiracy, sedition, murder, manslaughter, incest, rape, and adultery, were to be tried by juries.[2]

Trial by jury was introduced into the Massachusetts Bay Colony by 1628.[3] The Massachusetts Body of Liberties, adopted by the General Court of Massachusetts on December 10, 1641, contains detailed and unusual provisions concerning trial by jury. The following are those provisions:

> Art. 29 — In all actions at law it shall be the libertee of the plaintife and defendant by mutual consent to choose whether they will be tryed by the Bench or by a Jurie, unless it be where the law upon just reason hath otherwise determined. The like libertie shall be granted to all persons in criminall cases.

> Art. 30 — It shall be in libertie both of Plaintife and defendant, and likewise every delinquent (to be judged by a Jurie) to challenge any of the Jurors and if his challenge be found just and reasonable by the Bench, or the rest of the Jurie, as the challenger shall choose, it shall be allowed him. And tales de cercumstantibus impaneled in their room.

Art. 31 — In all cases where evidence is so obscure or defective that the Jurie cannot clearly and safely give a positive verdict, whether it be a grand or petit Jurie, It shall have libertie to give a nonLiquit, or a spetiall verdict, in which last, that is in a spetiall verdict, the Judgment of the cause shall be left to the Court, and all Jurors shall have libertie in matters of fact if they cannot finde the maine issue, yet to find and present in their verdict so much as they can, If the Bench and Jurors shall so differ at any time about their verdict that either of them cannot proceede with peace of conscience the case shall be referred to the General Court, who shall take the question from both and determine it.

Article 57 provided for the summoning of a jury of 12 freemen to inquire into the cause of death. Article 49 limited jury service to two courts a year, except grand jurors were required to hold at least two courts a year. The Jurors, pursuant to Article 50, were chosen by the freemen of the town where they lived. Finally, there were these two interesting provisions:

Art. 76 — Whensoever any Jurie of trialls or Jurors are not cleare in their Judgments or conscience conserning any cause wherein they are to give their verdict, they shall have libertie in open Court to advise with any man they think fitt to resolve or direct them before they give in their verdict.

Art. 77 — In all cases wherein any freeman is to give his vote, be it in point of Election, making constitutions and orders, or passing sentence in any case of Judicature or the like, if he cannot see reason to give it positively one way or an other, he shall have libertie to be silent, and not be pressed to a determined vote.[4]

The Concessions and Agreements of West New Jersey (1677) contained the following guarantee of trial by jury:

Chp. XVII — That no Proprietor, freeholder or inhabitant of the said Province of West New Jersey, shall be deprived or condemned of life, limb, liberty, estate, property or any ways hurt in his or their privileges, freedoms or franchises, upon any account whatsoever, without a due tryal, and judgment passed by twelve, good and lawful men of his neighbourhood first had: and that in all causes to be tryed, and in all tryals, the person or persons, arraigned may except against any of the said neighbourhood, without any reason rendered, (not exceeding thirty-five) and in case of any valid reason alleged, against every person nominated for that service.[5]

When the English occupied New Amsterdam in 1664 and renamed it New York, they again brought the jury with them. In early cases on Long Island, an appeal was permitted from a jury verdict to a court of equity.[6] Jury trials were held in Pennsylvania under the Duke as early as 1673, and in that year, county courts were instituted with juries of six or seven, where a majority could render a verdict.[7] The Frame of Government of Pennsylvania (1682), the year after William Penn was made proprietor of the colony, contained this provision:

VIII. That all trials shall be by twelve men, and as near as may be, peers or equals, and of the neighbourhood, and men without just exception; in cases of life, there shall be first twenty-four returned by the Sheriffs, for a grand inquest, of whom twelve, at least, shall find the complaint to be true; and then the twelve men, or peers, to be likewise returned by the sheriff, shall have the final judgment. But reasonable challenges shall be always admitted against the said twelve men, or any of them.[8]

In early Connecticut upon the continual failure of the jurors to agree, the verdict could be decided by a majority vote; if it was a tie, the magistrate presiding cast the deciding vote.[9] By at least 1693 a jury could be waived in misdemeanor cases in Baltimore,[10] and even admiralty cases were tried by juries in some states.[11] During colonial times trial judges were generally unpopular, incompetent, and without legal training.[12] It may be by reason of these considerations that their powers at trial were limited in both civil and criminal cases.[13] Lawyers were as unpopular as judges. Chapter XXII of the Concessions and Agreements of West New Jersey provided that, ". . . no person or persons shall be compelled to fee any attorney or counciller to plead his cause, but all persons have free liberty to plead his own cause, if he please. . . ."[14] It is reasoned that the absence of lawyers made impossible a highly developed system of law.[15]

Trial by jury had its setbacks during colonial times. It was not adopted initially in New Haven.[16] After the early settlement of Virginia, the jury system had been restrained by laws contrary to the common law of England, although this problem was corrected by legislation in 1661-62.[17] During the late colonial period, British procedures did not provide for jury trial for crimes relating to liquor, labor, smuggling, and assaults.[18]

The charge of attaint was a problem to jurors in America as it was in England, and was used, for example, in Rhode Island.[19] The Massachusetts General Court passed an act requiring every verdict of a jury to be accepted unless the party which lost attainted the jury, whereupon the court would impanel a jury of 24 upon whose verdict final judgment was rendered.[20] This remedy became so popular by 1684 that another statute was passed providing that if the person bringing the attaint lost, he would be fined 34 pounds and the jury against which the attaint was brought could prosecute him for slander.[21] The remedy became less popular.[22] Alexander Hamilton, in *The Federalist*, makes reference to appeals from one jury to another in Georgia, Rhode Island, Connecticut, New Hampshire, and Massachusetts, until one party had two verdicts.[23] He was probably referring to attaint. By Hamilton's time the remedy was nearly as obsolete in the colonies as in England.[24]

As in England, the practice of ordering a new trial in civil cases when the trial judge disagreed with the verdict made attaint unnecessary. When the order was made by a court of appeal, the order for a new trial was called a *venire facias de novo.*[25] Special verdicts were used as early as 1657 in Massachusetts,[26] and a number of examples of new trials are reported for Pennsylvania for the 1760's.[27]

For minor crimes, conviction and punishment could be had without a jury. Punishment by whipping (up to 10 strokes), the stocks (up to three hours), the ducking stool, and fines and imprisonment could all be imposed by magistrates in Massachusetts without a jury. If, however, bond was posted, a jury could be had on appeal.[28]

The importance of jury trial to the colonists and early citizens of the newly formed American republic is proved by the frequency to which it was referred in their revolutionary and constitutional documents. The Declaration of Rights of the First Continental Congress, issued on October 14, 1774, included this passage:

> . . . the respective colonies are entitled to the common law of England, and more especially to the great and inestimable privilege of being tried by their peers of the vincinage according to the course of law.[29]

On October 19, 1775, The First Session of the American Stamp Act Congress issued resolutions considered to contain " . . . the most essential rights and liberties of the colonists . . . " among which was the clause, "That trial by jury is the inherent and invaluable right of every British subject in these Colonies."[30] Nine of the thirteen colonies supported this principle,[31] and in fact, it became an increasingly influential argument in the debate against English rule. On July 6, 1775, as one of the reasons for taking up arms, it was claimed that the colonists had been deprived ". . . of the accustomed and inestimable privilege of trial by jury, in cases affecting both life and property." This statement was contained in the "Declaration of the Causes and Necessity of Taking Up Arms."[32]

The Constitution of Virginia was published on June 12, 1776 and adopted June 29, 1776, and can be considered the first written constitution of a modern republican goverment. These guarantees of trial by a jury were contained in Virginia's Bill of Rights:

> Sec. 8. That in all capital or criminal prosecutions a man has a right, to a speedy trial by an impartial jury of twelve men of his vincinage, without whose unanimous consent he cannot be found guilty, . . . that no man be deprived of his liberty, except by the law of the land or the judgment of his peers.

> Sec. 11. That in controversies respecting property, and in suits between man and man, the ancient trial by jury is preferable to any other, and ought to be held sacred.[33]

The reference to "judgment of his peers" was a clear reference to the Magna Carta, which, regardless of the scholars, is still regarded as the original guarantee of the jury trial. Section 11 of Virginia's Bill of Rights was in fact a specific guarantee of jury trial in civil cases, and the lack of such a guarantee was one of Thomas Jefferson's objections to the United States Constitution before the Bill of Rights was passed.[34]

The Declaration of Independence, on the matter of jury trial, was brief but to the point, declaring that one of the reasons necessitating the separation of the colonies from England was, "For depriving us, in many cases, of the benefits of Trial by Jury."[35] The Articles of Confederation, drafted in 1777, contained no provision establishing a judiciary system,[36] but when the Continental Congress did have an opportunity to establish a system of trial, it provided for trial by jury. The Ordinance For the Government of the Territory of the United States Northwest of the Ohio River was passed on July 13, 1787, and revived under the new Constitution, dated August 7, 1799. It provided:

Art. 11 — The inhabitants of the said territory shall be entitled to the benefits of the writs of habeas corpus and of the trial by jury. . . . No man shall be deprived of his liberty or property, but by the judgment of his peers, or the law of the land. . . .[37]

For the most part the states were quicker to incorporate the right to trial by jury into formal documents. Pennsylvania, on August 16, 1776, adopted provisions relative to jury trial which were very nearly identical to those contained in the constitution of Virginia.[38] The provision adopted by Delaware in September of the same year was also much the same as Virginia's guarantee of jury trial in criminal cases.[39] On November 3, 1776, Maryland adopted the following constitutional provisions guaranteeing trial by jury:

III. That the inhabitants of Maryland are entitled to the common law of England and the trial by jury. . .

XIX. That in all criminal prosecutions, every man hath a right to . . . a speedy trial by an impartial jury, without whose unanimous consent he ought not to be found guilty.

XXI. . . . or deprived of his life, liberty or property, but by the judgment of his peers, or by the law of the land.[40]

On December 14, 1776, the constitution of North Carolina achieved much the same objectives with substantially different language:

> IX. That no freeman shall be convicted of any crime but by the unanimous verdict of a jury of good and lawful men, in open court as heretofore used.

> XIV. That in all controversies at law, respecting property, the ancient mode of trial, by jury, is one of the best securities of the rights of the people, and ought to remain sacred and inviolate.[41]

The word "freeman" was no doubt a reference to the institution of slavery as it existed in America, but it is also reminiscent of the language of the Magna Carta and the dual status with regard to the condition of freedom that also existed in England at that early time.

Vermont, on July 8, 1777, adopted constitutional provisions insuring trial by jury in both criminal and civil causes much like those adopted by Virginia.[42] In the same year Georgia adopted constitutional provisions guaranteeing trial by jury with this addition: ". . . the jury shall be judges of law, as well as fact, and shall not be allowed to bring in a special verdict."[43]

Massachusetts adopted its constitution on October 25, 1780, and guaranteed trial by jury in language differing from the rest:

> XII. . . . And no subject shall be arrested, imprisoned, despoiled or deprived his property, immunities, or privileges, put out of the protection of the law, exiled, or deprived of his life, liberty, or estate, but by the judgment of his peers or the law of the land.

> And the legislature shall not make any law that shall subject any person to a capital or infamous punishment, excepting for the government of the army or navy, without trial by Jury.

> XV. In all controversies concerning property, and in all suits between two or more persons, except in cases in which it has heretofore been otherways used and practiced, the parties have a right to a trial by jury; and this method of procedure

shall be held sacred, unless, in causes arising on the high seas, and such as relate to mariners' wages, the legislature hereafter find it necessary to alter it.[44]

This constitution, while substantially similar to the language of Article 39 of the Magna Carta, seems concerned that the protection not be too broad, hence the exceptions for the military, past practice, and mariners' wages. Of the models available in 1774, New Hampshire chose to substantially adopt Massachusetts' jury guarantees.[45]

Connecticut, despite its lack of actual constitutional provisions for trial by jury, made perhaps more use of the jury than many of the other states because they did not have distinct courts of chancery and admirality.[46] Rhode Island, on the other hand, did not adopt a constitution until 1843, but continued under the Colonial Charter of 1663.[47]

The effort to preserve the jury in a pure form is highlighted by a case decided by the Supreme Court of New Jersey in the year 1780. The legislature had passed a statute providing for a jury of six. The court held this provision unconstitutional, saying, ". . . the inestimable right of trial by jury shall remain confirmed as part of the law of this colony without repeal forever." This was the first piece of legislation to be held unconstitutional in the United States.[48]

When the Federal Constitution became effective on March 4, 1789, it contained this provision guaranteeing trial by jury in criminal cases:

> Art. 3, Sec. 2 (in part) — The Trial of all Crimes, except in cases of Impeachment, shall be by Jury; and such Trial shall be held in the State where the said Crime shall have been committed; but when not committed within any State, the Trial shall be at such place or places as the Congress may by Law have enacted.[49]

This laconic provision was deemed insufficient, as it was objected that it contained no provision for the trial of civil cases by the jury. This prompted Alexander Hamilton to devote number 83 of the *Federalist* papers to this subject. He observed:

The objection to the plan of the convention, which has met with most success in this State, and perhaps in several of the other States, is *that relative to the want of a constitutional provision* for the trial by jury in civil cases. [Emphasis Hamilton's][50]

He was quick to note that all concerned valued the jury:

The friends and adversaries of the plan of the convention, if they agree in nothing else, concur at least in the value they set upon the trial by jury; or if there is any difference between them it consists in this: the former regard it as a valuable safeguard to liberty; the latter represent it as the palladium of free government.[51]

Hamilton's own view held the criminal jury in "high estimation,"[52] but he could not". . . readily discern the inseparable connection between the existence of liberty, and the trial by jury in civil cases."[53]

While the opponents did not defeat the adoption of the Constitution, they did suceed in having it amended to insure the preservation of the right to trial by jury. They were so successful in this respect that when the Bill of Rights was sent to the legislatures of the states for ratification, no less than three out of 10 of the proposed amendments contained guarantees of various aspects of trial by jury:

Amendment V — No person shall be held to answer for a capital, or otherwise infamous crime, unless on a presentment or indictment of a Grand Jury, except in cases arising in the land or naval forces, or in the Militia, when in actual service in time of War or public danger; . . . .

Amendment VI — In all criminal prosecutions the accused shall enjoy the right to a speedy and public trial, by an impartial jury of the State and district wherein the crime shall have been committed, which district shall have been previously ascertained by law, and to be informed of the nature and cause of the accusation; to be confronted with the witnesses against him; to have compulsory process for obtaining witnesses in his

favor, and to have the assistance of Counsel for
his defense. . . .

Amendment VII — In suits at common law, where the
value in controversy shall exceed twenty dollars,
the right of trial by jury shall be preserved, and no fact tried
by a jury shall be otherwise re-examined in any court of
the United States, than according to the rules of the
common law.

In the Penn-Mead trial, (discussed in the last chapter) the defendants were not clearly informed of the nature of the charge before
their plea was taken, they were not permitted to call witnesses, and
they were not permitted counsel for their defense. Counsel for the
defense did not have a full right of participation even in England at
this time, although they were allowed to cross-examine witnesses of
the crown. Counsel could not address the jury in criminal cases, although in "all criminal prosecutions" the defendant was to have a
right to trial by jury. No doubt, latent memories of the Star Chamber
suggested the provision regarding grand juries. The jury trial guaranteed in the Bill of Rights was therefore something more than the
right enjoyed by Englishmen in 1791.

It was seen in the last chapter how juries had obtained the right
to decide law as well as facts after the Glorious Revolution of
1688 and how that privilege had been lost by the middle of the
eighteenth century. At the time of the American Revolution the
juries in the colonies generally had the prerogative to decide law
and fact in civil as well as in criminal cases. In cases decided in 1692,
1764, 1767, and 1773 in Pennsylvania, it was held that the jurors had
this right.[54] In a case in Pennsylvania in 1784 opposing counsel
argued different law and the jury was charged to make up its own
mind as to which was correct.[55] There was only one judge in the
United States who, between 1776 and 1800, was to deny the jury the
right to decide law in criminal cases. This judge presided in a court
of common pleas in Pennsylvania and made this ruling in 1793 in
the case of *Pennsylvania v. Bell*. He was afterwards impeached by the
House of Representatives of Pennsylvania and removed by the
Pennsylvania Senate, on the grounds of interference with the
rights of a fellow judge in the charging of grand and petit juries.[56]
The judge was also disqualified to hold any judicial office in the

state. By constitutional provision Pennsylvania provided in 1790 that, ". . . in all indictments for libels the jury shall have a right to determine the law and the facts under the direction of the court, as in other cases."[57] The words "as in other cases" must have been attached to make sure the provision was not taken to imply the absence of the right in non-libel cases. This is an example of the concern which libel cases stirred up.

New York juries had the right to decide law in criminal cases between 1776 and 1800. Although their right was not clear in civil cases, as the New York Court of Appeals was divided on this question in 1804.[58] The trial of John Peter Zenger for libel in 1735 gives some idea of how the colonial juries came by the right to decide law.[59] Zenger, a printer, had accused the governor of New York with maladministration, corruption, and taking the right of trial by jury from the citizens. The preliminaries included a dispute over the jurors' qualifications; however, forty-eight freeholders were chosen and Zenger was permitted to strike 12 of them. Finally, the twelve remaining jurors were chosen for the trial. By this time Zenger was represented by Andrew Hamilton of Philadelphia (Zenger's first two lawyers had been disbarred because their defense was too effective). The words and the publication in question were admitted. Counsel for the crown thought nothing remained but for the jury to return a verdict for the king, but Hamilton argued that they should be permitted to prove the truth of the charges made by Zenger, and in the event his proof was accepted, the words would not be held libelous.

Hamilton's position drew the comment from the presiding Chief Justice, "You cannot be admitted, Mr. Hamilton, to give the truth of a libel in evidence. A libel is not to be justified; for it is nevertheless a libel that it is true."

The judge was clear that this point of the law was for him and not for the jury to decide. Hamilton, however, was determined to win his case, and thus immediately addressed the jury:

> I thank your honour. Then gentlemen of the jury, it is to you we must now appeal, for witnesses to the truth of the facts we have offered and are denied the liberty to prove. . . . The law supposes you to be summoned out of the neighborhood where the fact is alleged to be

committed; and the reason of your being taken out of the neighbourhood is because you are supposed to have the best knowlege of the fact that is to be tried. . . . That the suppressing of evidence ought always to be taken for the strongest evidence. . .

The Chief Justice could not be blamed for thinking he had not made his position clear. He interrupted:

No, Mr. Hamilton; the jury may find that Mr. Zenger printed and published those papers, and leave it to the court to judge whether they are libelous. You know this is very common; it is in the nature of a special verdict, where the jury leave the matter of law to the Court.

Hamilton replied:

I know, may it please your honour, they may do so; but I do likewise know they may do otherwise. I know they have the right, beyond all dispute, to determine both the law and the fact, and where they have no doubt of the law, they ought to do so. . . .

He continued to the jury:

Gentlemen, the danger is great, in proportion to the mischief that may happen through our too great credulity. A proper confidence in a court is comendable; but the verdict (whatever it is) will be yours, you ought to refer no part of your duty to the discretion of these persons. If you should be of opinion that there is no falsehood in Mr. Zenger's papers, you will, nay (pardon me for the expression) you ought to say so. . . . It is the best cause; it is the cause of liberty. . . .

The Chief Justice charged the jury:

Gentlemen of the jury, the great pains Mr. Hamilton has taken to shew how little regard juries are to pay to the opinion of the judges, and his insisting so much upon the conduct of some judges in trials of this kind, is done, no doubt, with a design that you should take very little notice of what I may say upon this occasion. I shall therefore only observe to you that, as the facts or words in the information are confessed, the only thing that can come in question before you is whether the words, as set forth in the information, make a libel, and that as a matter of law, no doubt, and which you may leave to the court. . .

The jury was out a short time and returned with a verdict of not guilty, and this result was greeted by cheers from a large crowd. Andrew Hamilton was given the freedom of New York City together with a gold box engraved with the seal of this freedom.[60]

At no time during the trial did the judge concede the right of the jury to decide law, nor did he stop Hamilton from arguing the question to the jury. No doubt the great leeway given to juries after the Glorious Revolution was grounds for the restraint of the court. However, this conduct by counsel would not have been condoned in England, where the accused's counsel was still not permitted to address the jury. The colonies were molding their own idea of jury trial.

Massachusetts jurors were allowed the right to decide law in a case in 1641, although this right was successively repealed and re-granted by enactments in 1642, 1657, and 1660.[61] One of the reasons why Massachusetts jurors were allowed this privilege could be found in the oath incorporated in their jury instructions, cautioning them to deliver their verdict " . . . according to law and the evidence given you." English jurors on the other hand, were sworn to give their verdict " . . . according to the evidence." The oath of the Massachusetts jurors was affirmed by the King in 1724.[62]

If there was sometimes doubt in theory that juries had the right to decide law, there was no doubt in practice. In 1761 a case, *Erving v. Cradock,* was brought for trespass against a custom house officer for the detaining of a Brigantine and its cargo. The defendant, in the lower court, pleaded the general issue and the plaintiff obtained judgment. The defendant appealed and the question was submitted to a jury which found in favor of the plaintiff in the amount of 740 pounds.

In a letter to the Lords of Trade, Governor Bernard wrote:

The whole Bench directed the jury, as strongly as they could, to find for the defendant. Nevertheless they found for the plaintiff and gave upwards of 550 pounds sterling in damages, being all he said he was out of pocket. This was no surprise to those that were acquainted with the violence with which there proceedings are carried on. It was remarkable that Mr. Erving according to the Usage of there courts, spoke a great deal for himself, when he had admitted everything neccessary to prove that he had incurred a forfeiture and declared he acquiesced only in expectation that a time should come when he should have his *revenge;* a word he used several times to express the purpose of his conduct. . . . A custom house officer has no chance with a jury, let his cause be what it will.

The case was appealed, and the plaintiff, on February 27, 1762, signed a satisfaction of judgment in order that the matter would be moot, and he could therefore avoid answering the appeal.[63] In this case, as in the Zenger case, it was not so much a matter of the court recognizing the jury's right to decide law, but deferring to their decision of it. In other words, if the jury had held a prerogative actually enforceable by the courts, then the appeal would have been no threat to the verdict. Present day counsel will sympathize with Erving's lawyer for having a client who took so much on himself.

This was not an isolated case. *Goodspeed v. Gay* (1763) was an action of trover against a military officer who allegedly recruited the plaintiff's slave. The plaintiff gained the verdict. Again we have Governor Bernard's comment, " . . . upon tryal the Judges told the jury that there was no evidence against the defendant, not the least pretence to charge him in such an action."[64]

Both these cases were civil. We can presume that the jury's right (or usurpation of right) was given even greater deference in criminal cases. The jurors of Massachusetts, however, could be reasonably fair. A case in point is that of eight British soldiers who were indicted as the sequel of the Boston Massacre. Five of the soldiers were acquitted by the jurors, and the remaining two, Kilroy and Montgomery, were found guilty of manslaughter only. The eighth defendant, Preston, was tried seperately and was also acquitted.

The chief presiding judge was Trowbridge, who instructed the jurors to decide the law in issue as well as the evidence. Josiah Quincy, grandfather of the editor of the work cited in this chapter, was associated with John Adams in the defense. According to Quincy's reasoning, since the judge's summing up was for the defense, the jurors must take their law from the bench. Adams, consistent with his principles, still argued that the law was for the jurors, although in that course lay the real danger to his clients.[65] (This was four years before Adams was appointed chief justice of Massachusetts' revolutionary goverment, to succeed Trowbridge. He resigned, however, without taking his seat.[66]) Quincy says that even in civil matters, Massachusetts juries still had the right to decide law at the turn of the nineteenth century.[67]

Connecticut judges had been given the power to direct juries to find in accordance to the law, although a revision of 1702 did not contain this provision.[68] At the time of the revolution the jurors of this state had the right to decide law and fact in both civil and criminal cases.[69] A case in 1788 held that the jury could not be mistaken in their verdict because the jurors were judges of both fact and law.[70] Their right in civil cases did not last long past 1800,[71] however.

Georgian jurors had the right to decide law by the constitutional enactment of 1777, but their constitution of 1789 did not retain this provision.[72] New Jersey had the right by a statute of 1676.[73] Juries had the right to decide law in New Hampshire[74] and early in Rhode Island[75], while in Vermont, the judges had very limited powers in both civil and criminal trials.[76] The right of the juries to decide law existed in Virginia, although it deteriorated in later years.[77] A judge in Maryland could send the jury back to deliberate if he thought the verdict wrong, or he could impanel another jury. If the second jury found contrary to the first, the judge could fine the first jury.[78] Maryland denied the privilege altogether in 1804,[79] but at least, at the time of the Revolution in 1776, 10 of the 11 states for which we have found authority held that the jurors had the right to decide law.

The jury that we have today has its foundation in the Constitution of the United States, including the Fifth, Sixth, Seventh and Fourteenth Amendments. Upon that foundation, there has been much building and erosion, and the chief factor in shaping the jury system which we have in the 1980's has been the Supreme Court of the United States. We will have a close look at that process and the result in Chapter X.

Chapter VII Footnotes

1. *Sources of Our Liberties,* Perry and Cooper, editors (American Bar Foundation, 1959), p. 44.

2. *Id.* at p. 34.

3. "The English Common Law In The Early American Colonies," collected in *Select Essays in Anglo-American Legal History* (Cambridge, 1899), p. 378.

4. Perry and Cooper, *op. cit.* at note 1, at pp. 151-56.

5. Perry and Cooper, *op. cit.* at note 1, at p. 185.

6. "The English Common Law," *op. cit.* at note 3, at pp. 390, 393.

7. *Id.* at p. 398.

8. Perry and Cooper, *op. cit.* at note 1, at p. 217.

9. "The English Common Law. . . ," *op. cit.* at note 3, at p. 386.

10. *The American Jury,* Harry Kalven, Jr., and Hans Zeisel (Little, Brown and Company, Boston, 1966), p. 22.

11. *The Federalist,* Number 83, Alexander Hamilton (National Home Library Foundation, 1937), p. 546.

12. "Trial by Jury and the Reform of Civil Procedure," Austin Wakeman, 31 Harv. L. Rev. 669, at 676 (1918).

13. "Juries as Judges of Criminal Law," Mark DeWolfe Howe, 52 Harv. L. Rev. 582, at 591 (1939).

14. Perry and Cooper, *op. cit.* at note 1, at pp. 187-88.

15. "The English Common Law. . .," *op. cit.* at note 3, at p. 385.

16. "The English Common Law. . .,"*op. cit.* at note 3, at p. 386.

17. "The English Common Law. . .,"*op. cit.* at note 3, at p. 403.

18. *Duncan v. Louisiana,* dissent by Justice Harlan, 391 U.S. 145, at 191 (1968).

19. Wakeman, *op. cit.* at note 12, at p. 681.

20. *Report of Cases Argued and Adjudged in the Superior Court of Judicature of the Province of Massachusetts Bay,* Josiah Quincy, Jr. (Little, Brown and Company, Boston, 1865), p. 559.

21. "The English Common Law. . .," *op. cit.* at note 3, at p. 378.

22. Quincy, *op. cit.* at note 20, at p. 559.

23. *The Federalist, op. cit.* at note 11, at pp. 546-47.

24. Quincy, *op. cit.* at note 20, at p. 560.

25. *Capital Traction v. Hof,* 174 U.S. 1, at p. 9 (1898).

26. "The English Common Law. . .," *op. cit.* at note 3, at p. 378.

27. For example, *Ashton v. Ashton,* 1 Dallas 4 (1760), and *Tother v. Christian,* 1 Dallas 6 (1763).

28. *Duncan v. Louisiana, op. cit.* at note 18, at pp. 191-92.

29. *Sources of Our Liberties, op. cit.* at note 1, at p. 288.

30. Perry and Cooper, *op. cit.* at note 1, at p. 270.

31. Perry and Cooper, *op. cit.* at note 1, at p. 266.

32. Perry and Cooper, *op. cit.* at note 1, at pp. 290, 292, 295.

33. Perry and Cooper, *op. cit.* at note 1, at p. 312.

34. *The Complete Jefferson,* Saul K. Padover, editor (Duell, Soan & Pearce, Inc., New York, 1943), pp. 120-21; *Jefferson,* Saul K. Padover (London, 1942), p. 157.

35. *Federal Code Annotated,* (Bobbs-Merrill Co., 1950), Constitution vol. p. 7.

36. *Id.*at p. 9.

37. *Federal Code Annotated, op. cit.* at note 35, at pp. 14, 17.

38. Perry and Cooper, *op. cit.* at note 1, at pp. 328, 330.

39. Perry and Cooper, *op. cit.* at note 1, at pp. 338-39.

40. Perry and Cooper, *op. cit.* at note 1, at pp. 346, 348.

41. Perry and Cooper, *op. cit.* at note 1, at pp. 355-56.

42. Perry and Cooper, *op. cit.* at note 1, at pp. 362, 366.

43. Wakeman, *op. cit.* at note 12, at p. 678.

44. Perry and Cooper, *op. cit.* at note 1, at pp. 374, 376.

45. Perry and Cooper, *op. cit.* at note 1, at pp. 382, 384-85.

46. *The Federalist, op. cit.* at note 11, at p. 55.

47. *Constitutions of the United States, National and State,* for Columbia University (Oceana Publications, New York) under listing for Rhode Island.

48. Wakeman, *op. cit.* at note 12, at pp. 672-73.

49. *Federal Code Annotated, op. cit.* at note 35, at p. 25.

50. *The Federalist, op. cit.* at note 11, at p. 538.

51. *The Federalist, op. cit.* at note 11, at pp. 542-43.

52. *The Federalist, op. cit.* at note 11, at p. 543.

53. *Ibid.*

54. Howe, *op. cit.* at note 13, at p. 594.

55. Quincy, *op. cit.* at note 20, at p. 568.

56. Quincy, *op. cit.* at note 20, at p. 569.

57. Howe, *op. cit.* at note 13, at p. 587.

58. Quincy, *op. cit.* at note 20, at p. 568.

59. *A Complete Collection of State Trials and Proceedings For High Treason,* T.B. Howell, editor (T.C. Hansard, London,1816), XVII-692.

60. *Id.* at XVII-672-692.

61. Quincy, *op. cit.* at note 20, at p. 558.

62. Quincy, *op. cit.* at note 20, at pp. 560, 565-66.

63. Quincy, *op. cit.* at note 20, at pp. 553-557.

64. Quincy, *op. cit.* at note 20, at p. 558.

65. Quincy, *op. cit.* at note 20, at pp. 564-65.

66. Quincy, *op. cit.* at note 20, at p. 567.

67. *Ibid.*

68. Howe, *op. cit.* at note 13, at p. 601.

69. Quincy, *op. cit.* at note 20, at p. 568.

70. Howe, *op. cit.* at note 13, at p. 601.

71. Howe, *op. cit.* at note 13, at pp. 601-02.

72. Howe, *op. cit.* at note 13, at p. 598.

73. Quincy, *op. cit.* at note 20, at p. 568.

74. "The English Common Law. . .," *op. cit.* at note 3, at p. 387.

75. Quincy, *op. cit.* at note 20, at p. 568.

76. Howe, *op. cit.* at note 13, at p. 591.

77. Quincy, *op. cit.* at note 20, at p. 569.

78. "The English Common Law. . .," *op. cit.* at note 3, at p. 400.

79. Quincy, *op. cit.* at note 20, at p. 569.

VIII
The Gift Rejected

According to Brunner, prior to 1790 the English jury had been confined to England and its sister systems.[1] Repp, in 1832, noted that the various constitutions which had been established in the nineteenth century were dissimilar in most respects except that the jury ". . . was a vital point."[2] The first jury came to France after the revolution of July, 1789, and by September 16, 1791, the Constituent Assembly adopted trial by jury in criminal cases.[3] Robespierre urged the adoption of the civil jury, but it was rejected.[4] During the Reign of Terror, juries became permanent commissions, although even this formality of a trial was soon eliminated.[5]

When the "terror" had ended, the jury was re-established.[6] Napoleon retained the criminal jury in his Code of 1808, but there was no grand jury in France except for the period from 1791 to 1808. Criminal proceedings were commenced by the prosecutor who presented crimes to the Judge d'Instruction (generally three judges who could bring charges on their own initiative).[7] At this time a unanimous verdict was required except when the jury had deliberated for more than 24 hours.[8] Jurors were required to be at least 30, and service was limited to those with the electoral franchise, and those from selected categories including retired military officers, physicians, lawyers, and notaries.[9] It was said that Napoleon required his officers to select jurors for service that were predisposed in his favor.[10]

After the Revolution of 1848 participation in jury service was extended. It was still required, however, that jurors be 30 years of age and able to read and write. Bankrupts, felons, and state employees were excluded, and persons over 70 and those dependent upon their daily labor could be excused upon request.[11] Beginning in 1832 the jury was permitted to accompany a verdict of "guilty" with an additional claim of extenuating circumstances.[12] The difficulty with this type of verdict is that the quantum of proof necessary for conviction is reduced by inducing juries to compromise. The jury survived Louis Napoleon, with alteration; e.g., judges were instructed in 1880 to dispense with summing up,[13] and unanimity had been dispensed with, first for two-thirds and then, in 1853, for a simple majority.

The French jury was reduced in number in 1932, and, after the verdict, the jurors were permitted to consult with the judge on the penalty if there had been a conviction. As a result of this last provision, the percentage of convictions rose.[14] The Vichy government enacted laws in 1943 which provided that the jury would thereafter deliberate on guilt or innocence with the judge. From this time, although called jurors, the lay members of the court were really assessors. This system was retained after the war. Today the French jurors or lay assessors sit with three professional judges, and the decision is made by a simple majority. The Jurors are still required to be over 30 and able to read and write.[15]

As can be seen from the material in the first three chapters, in early times Germany had institutions in which the lay element was present in the judging process in various degrees. For example, there were vestiges of northern juries in Germany in the late Middle Ages. Also, Hauenstein's charter of 1442 secured the right of being tried by a jury of 24 jurors in both civil and criminal cases.[16] A Swabian ordinance of 1562 provided for trials by a jury of 12, whereas Emmendinger had trials by a tribunal of 12 headmen. As late as 1748, a criminal jury trial was held at Purlach in the Grand Duchy of Baden.[17] Gradually, however, trial by judge alone became the rule. The judge relied on secret investigations, written records, and interrogation of the accused, alone and without counsel. The process lasted as long as one and one-half years and the accused often spent that time in jail.[18] A comparison with Kafka's *Trial* indicates that this novel about judicial terror was based upon fact.

The German jury of the nineteenth century did not descend from these earlier German models. Instead, the modern jury came to the German Rhineland when it was invaded by the French in 1798, and after the French left, the Rhenish people continued the tradition. Prussia, however, was opposed to the jury because of its French origin. A commission composed of two Rhenish and three Prussian members investigated the jury in 1819 and unanimously recommended that it be retained. This was done although political offenses were exempted from its jurisdiction.[19]

As a consequence of the political disturbances of 1848, trial by jury was adopted in various German states, such as Bavaria Hesse in 1848, Wurtemburg in 1849, and Austria in 1850. These juries were similar to the French model; i.e., the jurors had to be taxpayers of a certain level or members of certain professions and at least 30 years old. There was no grand jury. A verdict agreed by seven out of 12 was sufficient. If the court thought a verdict of guilty to be erroneous, it could order a new trial, although only once.[20]

Germany dispensed with the jury in 1924. Serious crimes were then tried by a court consisting of six members and three judges.[21] They made one bench, voting jointly with majority rule. Jurors, or assessors, on this court sat one time only. For less serious charges one judge sat with two lay assessors who served for two-year terms. These last assessors were appointed only with a view to their qualifications. These tribunals continued to dispense justice in Germany until the present day, with the exception of World War II, during which all courts were finally abolished.[22]

Elsewhere in Europe, Belgium introduced jury trial in 1830, at which time the chances of acquittal immediately doubled. Holland had the jury for awhile after 1831,[23] while Portugal introduced the jury to some degree in 1832 and more fully in 1837. The number of jurors was limited to six in 1840, and a vote of two-thirds was sufficient for a verdict. In addition the judges could review the verdicts and order new trials if they were not satisfied.[24] Modern Greece first used the jury trial in 1834 and retained it in the constitution of 1843. Geneva obtained trial by jury in 1844 and Sardinia in 1850,[25] ten years before Italy,[26] where it was abolished in 1931.[27] Russia established jury trial in 1864[28] and abandoned it under Communist rule as did her satellites and Yugoslavia.[29]

Denmark seems to have a type of jury where the judge may insist upon acquittal if he disagrees with a verdict of guilty.[30] Sweden makes use of lay judges in the way the English use justices of the peace, and the jury was only used when the case involved freedom of the press.[31] Japan adopted the jury along with other western innovations, but suspended it in 1943 and never revived it after the war.[32]

We would expect to find the jury introduced into most countries where British influence was strong. For example, an attempt was made to introduce the jury to India in 1832.[33] Canada, naturally, uses the jury, but in modern times, except in Ontario, the civil jury has ceased to exist for the most part.[34] In Australia a jury is used in personal injury cases except in South Australia and New South Wales. A majority verdict was used in Tasmania and New South Wales before it was introduced into England in the late 1960's.[35] In South Australia a majority of 10 out of 12 is sufficient for conviction or acquittal after four hours of deliberation, and in Tasmania after two hours of deliberation.[36]

The jury adopted by Malta in 1854 consisted of nine jurors who could reach a verdict when six agreed, and the judge was permitted to order a new trial if he thought the verdict erroneous.[37] The descretion lies with the government in Nyasaland to decide whether an offense requires a jury.[38] The membership of a Kenyan jury is restricted to the Europeans in those cases in which the accused is European, while, on the other hand, South Africa prohibits non-Europeans from serving on juries. When non-whites are defendants or accusers, the Minister of Justice has authority to order the case tried to a judge and two assessors, although the usual South African criminal jury consists of nine members, seven of whom must concur for a verdict.[39]

Regarding the British Isles, the Scots had used the jury almost as early as England, but the civil jury was gradually lost through lack of use. A case involving the right to land was tried by 12 persons who were sworn and gave a verdict in 1469, although in 1532, the Scotland Court of Session, consisting of 15 members, was instituted, and it was thought to have a large enough membership so that a jury would not be needed. The Sheriff's Court at Orkney, however, tried both civil and criminal cases by jury during the years of 1602 to 1604. Although the early Scots retained the criminal jury, they only required a bare majority for a verdict.[40]

Civil juries were reintroduced into Scotland in 1807, and a general statute was enacted in 1815 as an experiment which proved successful, and trial by jury was therefore made permanent after seven years. The civil jury consisted of 12 members whose verdict was required to be unanimous, contrasting with the criminal jury which had 15 members and it could render a verdict by a bare majority. If the civil jury deliberated for more than 12 hours, it was discharged unless the jurors requested more time. In 1852 the length of required deliberation was reduced to six hours. One of the main reasons for reintroducing civil juries into Scotland was to discourage appeals.[41]

Although the civil jury has not proven popular in Scotland, personal injury cases there are still tried by a jury, although not in England. In criminal cases the jurors have the choice of three verdicts: guilty, not guilty and not proven.[42] The jury is also used in Scotland in certain cases in almost the same form as the original Frankish and Norman inquisitions. For example, after six teenagers died on the slopes of the Cairngorm Mountains in central Scotland in late November, 1971, the investigation of the tragedy was conducted by a sheriff before a jury of seven.[43]

Not unexpectedly, the jury thrived in a special way in Ireland. That country had the highest rate of acquittals,(45.3%) of the criminal juries rendering verdicts during 1850. This was more than double the acquittal rate for England and almost double the acquittal rate for Scotland for the same year.[44] There can be little doubt that this high percentage of acquittals can be attributed largely to the political disaffection of the Irish.

A group of American attorneys visited the Soviet Union in the summer of 1983, and were permitted to take a look at the Soviet legal system. The closest practice they found to the American conception of a jury was the lay assessor system. Each trial was presided over by a judge who sat with two lay assessors. The assessors were elected for two week terms by their co-workers or neighbors. Supposedly, the assessors had an equal vote with the judge. Chief Judge Knostantin Bakhmanov said that in thousands of cases in his career he only had the assessors disagree with him once.[45]

It had seemed by the 1850's that the jury was going to become a hallmark of western civilization. In fact, over hundred years later, we find that even the criminal jury is very much restricted to countries that are still or have been dominated by England. The only non-Anglo-Saxon countries using the criminal jury in 1966 were Austria, Belgium, Denmark, Greece, Norway, and some parts of Switzerland and Latin America, with the limited use noted for Sweden.[46] Even at the height of the jury's popularity, no continental country introduced the jury as a mode of trial for civil cases.[47] The lay assessor system, which we have seen is popular in criminal cases on the continent, is quite a different thing than the English jury. What remains now is to trace the development of the jury in England and the United States during the nineteenth and twentieth centuries.

Chapter VIII Footnotes

1. *The Origin of Juries,* Heinrich Brunner (Berlin, 1872), p. 78.

2. *Trial by Jury, Wager of Law and Co-ordinate Forensic Institutions,* Thorl. Gudn. Repp (Thomas Clarke, Edinburgh, 1832), p. 59.

3. *History of Trial By Jury,* William Forsyth (John W. Parker and Son, London, 1852), p. 347.

4. *Id.* at p. 364.

5. Forsyth, *op. cit.* at note 3, at p. 347.

6. *Ibid.*

7. Forsyth, *op. cit.* at note 3, at p. 348.

8. Forsyth, *op. cit.* at note 3, at p. 347.

9. Forsyth, *op. cit.* at note 3, at p. 352.

10. *Democracy In America,* Alexis Clerel DeTocqueville, translated by Henry Reeve (New York, 1838), p. 283.

11. Forsyth, *op. cit.* at note 3, at p. 354.

12. "The Jury Abroad," anonymous, 221 The Law Times 118 (1956).

13. *Ibid.*

14. *Ibid.*

15. *Ibid.*

16. Forsyth, *op. cit.* at note 3, at p. 370.

17. *Id.*

18. Forsyth, *op. cit.* at note 3, at pp. 371, 373-75.

19. Forsyth, *op. cit.* at note 3, at pp. 382-83.

20. Forsyth, *op. cit.* at note 3, at pp. 384-85.

21. *The Jury,* W.R. Cornish (The Penguin Press, London, 1968), p. 269.

22. "The Jury Abroad," *op. cit.* at note 12, at p. 118.

23. Forsyth, *op. cit.* at note 3, at pp. 365, 460.

24. Forsyth, *op. cit.* at note 3, at p. 366.

25. Forsyth, *op. cit.* at note 3, at p. 366-67.

26. "The Jury Abroad," *op. cit.* at note 12, at p. 118.

27. Cornish, *op. cit.* at note 21, at p. 135.

28. *The American Jury,* Harry Kalven, Jr. and Hans Zeisel (Little, Brown and Company, Boston, 1966), p. 4.

29. *The Proof of Guilt,* Glanville Williams (Stevens and Sons, 1963 ed, 1st Ed. 1955), p. 255.

30. Williams, *Id.* at p. 334.

31. Williams, *op. cit.* at note 29, at pp. 256, 298.

32. Williams, *op. cit.* at note 29, at pp. 254-55.

33. Forsyth, *op. cit.* at note 3, at p. 448.

34. "Preservation of the Civil Jury," Stanley E. Stacks, 22 Wash. & Lee L. Rev. 76, at 80-81

35. "Address by The Right Honourable Lord Denning," 11 Australian L.J. 224, at 226 (1967).

36. Williams, *op. cit.* at note 29, at p. 320.

37. *Ibid.*

38. Williams, *op. cit.* at note 29, at p. 262.

39. Williams, *op. cit.* at note 29, at pp. 262-63, 320.

40. Forsyth, *op. cit.* at note 3, at pp. 303-06, 332.

41. Forsyth, *op. cit.* at note 3, at pp. 303, 308-11, 323, 325.

42. Cornish, *op. cit.* at note 21, at pp. 259, 292.

43. *Manchester Guardian,* February 9, 1972, p. 6.

44. Forsyth, *op. cit.* at note 3, at pp. 458-9.

45. "A Rare Look into Soviet Courts," by Timothy Harper, Am. Bar Assoc. Jour., October 1983, p. 1492-95.

46. Kalven and Zeisel, *op. cit.* at note 28, at p. 13.

47. Forsyth, *op. cit.* at note 3, at p. 434.

The first photograph of a jury. It was taken in 1873 of the jury that convicted the defendant in the Tichborne case which was tried in London, England, in 1873. Photograph courtesy of S.F. Spira.

IX
Inconvenient Relic
(England — 1789-1985)

At the time of the French Revolution, the starting point for the worldwide spread of the jury, the English still had other ancient modes of trial. Although seldom used, such practices as wager of law (compurgation), trial by battle, the possessory assizes, and other ancient trappings had never been officially repealed. During the remaining two centuries of the jury's story, almost all ancient procedures were eliminated.

Judicial combat was abolished in 1819.[1] The last trial by wager of law was held in 1824, and this form of trial was eliminated by statute in 1833.[2] Attaint, seldom used for more than a century, was revoked in 1825, and thus would no longer be a threat to jurors.[3] Fifty-six courts of the hundreds still existed in the 1830's, but they were little used. The Leet Court of Manchester became the goverment of the city of Manchester, although it was still the property of a private lord. The town council bought the court from the lord who owned it for the hefty price of 200,000 pounds, and it was allowed to disappear.[4]

The possessory assizes (novel disseisin, mort d'ancestor, darrein presentment) were eliminated in 1833, but, because of a pending action, the last meeting of the Grand Assize was held in 1838. Four knights, together with swords, and 12 other recognitors acted as the jury in common pleas court.[5] The unique jury for foreign parties, the jury *per medietate linguae*, was permitted to pass out of existence.[6] Special juries, both praised and criticized, were to remain for a longer time. In order to become a special juror, it was necessary to be a person legally entitled to be called esquire, or a person of high degree, such as a banker, a merchant, the head of a dwelling rated at not less than 100 pounds in a town of 20,000 or 50 pounds elsewhere, and so on.[7] Special jurors were more likely to vote with the crown than the ordinary juror in the hope of being chosen again in order to earn more money — thus the name "guinea men."[8]

Special juries were abolished, however, in 1949 with limited exceptions.[9] No trial with a special jury has been held since 1954.[10]

The remaining ancient mode of trial, trial by jury, seemed to have a more promising future. Fox's libel bill, passed in 1792, gave English juries an absolute right to deliver a general verdict in libel prosecutions. It is not clear that this changed the law at all, aside from preventing the forcing of a special verdict upon the jury by an overbearing judge. In part, it reads:

> the jury . . . may give a general verdict of guilty or not guilty upon the whole matter put in issue [providing the court or judge] shall, according to their or his discretion give their directions to the jury on the matter in issue . . . in like matter as in other criminal cases.[11]

Confidence in the jury was on the rise, and in 1837 the jury was chosen to set values in cases of eminent domain.[12] As contrasted with American practice, divorce cases were tried by jury at this time. For example, juries in England tried divorce cases in 1857. Probate matters were also tried to juries on request by 1857, and the chancery court could order a jury if requested by a party as early as 1858. In fact, by 1900, 50 percent of the divorce cases were tried by jury. However, although a jury trial in a divorce case is still a possibility, the last time this occurred was in 1956.[13]

The jury's jurisdiction was expanded in 1888 when minor civil suits in county courts could be tried to juries upon demand.[14] The next century found the jury struggling to hold its ground rather than develop new areas. After the abolition of juries in civil cases in 1918, jury trial was restored with certain exceptions in 1925. This restoration was to last only until 1933 when a general right to a civil jury was again abolished, except in matters involving fraud.[15]

There were more losses than gains as far as jury trial was concerned. A seemingly insignificant statute was passed in 1854 giving parties the right to waive juries in common pleas court.[16] (Previously, the only trials in this court were jury trials.) This statute was enacted in the hope that other ends could be achieved by limiting jury trials. But even such statutes as this one put some pressure on counsel to choose court trial, not as the most desirable mode of trial, but in order not to offend the judiciary.

On the criminal side of the docket, summary trial before a magistrate was permitted by an 1855 statute, if the defendant waived the jury when charged with stealing, where the value involved was less than five shillings. The amount was raised to two pounds in 1879, 20 pounds in 1915, and removed entirely in 1962 when summary trial of other crimes was also permitted.[17] Devlin claimed in the 1966 edition of *Trial by Jury* that 85 percent of the indictable offenses were tried summarily by magistrates without a jury at the defendants request.[18] (Occasionally, the consent of the prosecution was also obtained, although it was not mandatory).[19]

According to Cornish, in 1965, 88 percent of offenders were handled in magistrate court without a jury.[20] These figures most certainly include guilty pleas, but, even so, they appear to indicate that the jury is not popular with criminal defendants. This is misleading, however, as the defendants are offered an enticement to choose summary trial. The sentencing power of magistrates court is generally limited to a maximum of six months and a 400 pound fine. A case could be referred to Quarter Sessions for a stiffer sentence, but this does not seem to be the rule.[21] Quite apart from any jurisdictional sentencing differential, it is common practice in the United States for defendants to waive a jury trial in the hope of a lenient sentence. This is well known to the lawyers and is one of the chief considerations in inducing pleas of guilty. Logically, however, there can be no equitable reason for requiring a stiffer penalty in the one case than in the other.

In 1873, the common pleas courts were given power to refer to referees matters requiring prolonged examination, such as the investigation of documents, accounts, or scientific and other investigation.[22] In point of theory, this could have diminished the jurisdiction of the jury, but it does not appear that this power was widely used. After 1883, jury trial was used in ordinary course only in cases of libel, slander, malicious prosecution, seduction, false imprisonment and breach of promise. In other cases a party desiring jury trial had to request it, the aim being to reduce the number of jury trials necessary. As a result of this act, in the areas where a request was necessary, jury trials fell from 80 percent to 50 percent of the total.[23]

As a war measure, jury trial in civil cases was abolished except in the six cases mentioned in the 1883 act.[24] Jury trial was restored in 1925, but this lasted only until 1933 when this statute became law:

Sec. 1 . . . grand juries are hereby abolished. . . .

Sec. 6. (1) Subject as hereinafter provided, if on the application of any party to be tried in the King's Bench Division of the High Court made not later than such time before the trial as may be limited by rules of court, the court or a judge is satisfied that—

(a) A charge of fraud against that party; or

(b) A claim in respect libel, slander, malicious prosecution, false imprisonment, seduction or breach of promise of marriage is in issue, the action shall be ordered to be tried with a jury unless the court of judge is of the opinion that the trial thereof requires prolonged examination of documents or accounts or any scientific or local investigation which cannot conveniently be made with a jury; but save as aforesaid, any action to be tried in that division may, in the discretion of the court or a judge, be ordered to be tried either with or without a jury:

Provided that the provisions of this section shall be without prejudice to the power of the court or a judge to order in accordance with rules of court, that different questions of fact arising in any actions be tried by different modes of trial, and where any such order is made the provisions of this section requiring trial with a jury in certain cases shall have effect only as respects questions relating to any such charge or claim as aforesaid.[25]

Nothing in this statute seems to require the virtual elimination of jury trials, but that was to be its effect.

From about 1939 the great majority of accident-injury cases was tried by judge alone,[26] and in fact, from 1954 to 1964, less than 20 such cases were tried by juries in England.[27] In these cases the jury awards generally ran higher than similar awards by judges,[28] and Cornish estimated that in approximately one-third of the cases the jury awards were markedly higher than those by a judge alone, while in about one-third of the cases, jury awards were lower.[29]

Verdicts for quadreplegic cases in 1962-63 were about 50,000 pounds ($120,000), it being estimated that judges would have rendered awards for such cases ranging from 30 to 35,000 pounds.[30] In 1972 a 17-year-old girl was awarded 59,000 pounds for permanent brain injuries which would prevent her from performing all but the simplest household tasks.[31] This trial was held without a jury, like all such cases since 1964.

Among the reasons considered as rendering juries unfit to try personal injury cases were: (1) the cases were overly complicated; (2) the time and expense were greater with a jury; (3) it was impossible to achieve uniformity with juries; (4) it was difficult to control a jury verdict on appeal; and (5) it is improper for the jury to consider the fact that the defendant is insured as this fact often prejudices the jurors.[32] Referring to that part of the 1933 statute which provided that trial could be had by jury at the discretion of the trial judge, Judge Salmon, concurring in the Watts decision, said:

> I must confess that, if I were approaching the matter *res integra*, I should have thought that the section, and the rules passed in pursuance of it, confer an unfettered discretion on the judge to order or refuse a jury as he thought fit. In 1937, this court, . . . decided . . . that that was exactly what the section did mean.

Judge Salmon would have overruled *Sims v. William Howard* (the first case holding that juries were not proper tribunals for personal injury cases),[33] but he joined in the instant decision which merely affirmed the decision of the trial court to sit without a jury.[34] The *Sims* and *Watts* decisions put an end to trials of personal injury cases by juries in England. The atrophy of trial by jury was not limited to personal injury. Even in 1963, only one and one-half percent of the cases tried by the Queen's Bench were tried by a jury. (This court does not ordinarily try criminal cases.)[35] This percentage was approximately the same in 1965 and 1966.[36]

Statutes were passed making conditions better for the jurors who still served. At the discretion of the judge, after 1870, jurors were permitted to use a fire when out of the courtroom and to have reasonable refreshments at their own expense.[37] After 1897, the jury was permitted to separate at night except in murder cases, although after 1940 they were allowed to do so except during the summing up and deliberation period.[38] In 1949 jurors were finally paid travel and subsistence expenses, plus an allowance for loss of earnings, not to exceed 20 shillings a day.[39] The limit on the amount allowed for loss of earnings was removed in 1954,[40] and by 1968 the jurors could get up to six pounds and 10 shillings a day for loss of earnings.[41]

A number of statutes relating to the jury were purely administrative in character. A statute of 1825 specified qualifications for jurors, such as an age requirement between 21 and 60, a property requirement, and the provision that the juror must be a resident of that county. A view could be held with the stipulation that, although a majority of jurors must be present at the view, the entire number was not necessary. In addition jurors would receive a certificate of service in return for payment of a shilling to the sheriff.[42] Many courts in the United States give similar certificates to jurors at the conclusion of their term. Also, the practice of the king asking jurors to stand aside in lieu of challenging was reaffirmed,[43] although peremptory common law challenges in murder, treason, and piracy cases were limited to 20.[44] The Criminal Justice Act of 1947 provided that the defendant could only have seven peremptory challenges.[45] A defendant remaining silent when charged with treason, a felony, or a misdemeanor was treated as though he had pleaded not guilty and the trial proceeded.[46] With the consent of the parties a verdict could be rendered by less than 12 jurors after 1851.[47]

Women, except in connection with determining pregnancy, were not permitted to serve on juries until 1919. That act provided:

> 1. . . . and a person shall not be exempted by sex or marriage from liability to serve as a juror: Provided that . . . (b) Any judge, chairman of quarter sessions, recorder or other person before whom a case is or may be heard may, in his discretion, on application made by or on behalf of the parties (including in criminal cases the prosecution and the accused or any of them, or at his own instance), make an order that the jury shall be composed of men only or women only as the case may require, or may, on an application made by a woman to be exempted from service on a jury in respect of any case by reason of the nature of the evidence to be given or of the issues to be tried, grant, such exemption.[48]

The statute also provided for exemption for those women jurors unfit for service because of medical reasons. Therefore juries continued to consist primarily of men, women amounting to only about 11 percent of those serving in the 1960's.[49] Women also lost their right to exclusively determine whether women convicted of capital crimes were pregnant. This question would be decided instead by the jury trying the principal offense; if this was impossible, another jury would be chosen for this purpose.[50] By a statute of 1965, at the discretion of the court, trial of a case could continue despite the illness or unavoidable inability of a juror to continue as long as nine jurors remained. This act amended a 1925 act which had required 10 jurors to be present and also required the consent of the defendant and the crown.[51]

Some changes in trial procedures had to do with the type of evidence the judge or jury could consider. One change was the increasing use of expert witnesses. A handwriting expert was permitted to testify in a criminal case in 1865 and in a civil case in 1854.[52] By a statute of 1907 the court of criminal appeals was given the power to appoint experts, although it never excercised the power.[53] In 1916 a chemist was permitted to testify in his expert capacity in a will contest case,[54] while in another case the results of an electroencephalography test were permitted as expert testimony concerning epilepsy in 1940.[55]

Some changes seemed to have helped the crown more than the defense. Most defense counsel agree that the power of the judge to sum up facts and law, while giving his own opinion without binding the jury, is a procedure favorable to conviction. This power was granted by statute in 1841, although previously, in the eighteenth century, the practice had arisen whereby the judge summed up only the law.[56]

A change of the utmost significance was contained in the Criminal Justice Act of 1967. It provided for the possibility of a majority verdict; e.g., if there were 11 or 12 jurors, 10 could return a verdict, or, if there were only 10 jurors, nine could return a verdict. It was necessary for the jurors to have deliberated for at least two hours, at which time the judge at his discretion was permitted to authorize the jury to return a majority verdict.[57] This type of verdict helps the crown in two ways. It almost entirely eliminates the protection the unanimity rule gives to minority

populations. Even a minority as large as 20 percent of the population has only a small chance of being on the jury panel because of
property qualifications in England and because of the crown's
right to have jurors stand aside. Assuming that a member of the
defendant's minority group was impanelled, the majority verdict
nonetheless meant that he would have little influence on the
jury's final decision.

The other way that a majority verdict is favorable to the crown
is that it makes it more likely that a verdict will be reached.
Two hung juries are tantamount to acquital, not to conviction, and
often, a case is not retried after one hung jury. Since it is the
crown that is the moving party, the defense accomplishes most of
its objectives with a hung jury. The majority verdict decreases the
quantum of proof necessary for a conviction by reason of these
considerations. This same act (Act of 1967), also provided that the
defendant had to give advanced notice of his intention to use an
alibi.[58]

Some changes in procedure were in the defendant's favor. An
enactment in 1836 provided that the defendant could be fully represented by counsel at all stages of criminal proceedings, including
argument to the jury.[59] After 1848, justices were required to warn the
criminal defendant that he need not give evidence against himself,[60]
although the defendant himself was finally permitted to testify
under oath after 1898. From the dates of these last two statutes, it
would appear that the crown had somehow been permitted to
question the defendant even before the 1898 act. Prior to 1898, however, some justices had allowed defendants to make an unsworn
statement. After the act of 1898 was passed, the defendant was not
required to testify, but, if he did, he could be cross-examined by
counsel for the crown. The defendant can still make an unsworn
statement from the box, but this is not often done because such a
statement lacks credibility.[61] Also, by the nineteenth century, the
indigent defendant was provided counsel at the expense of the
government.[62]

Anyone attending a criminal trial at the Old Bailey at the
present time would immediately notice that the barristers and the
judge wear robes and wigs. The courtroom is arranged so that
solicitors are permitted to sit at tables on two sides between the

barristers and the jury, while the defendant and judge are seated on the other two sides. If the case is of some importance, there are generally two barristers for the crown and two for each defendant. The jurors are nearly all men, the greater number of them being past their forties. The jurors, contrary to most jurisdictions in the United States, are permitted to take notes and are provided with paper for this purpose. It is interesting to observe, however, that the jurors seldom make use of this privilege. Only one counsel stands at a time, and aside from going to the dock to talk with his client (who remains more or less caged during the entire trial), he seldom leaves his seat. If counsel desires a witness to examine a document, it is conveyed to the witness by an official of the court. The witness is required to remain standing during the delivery of his testimony.

English counsel tend to phrase their terminology differently than their American counterparts; for example, in contradicting a witness, an English barrister will say, "I put it to you that what really happened was. . . ." English lawyers make few objections to the proceedings, although the bench intervenes frequently for the sake of clarity, rather than for any need to keep order.

The senior counsel is called a Queen's Counsel, and he is required to associate himself with a junior. Generally, a barrister can apply to become Queen's Counsel after being in practice for about 10 years. This is not necessarily an attractive proposition, however, since it necessitates an increase in his fees, in addition to having to associate with a junior. The barristers do not belong to law firms as such, but they may share chambers and the services of a clerk with an assistant. Barristers receive their cases through the work of solicitors, who are not permitted to practice in High Court or at Old Bailey, although they can form partnerships and practice in the lower courts.

A difference in the approach to trial may also be noted from the time jurors are called to be sworn. If they are to be challenged, it must be before they are sworn. As opposed to American practice, challenges are infrequently used because barristers and clients lack information on which to challenge intelligently, and because the custom has developed of challenging only in exceptional cases. In 1964, out of 110 total cases, 25 jurors were challenged in 14 cases.[63] A similar report mentioned by Devlin alleged that challenges were used in 24 out of 341 cases (50 jurors challenged out of 4,092).[64] In an exceptional case at Old Bailey in October and November of 1971, there were multiple black defendants and all of their challenges (seven each) were used in order to obtain black jurors. Generally, however, the observation by an experienced barrister to the effect that, "In England, the trial begins when the jury is picked; in the United States, the trial is over when the jury is picked," has a great deal of truth.

The burden of proof in a civil case involves the "balance of probabilities,"[65] while in criminal cases, the burden of proof is "beyond a reasonable doubt."[66] This was not clear in the late forties and early fifties, when it was thought that the burden of proof was that the jury must be "satisfied of guilt," and so on.[67] The crown cannot cross-examine the defendant about his past record unless he has attacked the credibility of crown witnesses.[68] A wife cannot be compelled to testify against her husband, and in fact cannot testify against him at all except for the usual matters including offenses against her or her children.[69]

It is unusual for English juries to deliberate more than four to five hours, and the percentage of disagreements was small even before the introduction of majority verdicts.[70] The overall impression gained from observing both civil and criminal trials in London is the apparent detachment on the part of counsel, the judge, the jury, and even the parties. This atmosphere is looked upon as a great virtue by the English bar, but one can not help feeling that this low-key atmosphere works to the disadvantage of criminal defendants. This air of detachment begins even before the trial commences because the solicitor does most of the trial preparation, such as interviewing witnesses, which the barrister is generally forbidden to do (except for the client and expert witnesses). Even the solicitor, especially in criminal cases, must be very circumspect about interviewing witnesses. He most certainly would not interview persons known to be crown witnesses without notifying the police and counsel for the other side, as well as having a third party present. (This holds true despite the fact that the Law Society (the ruling association to which solicitors belong) has ruled that witnesses are not the property of either the Crown or the defendant, and both parties should have equal access to them.) Very rarely would a witness for the crown be interviewed out of court by the defense after the witness had testified at preliminary hearing.[71]

An article by James Driscoll in 1979,[72] states, " . . . jury trial in England and Wales has become circumvented in criminal cases by factors other than negotiated pleas and is also virtually extinct in civil litigation." Driscoll notes that Blackstone's "Bulwark against Tyranny" (that is, the jury) has been manned by " . . . a small and unrepresentative section of society, . . . " He did note that in 1972 all adults eligible to vote became eligible for jury duty. He cites a survey that shows, notwithstanding the criminal jury's decline, most defendants thought a jury was a better forum to demonstrate innocence.

In the capacity of a consultant, the writer was asked to sit in at a pre-trial conference in a barrister's office which was being held preparatory to trial. Those present were the barrister, a junior, two solicitors and the client, in addition to the writer, while a witness who showed up was asked to leave by the barrister. The barrister had already read the solicitor's brief, but did not have a firm grasp of the details of the case, although trial was to commence the following Monday. The barrister was shown for the first time several dozen police photographs which the solicitor had recently obtained, but nothing was done about having several photographs which were favorable to the defendant blown up for use as exhibits. The defendant was not questioned at all, but there was simply an exchange of views and information between the barrister, the solicitors and the client. The entire conference lasted about an hour and a half, and this constituted most of the trial preparation at which the client was present. In spite of what would have been inadequate preparation under American procedures, the client was acquitted.

As to the impact jury service makes upon the citizens, in 1964 approximately seven million citizens in England and Wales were eligible for service.[73] About 175,000 were actually called for service and 110,000 impanelled for duty,[74] while approximately 5,000 to 6,000 cases are tried a year.[75] By far the greater number of the cases tried are criminal cases, as the civil jury in England is practically extinct. It is likely that soon the property qualification will be extinguished and eligibility for jury service will begin at the age of 18 with the passage of the Criminal Justice Act of 1972.[76]

There would then be more jurors, but they would have less to do. Libel is one of the remaining strongholds of the civil jury, but the Law Society has recommended that the jury no longer be permitted to fix damages in libel cases.[77] In England there is no new trial in criminal matters if there is a conviction. (The right to order a new trial may have been recently enacted, but if so, it has not been acted upon.)[78] A judge, in contrast to a juror, has no maximum age unless he is newly appointed, in which case his maximum age is 75.

The coroner's jury has remained in very much the same form for many years, although the number of jurors serving on a particular coroner's jury has varied. Before 1926 it was between 12 and 23. Since then there are 7 to 11 members, and they can deliver a verdict if no more than two dissent from the verdict. Coroner's juries are responsible for returning verdicts in unexplained death such as murder, manslaughter, and infanticide. If indicated by a verdict, the coroner must issue arrest warrants. If criminal proceedings are instituted previous to a verdict, the coroner's proceeding is adjourned.[79]

We find an even purer form of the ancient jury existing in London at the present time. This is the Trial of the Pyx. The "Pyx" is a box in which samples of coins minted by the Royal Mint are placed. Once a year, a jury of goldsmiths is called upon to try the quality of the coin of the realm. The first record of such a trial in England was in 1248, but it became almost the exclusive responsibility of the goldsmiths from 1349. From the time of Elizabeth I the trial took the form that it still retains.[80] On March 10, 1972, this writer attended the Trial of the Pyx at the Goldsmith's Hall. On arriving, the armoured truck was already present and 30 some boxes containing coins and trial plates were being unloaded. The jurors soon began to assemble, including men in high positions such as heads of financial institutions, experts from the assay office, and some retired persons, but all free men of the Goldsmith's Company.

The 26 jurors seated themselves around a long table in a decorative, baroque room. The Queen's Remembrancer, an officer of the Exchequer and a high judicial officer, arrived precisely on time in wig and robe, accompanied by his aides. He administered an oath to the jurors who had been supplied testaments for this purpose.

The jurors elected a foreman, and the Queen's Remembrancer addressed the jurors regarding their duty. After this was done, the jury was adjourned until April 21, 1972, when their verdict would be delivered. Immediately upon adjournment, the members set at once to their task, opening packets of 10 and 50 pence pieces, counting them, and putting two of those coins from each packet into a wooden bowl to be later subjected to exacting tests. Part of the jury had departed to another room to count the five pence pieces with automatic machines, an innovation of the preceding year. Of the five pence pieces, only one from each packet was saved for further testing.

Other jurors were in another part of the Goldsmith's Hall operating huge and sensitive balances. They weighed all the coins and the trial plates. When they had completed these tasks, they had refreshments provided by the Goldsmith's Company. They would also be treated to a dinner after they returned their final verdict.

This then was the state to which the English jury had declined since the peak of its power in the last half of the nineteenth century. It seems that only in libel cases is the English civil jury alive and well. Even here its status is subject to continual challenge. *Cassell Et. Co. Ltd. v. Broome*, (1972) 1 All E.R. 801, was such a case. During World War II, Convoy PQ 17, consisting of 35 merchant ships was on its way to the Soviet Union. The British Admirality had ordered the convoy to scatter, not knowing that a German battleship was in the area. In the resulting disaster 24 of the ships were sunk. David Irvin wrote a book entitled *The Destruction of Convoy PQ 17* which was published by Cassell, both the writer and publisher being defendants in the subject case, but the writer gave up the struggle before the appeal.

The thesis of the book was that Captain Broome was substantially responsible for the loss of the ships. Unfortunately for the defense in the legal case, in Irvin's attempt to publish the book, one publisher had turned the work down because they considered it libelous. The trial to a jury took 17 days and resulted in a total verdict for Broome of £40,000, of which £25,000 was for exemplary damages. Only the exemplary damages were questioned on appeal. After a nine day hearing before the Court of Appeals, the appeal was dismissed, and the case was accepted by the law committee of the House of Lords where the hearing lasted 13 working days.

The majority of the Law Lords held to dismiss the appeal. This excerpt expresses the basis of the majority view, "I do not think the judiciary at any level should substitute itself for the jury, unless the award is so manifestly too large, . . . or manifestly too small, . . . that no sensible jury properly directed could have reached the conclusion." *Cassell Et. Co. Ltd., supra,* at 819.

On March 19, 1971, *The Times* carried an article under the headline, "Profit and Dishonour in Fleet Street." The article charged certain interests with heartlessly closing down a great newspaper for profit and needlessly bringing unemployment to hundreds. *The Times,* its editor and the reporter were sued for libel by Associated Newspapers Group and others, and the case is reported as *Rothermere et al* v. *Times Newspapers Ltd. et al.*[81]

The Times requested jury trial and, initially, the request was granted. An interlocutory appeal was allowed, however, and trial was directed to be by a judge sitting alone, on the ground that " . . . the trial would require a prolonged examination of documents and accounts which could not be conveniently made with a jury." *The Times* appealed from this order to the Court of Appeal.[82]

By a majority of two to one, the Court of Appeal held that *The Times* was entitled to a jury trial. Lord Denning and Lord Lawton wrote the majority opinions. Lord Lawton said,

> If the defendants lost their action and heavy damages were awarded against them, the newspaper scene in this country might never be the same again. The reputation which *The Times* had enjoyed for so long around the world for responsible journalism would be badly dented, if not destroyed. The destruction of its reputation would be the destruction of a national institution. A trial which could have that result should not be the responsibility of one man.[83]

Blackshaw v. Lord, (1983) 3 W.L.R. 283, was a libel action by Alan Blackshaw against Rodney Lord and the Daily Telegraph. Blackshaw complained that an article in the Telegraph falsely charged him with incompetency in connection with his duties as the official in charge of the Offshore Supplies Office. Specifically, the article claimed 52 million in grants were paid that should not have been paid and that the grants were unlikely to be returned.

A jury found: (1) The article was defamatory, (2) The article was not accurate or fair, and (3) The damages were £45,000. The appeal, questioning the amount of the damages was dismissed. Athough the appellate court thought the damages were higher than what they would have awarded, they concluded that that was not the test. They held that, " . . . this court must not interfere with such an award unless the damages are so large that no reasonable jury could have given them, or unless the jury were misled, or took into account matters which they ought not to have considered." *Blackshaw, supra,* at 313.

These English libel decisions are of immense importance to the limited retention of the civil jury in England. It appears that England's great libel trials will continue to be tried to 12 jurors. Perhaps Englishmen really do believe that the jury is the best tribunal for determining facts, but they only resort to trial by judge alone as a matter of convenience while reserving the jury for matters touching their honor.

Chapter IX Footnotes

1. *The History of English Law,* Sir Fredrick Pollock and Frederick William Maitland (2nd edition, Cambridge Univ. Press, 1895), I-150.

2. *A Preliminary Treatise on Evidence,* James Bradley Thayer (Sweet and Maxwell, London, 1898), pp. 33-34.

3. *Id.* at p. 152.

4. *A History Lay Judges,* John P. Dawson (Harvard Univ. Press, Cambridge, Mass., 1960), pp. 183, 253-54.

5. *History of Trial by Jury,* William Forsyth (John W. Parker and Son, London, 1852), p. 139.

6. *Id.* at p. 345, seemingly in conflict with the statement at p. 230, but this form of the jury was gone.

7. *The Statutes Revised,* 1870, 33 and 34 Vict. C77.

8. *The Jury,* W.R. Cornish (The Penguin Press, London, 1968), p. 131.

9. *The Statutes Revised,* Juries Act, 1949, Sec. 18(1) a.

10. Cornish, *op cit.* at note 8, at pp. 32-33.

11. "Juries as Judges of Criminal Law," Mark De Wolfe Howe, 52 Harv. L. Rev. 582, at 585 (1939).

12. *The Statutes Revised,* 1837 C. 94 sec. 19.

13. Cornish, *op. cit.* at note 8, at p. 75.

14. *Ibid.*

15. *Trial by Jury,* Sir Patrick Devlin (Stevens and Sons, London, 1966, first edition 1955), p. 130.

16. *Id.* at p. 130.

17. Forsyth, *op cit.* at note 5, at p. 57.

18. Devlin, *op cit.* at note 15, at p. 130.

19. Cornish, *op cit.* at note 8, at p. 60.

20. "The Jury Abroad," anonymous, 221 The Law Times 118 (1956).

21. Cornish, *op cit.* at note 8, at pp. 57-59.

22. Devlin, *op cit.* at note 15, at p. 130.

23. Cornish, *op cit.* at note 8, at p. 76.

24. Devlin, *op cit.* at note 15, at p. 130.

25. *The Statutes Revised,* 1933, C. 36.

26. *Watts v. Manning,* 2 All Eng. Rep. 267, 271 (1964).

27. Cornish, *op cit.* at note 8, at p. 231.

28. Devlin, *op cit.* at note 15, at p. 179.

29. Cornish, *op cit.* at note 8, at p. 231.

30. *Ibid.*

31. *The Evening News,* March 29, 1972, London, p. 1.

32. *Watts v. Manning,* 2 All Eng. Rep. 267, 269 (1964).

33. *Sims v. William Howard and Son Ltd.,* 1 All Eng. Rep. 918 (1964).

34. *Watts v. Manning,* 2 All Eng. Rep. 267, 272-73 (1964).

35. Devlin, *op cit.* at note 15, at p. 180.

36. Cornish, *op cit.* at note 8, at p. 76.

37. *The Statutes Revised,* 1870, C.77, sec. 23.

38. Cornish, *op cit.* at note 8, at p. 145.

39. *The Statutes Revised,* 1949, C. 27, sec. I(1).

40. *The Statutes Revised,* 1954, C. 41.

41. Cornish, *op cit.* at note 8, at p. 53.

42. *The Statutes Revised,* 1825, C. 50.

43. Forsyth, *op cit.* at note 5, at p. 232.

44. Forsyth, *op cit.* at note 5, at p. 231.

45. Devlin, *op cit.* at note 15, at p. 28.

46. *A History of English Law,* Sir William Holdsworth (Sweet and Maxwell, London, 1956 ed, 1st ed, 1903), I-327.

47. Forsyth, *op cit.* at note 5, at p. 241.

48. *The Statutes Revised,* 1919, C. 71.

49. Cornish, *op cit.* at note 8, at p. 28.

50. *The Statutes Revised,* 1931, C. 24.

51. *Public General Acts and Measures of 1965,* C. 26.

52. Cornish, *op cit.* at note 8, at p. 162.

53. *The Proof of Guilt,* Glanville Williams (Stevens and Sons, London, 1963 ed., 1st ed. 1955), p. 130.

54. Cornish, *op cit.* at note 8, at p. 162.

55. *Ibid.*

56. Williams, *op cit.* at note 52, at pp. 303-04.

57. *Public General Acts and Measures,* 1967, C. 80.

58. Cornish, *op cit.* at note 8, at p. 68.

59. Holdsworth, *op cit.* at note 46, at I-326.

60. Williams, *op cit.* at note 53, at p. 45.

61. Williams, *op cit.* at note 53, at pp. 11, 47, 71-72.

62. Cornish, *op cit.* at note 8, at pp. 72-73.

63. Cornish, *op cit.* at note 8, at p. 45.

64. Devlin, *op cit.* at note 15, at p. 169.

65. Devlin, *op cit.* at note 15, at p. 62.

66. Cornish, *op cit.* at note 8, at p. 91.

67. Williams, *op cit.* at note 53, at pp. 91-92.

68. Cornish, *op cit.* at note 8, at p. 91.

69. Williams, *op cit.* at note 53, at p. 72.

70. Devlin, *op cit.* at note 15, at pp. 51-52, 54.

71. Williams, *op cit.* at note 53, at pp. 101-04.

72. "The Decline of the English Jury," 17 American Business Law Journal 99 (1979).

73. Devlin, *op cit.* at note 15, at p. 166.

74. Cornish, *op cit.* at note 8, at p. 10.

75. Devlin, *op cit.* at note 15, at p. 166.

76. *The London Times,* March 7, 1972, p. 2.

77. *The Guardian,* February 14, 1972, p. 7.

78. "Early Opposition to the Petty Jury In Criminal Cases," Charles L. Wells, 30 Law Q. Rev. 97, 108 (1914).

79. Cornish, *op cit.* at note 8, at pp. 245-46.

80. *Royal Mint Annual Report,* 1963, pp. 7-8.

81. *The Times* (London), January 24, 1973, p. 11.

82. *Ibid.*

83. *The Times* (London), February 14, 1973, p. 14.

A Lawrence County, Ohio, jury in a criminal case minutes after returning a verdict of guilty in 1986. Photograph by author.

X
The Constitutional Jury
(The United States — 1791 to 1986)

1. The Constitutional Foundation

The first question is, where do you look to see what it is that we call a jury? In the federal system, whether the jury is civil or criminal, you start with the Constitution of the United States. In addition to that part of Article 3, Section 2, quoted in chapter VII of this book, the following language has been held to be significant: "The judicial Power shall extend to all Cases, in Law and Equity. . . ." As we shall see, in the application of the Seventh Amendment, the words "Law and Equity" are all important and are often taken to be the equivalent of "jury and court."

Also found in Section 2 of Article III, are the words "In all other Cases before mentioned, the Supreme Court shall have appellate Jurisdiction, both as to Law and Fact, with such Exceptions, and under such Regulations as the Congress shall make." The words, "Law and Fact" continue to have the distinctive meaning that they had under the common law of England, particularly after the adoption of the Seventh Amendment.

Article I Section 3 of the Constitution, although not often looked at in that light, contains a provision for a very special type of jury, that is, the Senate, sitting under the presiding Chief Justice of the Supreme Court in an impeachment trial. The senators are to be under oath or affirmation, and two-thirds of their number is required for conviction. President Andrew Johnson narrowly avoided conviction before the Senate acting as Jury in 1868. This comparison is more striking if we look back to the *Inquisitio* of Charlemagne and the early English juries. The members of those early juries had knowledge of the matters they were to investigate and, in the case of the *Inquisitio,* the number of jurors could be quite large.

While not directly affecting jury trial, the powers enumerated to Congress in Article I, Section 8, have had the effect of diminishing the jury's role by creating new rights and institutions to which jury trial is not applicable.

The Judiciary Act of September 24, 1789, provided that suits in equity could not be sustained where there was a plain and adequate remedy at law. That Act's language was important as indicating what had to be shown to avoid jury trial by the equity route. The first ten amendments to the Constitution became effective in 1791. Amendment V requires a Grand Jury for prosecution of federal crimes and also provides that "No person shall be . . . deprived of life, liberty, or property, without due process of law; . . ." The question arose after the enactment of the Fourteenth Amendment, do the words "due process," incorporate all the attributes of federal jury practice as a part of "due process."

Obviously important are the Sixth Amendment, which guarantees jury trial in all federal criminal prosecutions, and the Seventh Amendment, which requires a jury in suits at common law where the value in controversy exceeds twenty dollars. The language in the Seventh Amendment that ". . . no fact tried by a jury, shall be otherwise reexamined in any Court of the United States, than according to the rules of the common law," is particularly important. There is no book in existence that precisely lays down the "rules of the common law," so the courts looked to English practice, and to contemporaneous usage reflecting English practice. Thus, in *Parsons v. Bedford*, 28 U.S. 433 (1830), Justice Joseph Story said that the words "common law" are used in contradistinction to "equity and admirality," adding that the framers of the Seventh Amendment intended "law" to mean suits at common law in the same sense that the word "law" was used in Article III of the Constitution. He also mentioned the Judiciary Act of 1789, employing similar language, as being contemporaneous with the proposal of the Seventh Amendment.

The Fourteenth Amendment became effective on July 21, 1868. On its face it does not have any necessary connection with jury trial. To a large extent, as we shall see, that is the way it has worked out in civil cases. In criminal trials, however, it is a different story. The restriction against the states abridging ". . . the privileges or immunities of citizens of the United States . . ." and against depriving ". . . any person of life, liberty, or property, without due process of law; . . ." and against denying ". . . to any person within its jurisdiction the equal protection of the laws," did have an important impact on jury trials in state criminal cases.

Perhaps the clearest exposition of the historical approach to a definition of the jury is contained in *Patton v. United States*, 281 U.S. 276 (1930), where Justice Sutherland said that all the elements in a federal criminal jury are those which existed and were recognized in the United States and England when the Constitution was adopted. He listed the essential elements as being (1) twelve men, (2) the presence of a judge with power to instruct the jury on law, and (3) a unanimous verdict. He also said that it was beyond the power of the legislature to change the essentials, and that the purpose of the jury was primarily for the protection of the accused.

In regard to the Seventh Amendment and the federal civil jury, *Baltimore and Carolina Line v. Redman*, 295 U.S. 645 (1935) held that the right to trial by jury was the right that existed in England under the common law at the time of the Constitution's adoption. The emphasis was on substance, not form, particularly in the distinction between the province of the court and that of the jury.

2. Size

The number of members on a jury at the time the Constitution was adopted was clearly twelve, as seen by the foregoing authority. Depending on the political jurisdiction and the jury's function in a particular situation, juries of other sizes have been used. The smallest jury that has come to the writer's attention in the legal context is the three person jury that was empanelled by a judge in Utah to try challenges for cause in criminal cases. *Hopt v. Utah*, 110 U.S. 574 (1884).

An eight person jury was held constitutionally infirm in *Thompson v. Utah*, 170 U.S. 343 (1898). Although this was a state jury, this ruling had application to federal cases only. The defendant had been indicted for grand larceny when Utah was a territory. His first trial was by a jury of twelve which found him guilty. He was granted a new trial, but by that time Utah had become a state. The second trial was under state law to a jury of eight, to which the defendant objected after the verdict was received. (Utah's law even provided for juries in inferior courts to consist of four members.)

It was held in *Thompson, supra,* that the Federal Constitutional provisions pertaining to jury trial applied to federal territories, and that the defendant must be tried by the law applicable at the time the alleged crime was committed. At the time the crime was committed the only way he could have been convicted was by the unanimous verdict of twelve jurors, and he could not have consented to a jury of another number either by his silence or his express consent. This opinion was written by Justice John Marshall Harlan, who wrote many opinions that affected the jury.

Two years later, in *Maxwell v. Dow,* 176 U.S. 581 (1900), it was held that Utah could indeed try a person charged with a felony before an eight person jury. The defendant was found guilty, sentenced to 18 years, and he tested the result by *habeas corpus.* The holding was that the Fourteenth Amendment did not secure to all persons in the various states the jury of twelve guaranteed in federal criminal cases by the Sixth Amendment. Moreover, Justice Peckham added, "Trial by jury has never been affirmed to be a necessary requisite of due process." (*Maxwell, supra,* at 603)

The indication in *Maxwell* that the states might even dispense with juries altogether in criminal cases was not to be the final word. In *Duncan v. Louisiana,* 391 U.S. 145 (1968), the defendant was convicted of simple battery which had a maximum penalty of two years and a $300 fine. He had asked for a jury, but the request was denied because Louisiana only granted such requests when the penalty was either capital or imprisonment with hard labor. In actual fact, the defendant was sentenced to 60 days and a $150 fine.

Justice White, speaking for the majority, said that the Fourteenth Amendment, through the due process clause, looked increasingly to the Bill of Rights for guidance. Therefore, the Supreme Court held that a jury was guaranteed in all state criminal cases where, if the case were to be tried in federal court, the Sixth Amendment would guarantee a jury. The policy reasons for requiring a jury were listed as (1) protection against arbitrary action, (2) providing a safeguard against an overzealous prosecutor or a compliant, biased or eccentric judge, (3) the jury's common sense in comparison to the more tutored reaction of a judge, and (4) the federal and (in most instances) state constitutional decision to entrust the plenary power over life and liberty to a jury.

Justice White did indicate that there were arguments against jury trial, namely, juries were said to be (1) incapable of understanding evidence, (2) incapable of determining issues of fact, (3) unpredictable, (4) quixotic, and (5) ". . . little better than a roll of the dice." The opinion went on to suggest that crimes only carrying penalties up to six months did not require a jury trial if they otherwise qualified as petty offenses. The holding in *Duncan, supra,* was not retroactive. *Peters v. Kiff,* 407 U.S. 493 (1973)

Maxwell, supra, did not end the erosion of the size of the state criminal jury's size. *Williams v. Florida,* 399 U.S. 78 (1970), Justice White again writing the opinion, held that a defendant in a state felony case could be tried by a six person jury. He said that a twelve person jury is not a necessary ingredient of a jury trial. The values of a jury, namely, prevention of oppression, promotion of group discussion, freedom from outside intimidation, representation by a cross-section of the community, and reliability as a fact finder, he said, were not a function of size. He went on to say that the fact that the common law jury consisted of twelve persons was a "historical accident, unnecessary to effect the purposes of the jury system and wholly without significance except to mystics." Justice Marshall dissented, perhaps indicating that he is a mystic.

How far could the attrition of the right to a jury in state criminal trials go? The answer is contained in *Ballew v. Georgia,* 435 U.S. 223 (1978), which held, Justice Black writing the decision, that if the maximum penalty exceeds six months, a five person jury violates the Fourteenth Amendment due process clause and, through it, the Sixth Amendment.

It seemed for ever so long that the twelve person jury was just as safe in federal civil trials as it was in federal criminal trials. On December 20, 1937, the Federal Rules of Civil Procedure were adopted. Nobody dreamed at the time that this might be the first step in eliminating twelve person civil juries in federal court. Rule 83 of those rules gave the judges of District Courts the power to make and amend rules governing its practice not inconsistent with the Rules of Civil Procedure.

Rule 48 provided: "The parties may stipulate that the jury shall consist of any number less than twelve or that a verdict or a finding of a stated majority of the jurors shall be taken as the verdict or finding of the jury." On the face of it, this rule would seem to make the twelve person jury even more secure to a party that did not desire to waive it. However, it was held in *Coalgrove v. Battin*, 413 U.S. 149 (1973), that the Seventh Amendment and Rule 48 did not prevent District Courts from making a local rule, pursuant to their power under Rule 83, mandating six person juries in civil cases.

In less than six years after the *Coalgrove* decision, *supra*, at least 57 federal district courts adopted local rules reducing the size of civil juries to six members.[1] By now, the twelve person civil jury in federal court belongs right here in a history book.

3. Race

The question of racial representation on grand and petit juries has been almost exclusively concerned with blacks, and, as might be guessed, this concern did not develop before the end of the Civil War. Before that time, mention of blacks in Supreme Court opinions was more often than not in reference to their qualities as personalty rather than in reference to their almost nonexistent rights.

Typical of this era is *Bennett v. Butterworth*, 53 U.S. 361 (1850), where the suit was an action in a Federal District Court in Texas to recover the value of four negroes. The verdict was for $1,200 for the value of the negroes and six and one-half cents for damages.

Things changed with the Civil War and with the passage of the Fourteenth Amendment which guaranteed all citizens, including blacks, equal protection of the laws and due process. This Amendment became effective in 1868.

The first important case on the right to black representation on juries is *Strauder v. West Virginia*, 100 U.S. 303 (1879). A West Virginia statute passed in the 1872-73 session of their legislature required jurors to be white, male, and at least 21 years of age. This was the easy case because the statute was discriminatory on its face. Justice William Strong did use the unfortunate phrase "superior race" when referring to whites, but the court reversed the conviction and held that the Fourteenth Amendment was to be liberally construed.

That same year, a Virginia judge was charged under a federal law with failing to select jurors of the "African race" as grand and petit jurors. The judge's claim was that the United States District Court had no jurisdiction. He raised the issue in a *habeas corpus* action and lost. *Ex parte Virginia,* 100 U.S. 339 (1879). This was another opinion by Justice Strong.

The problem blacks had in raising the question of the systematic exclusion of blacks from jury service is illustrated by *Virginia v. Rives,* 100 U.S. 313 (1879). Rives, one of two blacks indicted for murder, moved the trial court to require the venire to be one-third black (it was all white). The procedure that the trial court followed was in accord with Virginia law. The Supreme Court said that discrimination in the selection of jurors was unconstitutional, but the fact that there had never been a black juror on a Patrick County jury and the fact that there was none on Rives' jury fell short of establishing discrimination in selecting the panel summoned to try the case. A mixed jury was not guaranteed. Justice Strong also wrote this opinion. One wonders what he meant in *Strauder, supra,* when he said that the Fourteenth Amendment was to be "liberally construed."

When the question of systematic exclusion of blacks is raised, the trial courts are required to hear evidence on pretrial motions to quash the indictment and to quash the petit jury venire, and the defendant must be permitted to subpoena witnesses to support his motion. *Neal v. Delaware,* 103 U.S. 370 (1880), announcing this holding, reversed Neal's conviction for rape and his sentence to be hung. To the same effect is *Carter v. Texas,* 177 U.S. 442 (1900), in which Justice John Marshall Harlan wrote the opinion.

Later cases addressed the issue of proof of discrimination. Supporting the claimed discriminatory exclusion by reason of race with an affidavit proved to be insufficient according to another opinion by Justice Harlan. *Charley Smith v. Mississippi,* 162 U.S. 592 (1896). Subsequent cases established that discrimination would not be presumed from the mere absence of blacks on the panel, *Tarrance v. Florida,* 188 U.S. 515 (1903), *Thomas v. Texas,* 212 U.S. 278 (1909), and that discrimination is an issue of fact to be tried to the judge, *Thomas v. Texas, supra.* Thus, the record in such a case must affirmatively show evidence or an attempt to introduce evidence on the issue of discriminatory selection. *Martin v. Texas,* 200 U.S. 316 (1906). The defendant has the burden of pleading and proof. *Franklin v. South Carolina,* 218 U.S. 161 (1910).

In 1935, blacks were still struggling to obtain the benefits of the Fourteenth Amendment. In *Norris v. Alabama,* 294 U.S. 587 (1935), the evidence showed that blacks had not been on a jury in Morgan County in over 50 years. In light of such a history of exclusion, the Supreme Court held in an opinion by Chief Justice Charles Evans Hughes, that even though the law was fair on its face it violated the equal protection clause in its implementation.

In *Pierre v. Louisiana,* 306 U.S. 354 (1939), it was established that the protection which the Fourteenth Amendment affords minorities in regard to petit juries applies to grand juries. In an opinion written by Justice Hugo Black, it was held that notwithstanding that the petit jury venire was quashed for excluding blacks, it was error not to quash the indictment because it was from the same venire as the petit jury. The defendant's conviction and sentence to death was reversed. *Pierre v. Louisiana,* 306 U.S. 354 (1939). Regardless of whether the discrimination in jury selection is done "ingeniously or ingenuously", a conviction in such a case cannot stand. *Smith v. Texas,* 311 U.S. 128 (1940).

Later cases again took up the issue of proof. In *Hill v. Texas,* 316 U.S. 400 (1942), a prima facie case of discrimination was established where the evidence showed that about 58,000 whites and 8,000 blacks paid the poll tax in Dallas County, and that for about 28 years there had been no black grand jurors and only a few black petit jurors. The United States Supreme Court in *Akins v. Texas,* 325 U.S. 398 (1945), reaffirmed that the burden is on the defendant to establish the discrimination and that mere inequality in the number selected does not establish discrimination.

A mere mathematical difference between the black-white ratios for the general population and for the list of prospective jurors may not be enough to show discrimination. Thus, showing only that the percentage of black population to the total population was 32.5 percent while the jury was drawn from the tax list of which the blacks comprised only 16 percent was not sufficient in *Brown v. Allen,* 344 U.S. 443 (1953). But, a system in a state court which puts white jurors' names on white slips and black jurors' names on yellow slips and ends up with no blacks on a 60 person panel established denial of equal protection. *Avery v. Georgia,* 345 U.S. 559 (1953). Neither will discrimination stand up when the jury commissioners have the effrontery to use a jury list that has already been condemned as discriminatory. *Whitus v. Georgia,* 385 U.S. (1967). Moreover, statistics alone, if strong enough, can establish discrimination. A conviction was reversed in *Sims v. Georgia,* 389 U.S. 404 (1967), when the evidence showed blacks comprised only 4.7 percent of the names on grand jury lists and 9.8 percent of the names on petit jury lists, while they comprised 24.4 percent of the population.

A class action was held unnecessary to correct *de facto* discrimination where the state law was fair on its face and the jury commissioners were already under a district court order not to systematically exclude blacks. *Carter v. Jury Commission,* 396 U.S. 320 (1970). In *Alexander v. Louisiana,* 405 U.S. 625 (1972), a black convicted of rape and sentenced to life in Louisiana had, prior to his trial, raised the issue of tokenism as to blacks on the grand jury and the issue of women being on the grand jury only on a voluntary basis. The Supreme Court held that he had made a prima facie showing of discrimination on the race issue and declined the female question.

The issue of standing to complain about blacks being systematically excluded from grand and petit juries was raised in a habeas corpus case by a white petitioner in *Peters v. Kiff,* 407 U.S. 493 (1972). It was held that the exclusion of a discernible class from jury duty injured all defendants because it denied them the possibility of a jury that would reflect a representative cross section of the community. Thus, anyone has standing to raise the issue.

In *Rose v. Mitchell,* 430 U.S. 545 (1979), Justice Blackmun, writing the opinion of the court, said that the criminal conviction of a negro could not be upheld under the Equal Protection clause of the Fourteenth Amendment if it was based on an indictment by a grand jury of which the foreman was picked so as to systematicallly exclude blacks from that position. Unfortunately for the defendant in that case, the Supreme Court also held that the evidence did not support his position.

Strangely, the discriminatory exclusion of blacks in federal court from the position of grand jury foreman did not invalidate a conviction of a white male charged with defrauding the government. The defendant also lost on the issue of exclusion of women from being foreperson of the grand jury. In 15 grand juries there had been no black or female forepersons. The discrimination was assumed, but it was held that nothing essential to a fair trial was affected. *Hobby v. United States*, 104 S.Ct. 3093 (1984). Dissenting from Chief Justice Burger's majority opinion, Justice Marshall was understandably bewildered, pointing out that the Chief Justice assumed the District Court would not discriminate while assuming that in this case it had discriminated.

It is widely assumed that prosecutors use their peremptory challenges to exclude racial and ethnic minorities in cases involving black defendants. This practice was condemned in *Illinois v. Payne*, 436 N.E.2d 1046 (1982), and in *People v. Wheeler*, 583 P.2d 748 (1978). The Supreme Court of the United States had ruled in *Swain v. Alabama*, 380 U.S. 202 (1965), that the use of peremptory challenges to strike minorities could not be shown to violate the equal protection clause unless a pattern over several trials was established. It was suggested in an article on the issues raised in *Payne, supra*, by Faye A. Silas,[2] that the adversary system results not in juror selection but in juror rejection, quoting trial lawyer Stanley Preiser of Charleston, West Virginia, not a new thought, as we will see later.

In *Batson v. Kentucky*, 106 S. Ct. 1712 (1986), the use of peremptory challenges to systematically exclude blacks when the defendant was a black was held to violate the fourteenth amendment after a prima facie showing that the prosecutor used peremtory challenges to exclude blacks the burden shifts to the prosecutor to show he had a neutral explanation (non-racial) or reason to challenge black jurors. It was held in *Turner v. Virginia*, 471 U.S. 1134 (April 30, 1986, no 84-6646), that a person accused of an interracial capital crime is entitled to have the jurors informed of the victims race and questioned on the issue of racial bias.[3]

4. Sex

Before the Nineteenth Amendment gave women the right to

vote in 1920, it was safe to say they were not on many voting lists from which prospective jurors were drawn. The pre-1920 cases discuss being entitled to a "jury of twelve men". *Capital Traction Company v. Hof,* 174 U.S. 1 (1899). However, the Nineteenth Amendment did not put an end to the idea that the Sixth Amendment jury was one that returned a unanimous verdict, under a judge, and consisted of twelve men. *Patton v. United States,* 281 U.S. 276 (1930).

Things began to change with *Glasser v. United States,* 315 U.S. 60 (1942). The defendant's objection to an all male jury in a United States District Court sitting in Illinois was overruled only because Illinois had only provided for women jurors as of July 1, 1939, and the federal practice (following the state practice where they sat in this regard) was considered as not having had time to catch up.

When a mother and her son were indicted for mail fraud and women were not permitted on the trial jury, the time had come and this conviction was reversed. *Ballard v. United States,* 329 U.S. 187 (1946). Still, in reviewing a New York conviction in 1947, the Supreme Court said that "... woman jury service has not so become a part of the texture or customary law of the land that one convicted of crime must be set free by this Court if his state has lagged behind...." *Fay v. New York,* 332 U.S. 261 (1947).

In 1974 the Supreme Court returned to the Louisiana law that excused women from jury service unless they had previously filed a written declaration of desire to be a juror, this being an issue which was present in *Alexander v. Louisiana, supra.* Once again a male raised the question. He was indicted on aggravated kidnapping and filed a motion to quash the venire because women had been systematically excluded from the jury. First, it was held that he had standing to raise the issue, that is, one did not need to be a member of the excluded group to raise the constitutional question. Second, the court held that women cannot be systematically excluded from panels from which petit jurors are drawn. The court used the occasion to note some of the reasons for keeping juries, namely: (1) to make available the common sense judgement of the community, (2) as a hedge against over-zealous or mistaken prosecutor, (3) in preference to a professional, over-conditioned, or biased judge. *Taylor v. Louisiana,* 419 U.S. 522 (1974).

5. Occupation

In *Rawlins v. Georgia*, 201 U.S. 638 (1906), five men were indicted for murder and convicted, four being sentenced to be hung and one to life imprisonment. Objection had been had to the jury pool because lawyers, preachers, ministers, doctors, engineers and firemen of trains, and dentists were excluded from service for the supposed reason that society benefited from their work not being interrupted. It was held that this statute did not violate the Fourteenth Amendment, although persons could not be excluded from jury service because of race or class. Oliver Wendell Holmes, Jr., who wrote the opinion, went on to say, "Even when persons are excluded, it is no ground for challenge to an array if a sufficient number of unexceptional persons are present." That did not sound complimentary to the jury system.

One of the more interesting cases to reach the Supreme Court, one where you can not help but admire plaintiff's counsel, was a case where the plaintiff had jumped off a moving train and sued the railroad company because they should have stopped him because they should have known he was insane. *Thiel v. Southern Pacific Co.*, 328 U.S. 217 (1946). The plaintiff won, at least in the Supreme Court. The plaintiff had moved to strike the jury because those working for wages were systematically excluded from service. The motion was overruled. Five persons who worked for wages actually sat on the trial jury. There was a defendant verdict on which judgment was entered. The Court of Appeals affirmed and the Supreme Court reversed. The Supreme Court said that it was an American tradition to have an impartial trial jury drawn from a cross-section of the community, and that court officials should not systematically and intentionally exclude any group.

6. Indifferent Jurors

The jurors are to come to their duty with an open mind and remain in that condition until the case is submitted to them. However, the fact that two jurors read newspaper accounts of the case they were trying did not entitle a defendant who was convicted of murder on the high seas to a reversal. *United States v. Reid*, 53 U.S. 361 (1851). Chief Justice Morrison R. Waite, while admitting that the juror was to ". . . be indifferent as he stands unsworn," (quoting Lord Coke), also noted that jurors often sought to excuse themselves on the ground that they had formed an opinion. Nonetheless, in such a case the burden of demonstrating that the juror does not have an open mind is on the party objecting to the juror. *Reynolds v. United States*, 98 U.S. 145 (1875).

However, in a trial that lasted three-fourths of an hour, in which the verdict was returned in five minutes, under mob atmosphere, there was no due process, and the judgment was reversed and remanded. The opinion of the court was written by Justice Oliver Wendell Holmes, Jr. *Moore v. Dempsey*, 261 U.S. 86 (1923). Likewise, in *Irvin v. Dowd*, 366 U.S. (1961), it was held that mob atmosphere prevented the defendant from having a panel of "indifferent jurors", and the case was reversed. See also, *Murphy* v. *Florida*, 421 U.S. 794 (1975).

In a case where jurors who believed in capital punishment were seated in the jury box, and jurors who had concientious scruples against capital punishment were excused by the court for cause (47 jurors, about half of the prospective venire), the resulting jury was not fit to perform the constitutional task demanded of it. *Witherspoon v. Illinois*, 391 U.S. 510 (1968). Of the 47 excused jurors who had scruples against capital punishment, only five had said that they would not bring back a death penalty verdict under any circumstances. The verdict of a jury so selected was not an indifferent verdict. Justice Stewart, writing the opinion of the court, said, "Whatever else might be said of capital punishment, it is at least clear that its imposition by a hanging jury cannot be squared with the Constitution." The conviction was reversed because the method of jury selection violated the defendant's right to due process.

In *Grigsby v. Mabry*, United States Circuit Court of Appeals, 8th Circuit, case No. 83-2113, discussed in the *National Law Journal*, Feb. 18, 1985, p 3, it was held that prosecutors could not systematically exclude jurors from the guilt-or-innocence phase of capital cases solely because they held absolute scruples against the death penalty. The writer of the article in *The National Law Journal*, David A. Kaplan, predicted that the case will be reviewed by the Supreme Court.

7. Sanity

Not many cases discuss the question, but it is probably assumed that the jurors should be sane. The issue was raised in *Jordan v. Massachusetts*, 225 U.S. 167 (1912) where the defendant filed a motion for a new trial on the ground that one of the jurors was insane. There was no question but what the juror was insane shortly after the verdict, but the court held that the burden was on the party raising the issue to show by a preponderance of the evidence that the insanity existed during the trial. In this the defendant failed, and his conviction was affirmed.

8. Peers

Much of the above material relates to obtaining a jury of one's peers. In a lighter vein, what may be the ultimate example of obtaining a jury of one's peers, occurred in Sonoma County, California, in March of 1984. The plaintiff was a lawyer suing for a fee of $7,500 allegedly due for work on a divorce case. There was a counter-claim for malpractice. The defendant's attorney had forgotten to post the required jury fee 12 days in advance under California practice. The defendant wanted a jury nonetheless, and the judge offered him a jury of lawyers which were standing around. The defendant accepted the offer.

The trial lasted two and one-half days; the jury returned a unanimous verdict of $5,001.35 in favor of the plaintiff.[3]

9. Unanimity

The common law jury requirement of unanimity was a requirement of federal juries, civil and criminal, from the beginning to the present time. In *American Publishing Company v. Fisher*, 166 U.S. 464 (1897), in an opinion by Justice Brewer, it was held that the Constitution secured to United States citizens in United States Courts the right to jury trial as at common law and that an essential feature of this type of trial was a unanimous verdict. Therefore, a 9-3 verdict for $20,844.75 for the plaintiff was reversed. That same year, Chief Justice Fuller wrote that unanimity was essential in civil cases in federal courts, notwithstanding the argument that Congress had delegated to the territory of Utah the discretion to dispense with unanimity. *Springfield v. Thomas*, 166 U.S. 707 (1897).

If the case was being tried in state court under federal substantive law, it was another matter. *Minneapolis and St. Louis Railroad Company v. Bombolis,* 241 U.S. 211 (1916), held that in a suit in state court under the Federal Employees Liability Act, a Minnesota law was constitutional which provided that after the jury had deliberated for twelve hours, and could not reach a unanimous verdict, they could reach a verdict when five-sixths of their number agreed. The reason, according to the opinion by Chief Justice White, was the first ten Amendments to the United States Constitution were not concerned with state action. Therefore, the Seventh Amendment did not bind the states to the federal concept of civil jury.

In state criminal cases unanimity came to the attention of the United States Supreme Court in the 1970's. *Johnson v. Louisiana,* 406 U.S. 356 (1972), Justice White writing the opinion of the court, held that the conviction of a defendant by the 9-3 verdict of a state court jury did not violate the due process clause of the Fourteenth Amendment. The same result but with verdicts of 11-1 and 10-2, was reached in *Apodaca v. Oregon,* 406 U.S. 404 (1972), with Justice White again writing the decision. However, the non-unanimous verdict of a six person jury in a non-petty case in *Burch v. Louisiana,* 441 U.S. 130 (1979), did in fact deprive the defendant of his constitutional right to trial by jury. Justice Rehnquist delivered the opinion of the court.

Vincent Bentivenga, judge in the Circuit Court of Cook County, Illinois, writing an article "Is 11 Enough" in the December, 1983, issue of the American Bar Association Journal, discussed a case in which the jury deadlocked in an 11-1 vote. The judge excused the jury after two and one-half days of deliberation. The judge calculated that the one stubborn juror (as he was told by the other jurors) who refused to listen to reason was the cause of the waste of over $60,000 it had cost to prosecute. The case was retired and resulted in a conviction after two and one-half hours of deliberation. The cure, as far as the judge was concerned, was for the United States to catch up with England and permit verdicts when 10 out of 12 jurors agreed.

That sounds fine on paper. This writer once represented a woman charged with trafficking in drugs. The first jury hung 11-1 for conviction. The second jury returned a 12-0 not guilty verdict. We do not always know if our clients are innocent, but I felt in my heart that that woman was not guilty. Obviously, the nine members of the grand jury thought she was guilty. That made the tally 20 for guilty and 13 not guilty. Non-unanimous verdicts change things — if you're a defendant — for the worse.

Perhaps the most convincing study indicating that the quality of the verdicts is better under the unanimity rule (quality simply meaning that the verdict is consistent with the law) is a study of 69 voluntary juries by Reid Hastie, Seven D. PenRod and Nancy Pennington who wrote *Inside the Jury* (Harvard University Press, 1984). They presented a condensed rerun of a murder trial. One third of the juries had to reach a unanimous verdict, one third a 10-2 verdict and one a 8-4 verdict. They concluded that the fairest verdicts were unanimous.

10. Presence of the Defendant

Generally speaking, in a criminal trial the presence of the defendant is mandatory. *Lewis v. United States,* 146 U.S. 370 (1892). In *Hopt v. Utah,* 110 U.S. 574 (1884), the trial court dispensed with the defendant's presence while a three person jury (not a part of the venire for the trial jury) separately tried six jurors who had been challenged for bias. The absence of the defendant was with the consent of his counsel. Justice Harlan wrote the opinion of the court which held that the presence of the defendant could not be dispensed with, even by the defendant or his counsel. However, this holding was based upon a state statute, rather than the federal Constitution.

An attorney, in *Howard v. Kentucky,* 200 U.S. 164 (1906), accused juror Alexander of having expressed an opinion on the case. The judge inquired of the juror privately, excused him and sent him to jail. Implying that the Fifth and Sixth Amendments would have required the defendant's presence during the judge's inquiry, those amendments were held not binding upon the states. The writer of this opinion, Justice Joseph McKenna, said, "The right to challenge is the right to reject, not to select a juror." This language echoes Justice Stephen Johnson Field who earlier had said, "The right to challenge is the right to reject, not to select." *Hayes v. Missouri,* 120 U.S. 68 (1887).

In *Frank v. Mangum,* 237 U.S. 309 (1915), a case in which the defendant was charged with murder, found guilty on a verdict and sentenced to death, the defendant was not in the courtroom when the verdict was received. His presence had been waived by his attorney. It was held that the due process clause of the Fourteenth Amendment did not impose upon the states any particular form or mode of procedure, but only required essentials such as notice, a hearing, and opportunity to be heard before a competent tribunal. Specifically, the presence of the defendant when the verdict is rendered is not such an essential part of the hearing.

Snyder v. Massachusetts, 291 U.S. 97 (1934), in an opinion by Justice Cardozo, held that the Fourteenth Amendment did not require the presence of a defendant at a view of the scene in a state criminal proceeding.

11. Right to Indictment by Grand Jury

Although the Fifth Amendment to the Constitution of the United States guarantees that no one will be charged under federal law for a capital or otherwise infamous crime except by the presentment or indictment of a grand jury, this in not binding upon the states. *Hurtado v. California*, 110 U.S. 516 (1884), held that a proceeding by information before a magistrate who certified the probable guilt of the defendant did not violate the due process clause of the Fourteenth Amendment. Later, Justice Pitney, speaking for the court in *Frank v. Mangum*, 237 U.S. 309 (1915), said that indictment by a grand jury is not essential to due process.

12. The Jury as an Element of Due Process

The civil jury is not by reason of the due process clause of the Fourteenth Amendment mandatory in state cases. In *Walker v. Sauvinet*, 92 U.S. 90 (1875), Sauvinet sued Walker claiming that Walker failed to serve him because he was "a man of color." This was illegal under Louisiana law and, if true, would have entitled Sauvinet to damages. Louisiana law provided for trial by jury, but, if the jury failed to reach a verdict, the judge then would make a decision upon the same evidence that was presented to the jury. That happened in this case, and the judge found for Walker. The fact that the Louisiana procedure did not meet the test for a Sev-

enth Amendment jury did not matter because the Seventh Amendment applied only to the federal government. Moreover, a civil jury trial
was not a privilege or an immunity of national citizenship which
the states were forbidden to abridge.

Even though the case is civil and is being tried in state court,
the state court may be required to grant a right to jury trial if the
right being protected is part of a right accorded by Congress. In *Dice
v. Akron, Canton & Youngstown R. Co.*, 342 U.S. 359 (1952), the court
had before it the issue of whether the question of fraud was for the
court as it was under the law of Ohio (the suit commenced in state
court) or for the jury as it was under federal law. It was held that the
right to trial by jury was "... too substantial a part of the right
accorded by the [Federal Employers' Liability Act] to permit it to be
classified as a mere 'local rule of procedure' for denial in the manner
that Ohio has here used."

Likewise, in criminal cases the first ten amendments do not
restrict state action. The question is one of due process. This is
determined by an examination of the settled usages and modes of
proceedings existing in the common law and statutes of England
"...before the immigration of our ancestors, and shown not to have
been unsuited to their civil and political condition by having been
acted on by them after settlement of this country." *Twining v. New
Jersey,* 211 U.S. 78 (1908). Justice Mahlon Pitney, writing the opinion
of the court in *Frank v. Mangum,* 237 U.S. 309, 340 (1915), said "Trial
by jury is not essential to be due process, either in civil cases, . . . or
in criminal cases." Justice Cardozo wrote that the right to trial by
jury was "... not of the very essence of a scheme of ordered liberty" and not "... to be ranked as fundamental." *Palko v. Connecticut,*
302 U.S. 319 (1937). *Brown v. New Jersey,* 175 U.S. 172 (1899), *Adamson v.
California,* 232 U.S. 46 (1903), and *Fay v. New York,* 332 U.S. 261 (1947),
also hold that the Fourteenth Amendment does not automatically
incorporate the first ten amendments to the United States
Constitution.

The United States Supreme Court did, however, finally come to
the conclusion that in non-petty criminal cases, the defendant has a
right to trial by jury in state cases. The denial of such a right was
held to be a denial of due process in *Duncan v. Louisiana,* 391 U.S. 145
(1968). In *Burch v. Louisiana,* 441 U.S. 130 (1979), the Supreme Court

went so far as to rule that a non-unanimous six person jury deprived a defendant in a state, non-petty, criminal case of his constitutional right to trial by jury.

13. Contempt

Contempt of court has traditionally been one of the surest ways to get to jail without the benefit of a jury. In *In Re Debs*, 158 U.S. 564 (1895), it was held that punishment for contempt of the court's orders without a jury was no invasion of the right to trial by jury. As a matter of fact, the opinion of the court stated, "To submit the question of disobedience to another tribunal, be it a jury or another court, would operate to deprive the proceeding of half of its efficiency."

In *Gomphers v. Bucks Stove & Range Co.*, 221 U.S. 418 (1911), the distinction was made that criminal contempt was punishment for disobedience of a court's orders, and civil contempt was punishment to require compliance with court orders. In *United States v. United Mine Workers of America*, 330 U.S. 258 (1947), the court held that the defendants were properly tried by the court without a jury for both civil and criminal contempt.

In another case, two of eleven defendants, who had been convicted of conspiring to teach and advocate the violent overthrow of the government in violation of the Smith Act and were fined $10,000 and sentenced to five years in jail, failed to surrender for execution of their sentences. They remained fugitives for four and one half years. Both were found guilty of contempt by the court and sentenced to serve three years to commence after they had served the original five years. The court held, in *Green v. United States*, 356 U.S. 165 (1958), ". . . beyond peradventure that criminal contempts are not subject to jury trial as a matter of constitutional right."

Ross R. Barnett, the governor of Mississippi, and Paul B. Johnson, Jr., lieutenant governor of Mississippi, had been charged with contempt by the United States Court of Appeals for the Fifth Circuit in connection with the effort to enroll James Meredith in the University of Mississippi. In *United States v. Barnett*, 376 U.S. 681 (1964), it was held that, except where specifically precluded by statute, the courts have power to proceed summarily in contempt matters.

In *Shillitani v. United States*, 384 U.S. 364 (1966), witnesses, even after a grant of immunity, refused to answer questions before a grand jury. Without an indictment and without a jury, the witnesses were sentenced to two years confinement subject to release upon testifying before the grand jury. The court held that since the prisoners carried "the keys of their prison" the action was essentially civil, for the benefit of the parties, and that no jury was required. Justice Clark's opinion noted that the contemnor must have the ability to comply with the court's order in a civil contempt and that the court must use the least power adequate to the end.

In *Cheff v. Schnackenberg*, 384 U.S. 373 (1966), in another opinion by Justice Clark, it was held that the federal courts had power in punitive contempt to issue sentences of up to six months incarceration. More time would require a jury. The distinction was that less than six months would constitute a petty offense. *Dyke v. Taylor Implement*, 391 U.S. 216 (1968), held that when the maximum sentence for contempt was ten days and $90, it was a petty offense triable without a jury, on the other hand *Bloom v. State of Illinois*, 391 U.S. 194 (1968) held that when a defendant faces a 24 months incarceration for contempt, he has a right to a trial by jury.

14. Petty Offenses

A proceeding was had in the District of Columbia wherein a man was charged with conspiracy to illegally conduct a boycott in connection with an effort to organize musicians. He was found guilty in a bench trial (although he had requested a jury) and sentenced to a $25 fine or 30 days in jail. Under the District of Columbia procedure he had a right to post a bond, and a jury trial de novo could be had at the next level. Justice Harlan, writing the opinion of the court in *Callan v. Wilson*, 127 U.S. 540 (1888), an action in habeas corpus, held that the defendant in a federal trial had a right to trial by jury except when petty offenses were involved. The fact that he had a right to a jury trial on appeal was insufficient. Thus, the conviction was reversed, and the petitioner (Callan), was discharged.

In *District of Columbia v. Colt,* 282 U.S. 63 (1930), the question was raised whether driving an automobile at a greater speed than was reasonable and proper (22 miles per hour) was inherently wicked *(malum in se)* or only wrong as forbidden by positive law *(malum prohibitum)*. The Supreme Court held that the act was *malum in se* at common law (e.g., if committed with a horse), the defendant was entitled to trial by jury, and his conviction was reversed. On the other hand, a person who sold the unused portion of railway excursion tickets without a license was held not entitled to trial by jury because the offense, at common law, was a petty offense.

Even the states could not dispense with jury trial in criminal cases unless the offense charged was petty. *Duncan v. Louisiana,* 391 U.S. 145 (1968). However, *Cheff v. Schnackenberg, supra,* seemed to limit petty offenses, even in contempt, to situations where the maximum penalty was six months or less. Thus, in a criminal case in New York where the maximum penalty was up to a year confinement, the defendant had a right to trial by jury under the Fourteenth Amendment. *Baldwin v. New York,* 399 U.S. 66 (1970).

15. Waiver

In civil and criminal cases, the parties can waive the right to trial by jury, but the conditions, method and effect of such waiver are established by a number of Supreme Court cases. Although *Graham v. Bayne,* 59 U.S. 60 (1855), held that the parties to a civil suit could waive a jury and submit the law and facts to the court, the parties could not make the court an arbitrator to find the facts; the facts had to be agreed. To the same effect was *Burr v. Des Moines,* 68 U.S. 99 (1863), which held that the parties could submit the case to the court, but two conditions had to be met, namely: (1) An agreement of submission must appear in the record, and (2) The statement of submission must be sufficient in itself without inferences or comparisons or balancing of testimony. None of the jury's fact-finding function was to be left to the court.

Norris v. Jackson, 76 U.S. 12 (1869), noted that a statute of March 3, 1865, provided a procedure for waiver of trial by jury. No doubt this statute was passed in part due to the confusion brought about by the two cases first cited in this section. Under that statute, the waiver had to appear of record and appear in writing. *Kearns v. Case,* 79 U.S. 275 (1870).

Hodges v. Easton, 106 U.S. 275 (1882), reversed a district court judgment which had been decided by the court partly upon facts found by a special jury and partly upon facts conceded or not disputed. It was held that the trial court could not constitutionally decide the case partly on facts submitted to a jury and determine others itself without a waiver of jury trial. Justice John Marshall Harlan, who wrote the opinion of the court, said that every reasonable presumption would be indulged against waiver.

Now of course, under the Federal Rules of Civil Procedure, pursuant to Rule 38(b), a party to a civil action may demand a jury trial of any issue triable of right by a jury by serving a written demand for the same any time after commencement of the action and not later than ten days after service of the last pleading directed to the issue. Otherwise, pursuant to Rule 38(d), there is a waiver of the right to trial by jury. The demand once made cannot be withdrawn except by mutual consent. Rules 38(d) and 39(a).

Concerning criminal actions, in *Thompson v. Utah,* 170 U.S. 343 (1898), in a situation where the federal Constitution applied, a defendant could not consent by silence or otherwise to be tried by a jury of eight. This case arose and was tried while Utah was a territory, and was reversed and retried after Utah was a state. It was held that federal jury requirements applied since they were in effect at the time of the alleged crime. Justice Harlan wrote, ". . . the wise men who formed the Constitution of the United States and the people who approved it were of the opinion that life and liberty, when involved in criminal prosecutions, would not be adequately secured except through the unanimous verdict of twelve jurors." *Thompson, supra,* at 353. As to the defendant not objecting to only eight jurors until after the verdict, Justice Harlan said, ". . . it was not in the power of one accused of a felony, by consent expressly given or by his silence, to authorize a jury of only eight persons to pass upon the question of his guilt." *Thompson, supra,* at 353. However, a defendant can waive jury trial in petty criminal cases. *Schick v. United States,* 195 U.S. 65 (1904).

While a federal criminal jury does consist of twelve persons, if a juror is excused because of illness, the defendant and the government can agree to submit the case to eleven jurors. *Patton v. United States*, 281 U.S. 276 (1930). Justice Sutherland, writing the opinion in that case, made clear that the waiver by the defendant must be express and intelligent. Even a defendant without counsel can waive jury trial in a felony case in federal court, provided that these conditions are met. *Adams v. United States*, 317 U.S. 269 (1942).

The criminal defendant in federal court does not, however, have a constitutional right to a bench trial. In a mail fraud prosecution, the defendant waived trial by jury and the government refused to consent to a bench trial. The defendant was tried to the jury and convicted. The convictions stood. Chief Justice Warren, speaking for the Court, wrote ". . . there is no federally recognized right to a criminal trial before a judge sitting alone . . . ." *Singer v. United States*, 380 U.S. 24 (1965). In *Serfass v. United States*, 420 U.S. 377 (1975), Chief Justice Burger, in a case where the issue was former jeopardy, said in the opinion of the court that waiver of jury trial required concurrence of the defendant, the government, and the court.

16. Control of the Jury by the Judge

There are numerous ways in which judges shape trial procedures which limit the input of the jury into the ultimate product of jury trial, the judgment of the court. The most important of the means available to the court to control or dispense with the jury in common law actions will be discussed in this section. The courts have come a long way in the direction of judge control.

Taking *Georgia v. Brailsford*, 3 U.S. 1 (1794), at face value, in the beginning of the constitutional period jurors were masters of law as well as of fact. After having first informed the jury (this was a jury case being tried before the Supreme Court) that generally facts were for the jury and law for the court, Chief Justice Jay continued ". . . you have nevertheless a right to take upon yourselves to judge of both, and to determine the law as well as the fact in controversy." This was a civil case between Georgia and private interests as to whether a debt belonged to the state or to the original creditors. If this much discretion is still left anywhere in the jury system, it is only in the jury's ability to find for the defense in criminal cases, in which there is no such thing as a directed verdict in favor of the prosecution.

Wigmore wrote in the twentieth century:

The doctrine has obtained in a few jurisdictions that the jury, in dealing with the local law applicable to the case, has in criminal cases a legal right to repudiate the instructions of the judge and to determine the law for themselves. But this ill-advised doctrine, defiant of the fundamentals of law, had only narrow acceptance.[4]

The air of pristine democracy which had existed at the beginning of the constitutional period and which had allowed in many cases for juries to decide both law and fact had faded so rapidly that by 1835 DeTocqueville could write:

It is the judge who sums up the various arguments which have wearied [the jury's] memory, and who guides them through the devious course of the proceedings; he points their attention to the exact question of fact that they are called upon to decide and tells them how to answer the question of law. His influence over them is almost unlimited.[5]

Notwithstanding both DeTocqueville and Wigmore, there were some serious questions about a jury having the right to decide both law and fact. In the state courts, New York's Court of Appeals split on the question in 1804,[6] and finally denied the right in 1863.[7] A Massachusetts attorney risked contempt by arguing law contrary to the direction of the court in 1808, and by doing so he obtained an acquittal for his client. The same year, the jury was given the right by statute to decide law as well as fact, but the jurors had the option to return a special verdict for a general verdict subject to the opinion of the court on a point stated. This statute was repealed in 1836, but it was held permissible for a lawyer to argue law contrary to the direction of the court in 1847, although the jury was charged to take its law from the court. A statute gave the jury the power to decide law in criminal cases in 1855, but, despite this statute, the supreme court of the state held that law was for the judge to decide.[8]

Pursuant to statutory rule-making authority, the Supreme Court of Connecticut made it a rule for the courts to declare their opinion of the law of the case to the jury. Another statute to the same effect was enacted in 1812, covering civil and criminal cases. Blunting this trend was an 1821 statute of that state which required the court to direct the jury on the law in civil cases but to only state the court's opinion in criminal cases. The jury, in criminal cases, was to consider both law and fact. The Supreme Court of Connecticut, 81 years later, held that, notwithstanding this statute, the jury must accept its law from the court. A statute buttressed this position in 1918.[9]

In early Illinois, the juries judged both fact and law, and this right was given by an 1822 statute. Until 1931 it was thought to be the law of the state that a lawyer could argue law to the jury.[10] New Hampshire had this right until 1843,[11] but Tennessee was unclear on the issue until 1852, when it was held that the court was the only witness to the law. The right to decide law in Tennessee was finally lost in 1881.[12] Maine had the right in 1860,[13] but later lost it,[14] and Vermont lost the right in 1897.[15] It appears that Pennsylvania did not clearly lose the right until 1923;[16] Rhode Island had the right initially but lost it by 1860.[17] The right was denied in Maryland in 1804, but even after the constitutional grant to the jury of the right to decide law and fact, the court still denied the jury the right to rule on the constitutionality of the statute.[18] Before 1860, the jury's right to decide law had been denied in Alabama, Kentucky, Mississippi, Missouri, North Carolina, Ohio, and Texas.[19] Virginia did not reject the right until 1881.[20]

Indiana denied the right in 1828, allowed it in 1830, denied it in 1851, and established it by constitutional provision in 1858.[21] Louisiana had the right by statute in the beginning, lost in in 1871 and obtained it in 1879 by this constitutional amendment: ". . . the jury in all criminal cases shall be the judges of the law and of the facts on the question of guilt or innocence, having been charged as to the law applicable to the case by the presiding judge." However, this provision notwithstanding, it was held in 1885 that Louisiana juries had to take the law from the judges.[22]

A Georgia statute of 1833 said that juries were to be judges of fact and law and were, in every case, to deliver a general verdict of guilty or not guilty. It was held in 1861 that the jury had to take its law from the judge, and this continued to be the law regardless of a constitutional provision of 1877 which purported to make the jury the judge of law and fact.[23] It is still provided in the Georgia constitution as follows:

> In all prosecutions or indictments for libel the truth may be given in evidence; and the jury in all criminal cases shall be the judges of the law and facts. The power of the judges to grant new trials in case of conviction is preserved.[24]

The constitution of Missouri still contains the passage, ". . . and suits and prosecutions for libel, the jury, under the direction of the court shall determine the law and the facts."[25] Still, it is said that the right of the jury to decide law has been repudiated in all states except Indiana and Maryland.[26]

That judges were aware of their control is made clear in *Pleasants v. Fant*, 89 U.S. 116 (1875). Justice Miller, speaking for the court, mentioned three ways in which judges controlled juries, to wit: (1) rulings on evidence, (2) instructions on law, and (3) setting aside verdicts which were rendered contrary to the evidence.

During Aaron Burr's treason trial before Chief Justice Marshall, it sounded at times as if the doctrine of *Georgia v. Brailsford, supra,* was still alive. Marshall instructed the jury that it must decide the issue of whether Burr was levying war as being "compounded of fact and law." 1 Burr's Trial 470, cited in *Sparf & Hansen v. United States,* 156 U.S. 51 (1895). But, it seems that Marshall was already leaning in the direction of judge control for he added, "The jury have now heard the opinion of the court on the *law* of the case. *They will apply that law to the facts* and will find a verdict of guilty or not guilty as their own consciences may direct." The emphasis is that supplied in *Sparf & Hansen, supra.* Thus, the jury was directed to take the law from the court, and it was only the combined effect of that law and the facts that was left to the jury.

With this introduction to judge control, we will explore its various aspects.

a. Law and Fact and the Court's Opinion

Not only does the federal judge have the right to decide issues of law, the court has the right to give the court's opinion on the facts. The integrity of the jury system, however, requires that this summing up by the court, this giving of the court's opinion on the facts, not be binding by its terms. For violation of this rule, the trial court was reversed in *M'Lanahan v. Universal Insurance Company*, 26 U.S. 469 (1828). The right of the court to give its non-binding opinion on the facts was reaffirmed in *Carver v. Jackson*, 29 U.S. 1 (1830). Justice Story wrote both of these opinions.

In *Reynolds v. United States*, 98 U.S. 145 (1878), a conviction for polygamy survived appeal notwithstanding the trial court's vivid description of the horrors of the practice of polygamy. In the court's opinion in *Vicksburg & Railroad v. Putnam*, 118 U.S. 545 (1886), Justice Horace Gray noted that both in the federal courts and in England the court can comment upon the evidence, call attention to what the court considers the important parts, and express an opinion on that evidence. Of course, all matters of fact must ultimately be left to the jury. Justice Gray noted the state practice prohibited judges from expressing to the jury an opinion upon the facts, but held that the federal courts were not controlled by the state practice. To much the same effect was *Rucker v. Wheeler*, 127 U.S. 85 (1887), and *Lovejoy v. United States*, 128 U.S. 171 (1888).

Balancing the picture were *Hicks v. United States*, 150 U.S. 442 (1893), and *Starr v. United States*, 153 U.S. 614 (1894). In *Hicks*, the defendant exercised his right to be a witness in his own defense. Hicks had been charged with encouraging another person to kill Colvard (a white man married to a Cherokee woman). After a summing up by the court which was to the effect that the testimony of the accused was to be received with great caution, the jury found the defendant guilty. Justice George Shiras, in the opinion of the Supreme Court, noted that juries give great weight to the word of the trial court, and that the right of the defendant to be a competent witness should not be defeated by hostile comments of the trial judge. Justice Shiras said, ". . . it must be remembered that men may testify truthfully, although their lives hang in balance . . . ." The conviction was reversed.

In *Starr, supra,* defendant Starr, a Cherokee Indian, had been the object of pursuit by the United States Marshal and one Floyd Wilson, whom the marshal had impressed to assist him. Wilson spotted Starr, threw his gun to his shoulder and fired at Starr, who had been standing with his gun in both hands pointed down. Starr had not necessarily known who Wilson was or what he was up to. Starr returned fire and killed Wilson. The marshal also fired at Starr, and Starr escaped on the marshal's horse. Later Starr was apprehended, tried and convicted before a jury and sentenced to be hung.

Chief Justice Fuller delivered the opinion of the court. He noted that the influence of the judge on the jury is necessarily of great weight, but that it was the practice in the federal courts and in England that the presiding judge could, at the court's discrection, sum up the case and express an opinion on the facts. As to the trial court's summation concerning Starr's background and its bearing upon his right of self-defense, the Chief Justice said, ". . . the possession of a conscience void of offense toward God and men is not an indispensable prerequisite to justification of action in the face of imminent and deadly peril. . . ." Commenting on the derogatory nature of the summation, the Chief Justice continued, ". . . argumentative matter of this sort should not be thrown into the scales of justice by the judicial officer who holds them." The case was reversed.

The power of the federal judge to express an opinion upon the facts, however, remained, subject only to the limitation that the power and duty remained with the jury to consider and weigh all the facts. *Hyde v. United States,* 225 U.S. 347 (1912).

b. Control of the Jury by Directed Verdicts and Similar Devices

Obviously, if the trial court does not submit the case to the jury for a decision, the jury is not a factor in the result. In the early days of jury trial in the United States, it was not so common for the courts to take cases away from juries. In *Elmore v. Grymes,* 26 U.S. 469 (1828), the trial court, in an ejectment action, entered a peremptory nonsuit against the plaintiff against the plaintiff's will (a plaintiff could often enter a voluntary non-suit which did not prejudice such party in a later action). Chief Justice John Marshall wrote the opinion reversing this decision.

In *Chinoweth v. Haskell's Lessee,* 28 U.S. 92 (1830), the result was different. At trial, the defendant had demurred to the evidence of the plaintiff and the jury found for the plaintiff, subject to the opinion of the court on the demurrer. The trial court overruled the demurrer and gave judgment to the plaintiff. Again, Chief Justice Marshall wrote the opinion of the Supreme Court, which reversed the trial court and sustained the defendant's demurrer. The Chief Justice observed that if by no fair contruction of the evidence the verdict for the plaintiff could be sustained, the judgment rendered by the trial court must be reversed.

In *Parks v. Rose,* 52 U.S. 362 (1850), the Court held that the trial court could give the jury peremptory instructions to find for a party, but that there must be a basis in the evidence for such instructions. Holding it proper for the trial court to instruct the jury to find for the defendant where there is no dispute about the facts and the facts and law are conclusive against the plaintiff are *Schuchardt v. Allens,* 68 U.S. 359 (1863), *Merchant's Bank v. State Bank,* 77 U.S. 604 (1870), *Bevans v. United States,* 80 U.S. 56 (1871), *Improvement Company v. Munson,* 81 U.S. 442 (1871), *Walbrun v. Babbit,* 83 U.S. 577 (1872), *Hendrick v. Lindsay,* 93 U.S. 143 (1876), *Railroad Company v. Jones,* 95 U.S. 439 (1877), *Herbert v. Butler,* 97 U.S. 319 (1878), *Bowditch v. Boston,* 101 U.S. 16 (1879), *Griggs v. Houston,* 104 U.S. 533 (1881), *Anderson County Commissioners v. Beal,* 113 U.S. 227 (1884), *Schofield v. Chicago & St. Paul Railway Co.,* 114 U.S 615 (1885), *Marshall v. Hubbard,* 117 U.S. 415 (1886), *People's Savings Bank v. Bates,* 120 U.S. 556 (1886), *Meehan v. Valentine,* 145 U.S. 611 (1892), and *Southern Pacific Company v. Pool,* 160 U.S. 438 (1896).

Moreover, although it is a much less frequent occurence, the trial court in a proper case may also enter a directed verdict against the defendant. Thus, a verdict on liability was directed against the defendant railroad in *Union Pacific Railroad v. McDonald,* 152 U.S. 262 (1894). In this case a child had been injured when it entered into an unfenced slag area belonging to the defendant.

The case of *D'Wolf v. Rabaud,* 26 U.S. 476 (1828), held that one important fact, namely, the question of citizenship, was for the court to decide before trial by a plea in abatement.

Pleasants v. Fant, 89 U.S. 116 (1875), perhaps most clearly gives the reason why a court can direct a verdict and prevent the jury from making an independent judgment on the facts. The court said, "It is the duty of a court in its relation to the jury to protect parties from unjust verdicts arising from ignorance of the rules of law and of evidence, from impulse of passion or prejudice, or from any other violation of his lawful rights in the conduct of the trial."

In *Slocum v. New York Life Insurance Co.,* 228 U.S. 364 (1913), the Court drew a fine distinction. The court of appeals had reversed the judgment of the trial court (which had entered judgment on a verdict) and directed a verdict for the opposite party in conformity with state practice. The Supreme Court noted that the federal court had to abide by the Seventh Amendment. The court of appeals could have set the verdict aside and ordered a new trial, but it could not itself determine the facts. When it had set the verdict aside, the right to trial by jury arose as when the suit was filed. It was within the power of the trial court to peremptorily instruct the jury, but the verdict of the jury could not be eliminated.

In a civil case, the court may reserve judgment on the defendant's motion to dismiss at the close of the plaintiff's evidence, and, after receiving a verdict for the plaintiff, enter judgment for the defendant on the defendant's motion. *Baylis v. Travellers' Insurance Company,* 113 U.S. 316 (1884). In *Baltimore and Carolina Line v. Redman,* 295 U.S. 654 (1935), it was made clear that a federal judge in civil cases could reserve a ruling on a defendant's motion for a directed verdict at the close of the evidence and enter judgment for the defendant on that motion after a verdict for the plaintiff.

In *Gasoline Products Co., Inc. v. Champlin Refining Co.,* 283 U.S. 494 (1931), the court observed that although at common law there was no practice of setting aside a verdict in part, it was permissible for the trial court to follow that procedure where the requirement for jury trial had been satisfied on a particular, severable issue, even though the separate issue must be tried again. In the case before the court the issues were not severable.

From early on, there were checks on the court's powers to direct verdicts and give peremptory instructions. Even a slight discrepancy in the facts required the judge to submit the case to the jury. *Barney v. Schmeider,* 76 U.S. 248 (1869). Even though the facts were undisputed, it was for the jury and not the judge to determine that the defendant was negligent. *Railway Company v. Stout,* 84 U.S. 657 (1873). A case should not be withdrawn from the jury unless the testimony is of such a conclusive character that a court would have to set aside a verdict in opposition to it. *Phoenix Ins. Co. v. Doster,* 106 U.S. 30 (1882), and *Montclair v. Dana,* 107 U.S. 162 (1882). A peremptory instruction to find for the defendant was improper where, giving the plaintiff the benefit of the permissible inferences from the evidence, the plaintiff was not guilty of contributory negligence. *Kane v. Northern Central Railway,* 128 U.S. 91 (1888). Likewise, where there was some evidence of care by the plaintiff, it was error to direct a verdict in favor of the defendant because of contributory negligence. *Jones v. East Tennessee Railroad Co.,* 128 U.S. 443 (1888).

When reasonable men may fairly differ as to whether there was negligence on the given facts, the matter is one for the determination of a jury. *Grand Trunk Railway v. Ives,* 144 U.S. 108 (1892). Thus, where uncertainty exists as to either negligence or contributory negligence, the question is one of fact for the jury, whether the uncertainty arises from a conflict of testimony or exists because fair minded people could draw different conclusions from the same facts. *Richmond & Danville Railroad v. Powers,* 149 U.S. 43 (1893), *Gunning v. Cooley,* 281 U.S. 90 (1930).

The Federal Rules of Civil Procedure, adopted in 1937, particularly Rule 50(b) giving the court authority to enter judgment contrary to a verdict instead of awarding a new trial, did not reduce the power of a jury to find the facts. *Berry v. United States,* 312 U.S. 450 (1941). Furthermore, just because a case is close is no reason for the court to usurp the function of the jury. *Jacob v. City of New York,* 315 U.S. 752 (1942).

Although a court cannot direct a verdict in favor of the government in a criminal case, it can of course direct a verdict for the defendant. *Famous Smith v. United States,* 151 U.S. 50 (1893). This was a murder case where it was incumbent upon the government to prove that the defendant was not an Indian in order to give the federal court jurisdiction.

A motion for summary judgment is similar to a motion for a

directed verdict, a new trial, judgment notwithstanding the verdict, peremptory instructions and peremptory nonsuits. However, instead of being based on the evidence submitted at trial, the decision in a motion for summary judgment is based upon the pleadings and affidavits, depositions, stipulations, and other evidentiary matters submitted with the motion for summary judgment, and the memorandum opposing it. The effect is much the same.

Summary judgment was not a usual common law procedure. An early federal case involving a similar procedure was *Hiriart v. Ballon*, 34 U.S. 156 (1835). In that case it was held that a summary proceeding on a surety bond in the United States District Court in Louisiana did not deprive a party of the right to jury trial. Likewise, a local rule of the United States District Court for the District of Columbia that provided for a procedure similar to summary judgment did not deprive the defendant of the right to trial by jury. *Fidelity and Deposit Co. v. United States*, 187 U.S. 315 (1902). The rule required a party to create an issue of fact by affidavit. Failing that, the court would render judgment.

Now, of course, Rule 56 of the Federal Rules of Civil Procedure governs motions for summary judgment in federal court. Rule 56(c) provides, in part, "The judgment sought shall be rendered forthwith if the pleadings, depositions, answers to interrogatories, and admissions on file, together with the affidavits, if any, show that there is no genuine issue as to any material fact and that the moving party is entitled to a judgment as a matter of law."

Another important aspect of the idea that facts are for the jury is illustrated by *United States v. Wonson*, 28 Fed. Cases 745 (Cir. Ct., Dist. Mass., 1812). In that case it was held that the only way a fact found by a jury could be reexamined was by a new trial ordered by the trial court, or, when reversed on appeal, when a *venire facias de novo* was awarded. The effect of the *venire facias de novo* was a new trial. Later, in *Justices v. Murray*, 76 U.S. 274 (1869), it was held that a federal court had no power to have a jury trial in a matter which had been removed from state court after a jury trial had already been held in the state court. This was notwithstanding a statute that appeared to give the federal court this power. The reason was that under the Seventh Amendment a fact once tried to a jury cannot be reexamined in any court of the United States.

A factually interesting case illustrating this principle was *Railroad Company v. Traloff*, 100 U.S. 24 (1879). Traloff, a subject of the Czar of Russia, had, while travelling in the United States, entrusted certain trunks to the defendant railroad. The trunks, it was claimed by the plaintiff, contained $75,000 worth of lace. The railroad managed to lose them. The jury returned a verdict in the amount of $10,000, and the railroad appealed. The Supreme Court held that facts once examined under correct instructions will not thereafter be reexamined by any court of the United States.

Another device courts have used to control juries is the special verdict, in which the jury finds certain facts and the court then applies the law to those facts. In *Suydam v. Williamson*, 61 U.S. 427 (1857), it was held that where a special verdict is utilized, the jury must find the facts and the judge is confined to the facts so found. The facts found by the jury must be ultimate facts and not simply a resumé of the various contentions. The verdict must thus state the jury's conclusion as to the facts. Rule 49(a) of the Federal Rules of Civil Procedure now governs special verdicts.

The case of *Sharon v. Time*, No. 83 Civ. 4660, United States District Court, Southern District of New York, demonstrated an interesting use of the special verdict. In this case the jury rendered three verdicts, but step-by-step. The first verdict found that Time's reporting concerning the plaintiff was defamatory. After deliberating two more days, the jury found that the reporting was false. A week later it found that there was no malice on Time's part. Thus, Time won the case. This use of a step-by-step verdict by Judge Abraham D. Sofaer is most unusual.[27]

A general verdict by the jury accompanied by answers to interrogatories is similar to a special verdict. It has long been held proper for a court, when the general verdict is inconsistent with answers to interrogatories, to enter judgment in conformity with the answers to the interrogatories. In *Walker v. New Mexico*, 165 U.S. 593 (1897), in approving this procedure, the court observed that special verdicts were not unknown to the common law. The statute providing that special interrogatories were to control over the general verdict did not violate the Seventh Amendment. This procedure is now codified in Rule 49(b) of the Federal Rules of Civil Procedure.

Another method for the court to modify the result of a jury verdict is by means of remittiturs and additurs. The reduction of an excessive verdict by means of a remittitur was approved in *Northern Pac. Rd., Co. v. Herbert*, 116 U.S. 642 (1885), and in *Texas and Pacific Railway Co. v. Cox*, 145 U.S. 593 (1891). But, in *Dimick v. Schiedt*, 293 U.S. 474 (1935), the Court held that an additur without the plaintiff's consent was not proper and that there should have been a new trial. It should be noted that this case was decided under the Seventh Amendment, which applies only in the federal courts.

There are times when the federal policy overrides state procedures on questions of jury trial in civil cases even when the case was tried in state court. In *Dice v. Akron, Canton & Youngstown R. Co.*, 342 U.S. 359 (1952), the case was originally tried in an Ohio court on the issue of fraudulent release under the Federal Employers' Liability Act. The Supreme Court of the United States held that ". . . the right to trial by jury is too substantial a part of the rights accorded by the Act to permit it to be classified as mere 'local rule of procedure' for denial in the manner that Ohio has here used." Under federal law, obviously, the manner of fraudulent release was a question for the jury.

In *Byrd v. Blue Ridge Rural Electric Cooperative, Inc.*, 356 U.S. 525 (1958), the federal policy in favor of jury trial again overrode state procedure. Under the state procedure, the question of whether the plaintiff was an employee of the defendant and so barred from suing for a personal injury was a question for the court. It was held that in a diversity case arising in the United States District Court the question was one for the jury.

17. Law and Equity

The distinction between law and equity existed at common law. Equity cases were triable to the court without a jury. Cases at law were tried to a jury. As to whether a case belonged in law or equity, recourse was often had to the common law of England as it existed at the time of the ratification of the United States Constitution in 1787 and the effective date of the first ten amendments to the Constitution in 1791.

Article III, Section 2, uses the words "Law and Equity" when referring to the judicial power of the United States. No provision was made for trial by jury in civil cases in the Constitution, but this was quickly remedied by the Judiciary Act of 1789 and by the Seventh Amendment to the Constitution. The right to a jury trial was, only applicable to cases triable at "law" as distinguished from "equity."

The federal courts had two distinct dockets and forms of action, one equity and the other law. This continued until the Federal Rules of Civil Procedure were adopted on December 20, 1937, to be effective in 1938. Rule 1 provided that the Civil Rules would govern the procedure in civil cases in the United States District Courts, whether at law, in equity, or in admiralty. Rule 2 provided that there should be one form of action, to wit "civil action." The importance of the distinction between law and equity was to continue in the matter of determining whether there was a right to trial by jury under the Seventh Amendment.

Just because there is a remedy at law does not necessarily defeat equity jurisdiction. So it was held in *Boyce v. Grundy*, 28 U.S. 210 (1830), where a complaint was filed in equity, alleged fraud, and asked for recission. The defendant was not entitled to have the equity action dismissed simply because the plaintiff might have sued at law. The remedy at law must be plain, adequate, and as prompt as the remedy in equity.

The framers of the Seventh Amendment meant by "law" what the Constitution means in Article II where "law" is used in contradistinction to "equity and admiralty." *Parsons v. Bedford*, 28 U.S. 433 (1830). Therefore, the "law" courts under the Seventh Amendment do not embrace the established and exclusive jurisdiction of equity and their jurisdiction is not concurrent with equity. *Shields v. Thomas*, 59 U.S. 253 (1855).

The absence of a plain and adequate remedy at law is the only test of equitable jurisdiction. *Watson v. Sutherland*, 72 U.S. 74 (1866). If there is a plain and adequate remedy at law equity will not entertain the case. *Thompson v. Railroad Companies*, 73 U.S. 134 (1867). Thus, a suit to restrain the collection of a state court tax is not maintainable in the United States District Court in equity because the party would have an adequate remedy at law. *Mathews v. Rodgers*, 284 U.S. 521 (1932).

Case law has established certain types of actions as being essentially equitable in nature. Thus an action for patent infringement for damages alone would be at law with a jury; when the action is for damages plus an injunction, the action is equitable. *Clark v. Wooster*, 119 U.S. 322 (1886). *Buzzard v. Houston*, 119 U.S. 347 (1886), listed an action for specific performance, removal of a cloud on a title, and the prevention of an injury for which damages could not be recovered as examples of equitable cases. Although there is no right to a jury trial in bankruptcy, a suit originally brought "in equity" to recover money claimed to have been paid by the bankrupt as a preference is properly transferred to the legal side of the docket and the defendant is entitled to a jury trial. *Schoenthal v. Irving Trust Co.*, 287 U.S. 92 (1932). And in a case of original jurisdiction in the Supreme Court between states over a boundary dispute, the Court held that it could ascertain facts with or without a jury, at its discretion, as other courts do in equity cases. *Rhode Island v. Massachusetts*, 37 U.S. 657 (1838).

The nature of the interest at issue in the suit is not controlling. Thus the assignee of a chose in action on which there is a complete and adequate remedy at law cannot sue in equity merely because the interest is equitable. *New York Guaranty Co. v. Memphis Water Co.*, 107 U.S. 205 (1882). Likewise, the fact that the claimed interest of the plaintiff was a bequest and therefore equitable under New York law did not deprive the plaintiff of the right to trial by jury in federal court. *Ex parte Simons*, 247 U.S. 231 (1918).

Further, the classification of an action as legal or equitable under state law is not controlling where the action is brought in federal court. While a suit by an owner of property in possession against the claims of parties not in possession is properly in equity, *Holland v. Challen*, 110 U.S. 15 (1883), where the claimant is not in possession of the property in a diversity case brought to recover property, a suit in equity will not be sustained in federal court even though the state law classified the action as equitable. *Whitehead v. Shattuck*, 138 U.S. 146 (1890). And the fact that an action in a Federal District Court in Mississippi was based on a state statute allowing a creditor to sue to set aside a fraudulent conveyance in chancery (equity) and subject the property to the debt as though there had been a previous judgment was not sufficient to deprive the defendant of a jury trial under the Seventh Amendment. *Scott v. Neely*, 140 U.S. 106 (1891).

Bennett v. Butterworth, 52 U.S. 669 (1850), was a suit in which the plaintiff sought the value of four negroes. Under state law the distinction between law and equity had been abolished. After the verdict for the value of the negroes in the amount of $1,200, the plaintiff elected to release the judgment and demand the negroes, which he could have done under state law. The trial court agreed and so rendered judgment. This was set aside by the Supreme Court, which said that the judgment of the court must follow the verdict and that state practice must not cause federal courts to confound the principles of law and equity. This case was still the law in *Slimer v. Conner*, 372 U.S. 221 (1963), where the court held that the federal courts in diversity cases must look to federal law on the matter of law or equity to see if a jury trial is required under the Seventh Amendment.

Where the issues before the court are of an equitable nature, a court of equity will decide all matters in dispute and decree complete relief. *Alexander v. Hillman*, 296 U.S. 222 (1935). Thus in an action by the Office of Price Administration to restrain price violations, the court had power to award complete relief even though a decree included relief that could have been conferred by a court of law. *Porter v. Warner Holding Co.*, 327 U.S. 395 (1946). And a Federal District Court had the power in an equity case to enter summary judgment against sureties in the case, and an action at law was therefore not necessary. *Pease v. Rathbun-Jones Eng. Co.*, 243 v. S. 273 (1917).

A number of cases have considered the right to a jury trial in "mixed" actions involving both legal and equitable issues. In *Beacon Theatres, Inc. v. Westover*, 359 U.S. 500 (1959), the fact that the plaintiff in an antitrust action asked for a restraining order was insufficient to deprive the defendant of the right to a jury on jury issues. However, in a suit against a foreign government in a Federal District Court under the Foreign Sovereign Immunities Act, the plaintiff's demand for damages did not convert the action into one at law under the Seventh Amendment where the legislative intent of the Act was clearly to require a trial without a jury. *Rex v. CIA Pervance DeVapores*, 660 F2d 61 (2nd cir., 1981).

In *Ross v. Benard*, 396 U.S. 733 (1970), the Court held that in a shareholders' derivative suit the right to trial by jury attaches to issues in the derivative suit respecting which the corporation, if it had sued, would have been entitled to a jury. The Seventh Amendment must be liberally construed; thus, the nature of the issues controls, not that of overall action. The Court noted that since 1938 and the merger of law and equity into one form of action, there has been an expansion of adequate legal remedies that correspondingly narrows the scope of equity.

In *Parkland Hosiery Co. v. Shore*, 439 U.S. 322 (1979), the Court held that a party to an equitable proceeding who has had the issues of fact adjudicated adversely in an equitable action may be collaterally estopped from relitigating the same issues before a jury in a subsequent legal action against it by a new party. Justice Stewart, who wrote the opinion of the court, observed that ". . . many procedural devices developed since 1791 that have diminished the civil jury's historic domain have been found not inconsistent with the Seventh Amendment."

18. The Complexity Issue

Recently, and especially since the case of *Ross v. Bernhard*, 396 U.S. 531 (1970), a number of courts and commentators have held or argued that in certain cases the factual issues are too complex for a jury to properly understand and decide, and that in such cases, the right to a trial by jury should not apply.

Prior to the *Ross* case, the Supreme Court of the United States had, from time to time, touched on the ability of the jury to handle complicated matters. Certainly, *Fowle v. Lawrason*, 30 U.S. 495 (1831), the opinion by Chief Justice Marshall, could be cited as a seminal case on the right to a jury trial in a complex case. The opinion, after noting that not every action on an accounting where a trustee was involved was necessarily in equity, stated, "But in transactions not of this peculiar character, greater complexity ought to exist in the accounts, or some difficulty at law should interpose, some discovery should be required, in order to induce a court of chancery to exercise jurisdiction."

While not mentioning "complexity," the opinion of the court in

Pleasant v. Fant, 89 U.S. 116 (1875), seems to share the same low opinion of the jury's abilities held by modern proponents of the complexity exception to the right to trial by jury. The opinion states, "It is the duty of a court in its relation to the jury to protect parties from unjust verdicts arising from ignorance of the rules of law and of evidence, from impulses of passion or prejudices or from other violation of his lawful rights in the conduct of the trial."

The argument for the complexity exception seems to be explicitly set forth in the opinion of the Court in *Kirby v. Lake Shore & Michigan, Southern Railroad Co.*, 120 U.S. 130 (1887).

> "The complicated nature of the accounts between the parties constitutes a sufficient ground for going into equity. It would have been difficult, if not impossible, for a jury to unravel the numerous transactions involved in the settlements between the parties, and reach a satisfactory conclusion as to the amount of drawbacks to which Alexander & Co. were entitled on each settlement . . . Justice could not be done except by employing the methods of investigation peculiar to courts of equity."

Later, in a criminal case, the defendant complained that the statute forbidding the monopoly of trade was so vague he could not anticipate that a jury, composed of persons less competent than himself, would interpret it correctly. However, Justice Holmes, who wrote the opinion of the court in that case, *Nash v. United States*, 229 U.S. 373 (1913), did not seem moved. He said, ". . . The law is full of instances where a man's fate depends on his estimating rightly, that is, as the jury subsequently estimates it, some matter of degree. If his judgment is wrong, not only may he incur a fine or a short imprisonment, as here, he may incur the penalty of death."

There has been, as the *Nash* case shows, some vacillation in the Supreme Court's views concerning the ability and importance of juries. For example, Justice Sutherland thought modern jurors were more intelligent than their predecessors. *Funk v. United States*, 290 U.S. 371 (1933). Justice Cardozo did not think that juries were essential to due process. *Palko v. Connecticut*, 302 U.S. 319 (1937).

The last important case on the complexity issue before *Ross, supra*, was *Dairy Queen v. Wood*, 369 U.S. 469 (1962). In this case *Dairy*

Queen had moved to strike the demand for a jury on the ground that the action was equitable. The court ruled that the right to jury trial was a matter of substance, not form, and that the right to a jury was not lost because the legal issue incidentally involved equitable issues. The court suggested that there could be two trials, first of the legal claim and then of the equitable issue. The court went on to suggest that the party desiring the issue in equity must show that ". . . the accounts between the parties are of such a 'complicated nature' that only a court of equity can satisfactorily unravel them. . . . " This opinion was written by Justice Black. Justice Harlan concurred, saying that to defeat a demand for jury trial, the thrust must be truly equitable or the accounts must be of such a 'complicated nature' that they can be satisfactorily unraveled only by a court of equity. These authorities seem to have within them the basis of an argument for a complexity exception.

Today, footnote 10 in *Ross v. Bernhard,* 396 U.S. 531 (1970) is usually given as the authority for striking demands for jury trial on the ground that the issue is too complex for a jury to understand. *In Re Boise,* 420 F.Supp. 99, 104 (U.S. Dist. Ct., W.D., at Seattle, Washington, 1976). *Ross* was a shareholders derivative suit in which the issue was law or equity, jury or court. The result in *Ross* was for the jury, but the question of complexity was raised in footnote 10, which suggested that the "legal" nature of an issue was determined by three tests: ". . . first, the pre-merger custom with reference to such questions; second, the remedy sought; and, third, the practical abilities and limitations of juries." By pre-merger, the court was referring to case law before the adoption of the Federal Rules of Civil Procedure in 1937, which merged law and equity into one "civil action."

Considerable litigation concerning the complexity issue has been stirred up by the *Ross* footnote. *In Re Boise Cascade Securities Litigation,* 420 F.Supp. 99 (W.D.Wa. 1976), the court sustained a motion to strike the jury demand because the case was too complex for a jury. In *Radial Lip Machine v. International Carbide Corp.,* 76 F.R.D. 224 (W.D.ILL. 1977), a motion to strike the demand for a jury was overruled because, among other reasons, no case was too complex for a jury. In *Bernstein v. Universal Pictures,* 79 F.R.D. 59 (S.D.N.Y. 1978), the demand for a jury was stricken because the court found ". . . that the trial of this case is beyond the 'practical abilities and limitations of juries.' " In *Ballew v. Georgia*, 435 U.S. 223 (1978), a criminal case, the Court appeared to think the jury is a competent body. The opinion stated, "Because juries frequently face complex problems laden with value choices, the benefits are important and should be retained." That is, complexity here seems to be an argument in favor of jury trial.

No complexity exception to the Seventh Amendment was found in *In Re U.S. Financial Securities Litigation*, 609 F2d 411 (9th Cir., 1979). The court, while holding that the jury was a competent finder of facts in complex cases, suggested that issues could be simplified by counsel, and that the court could appoint a master, pursuant to Rule 53 (b), and could utilize summaries pursuant to Rule 1006, to assist the jury.

In *Zenith Radio Corp. v. Matsushita Electric Industrial Co.*, 478 F.Supp. 889 (E.D.Pa. 1979), an extraordinarily complex case involving an alleged international conspiracy in violation of the antitrust laws, Judge Edward R. Becker rejected complexity as a constitutionally permissible ground for striking the plaintiffs' jury demands, reaffirming the "historical test" governing the right to jury trial based upon the law-equity distinction. Judge Becker looked to lawyers to improve the fact finding process by streamlining, clarifying, and teaching. As to the jury, the judge said, "One virtue of the jury is its 'black box' function; it gives results without reasons." The sum and substance for Judge Becker was that he thought the jury was at least as good as a judge in a complex case. However, in the same case on appeal, *In re Japanese Electronic Products Antitrust Litigation*, 631 F2d 1069 (3rd Cir. 1980), the court held that in a case where the facts and law were so complex that the jury could not rationally decide the case, the right to a rational decision under the due process clause of the Fifth Amendment overrides the right to trial by jury under the Seventh Amendment.

A lower court opinion to the contrary was *Kian v. Miro Aluminum Co.*, 88 FRD 351 (E.D. Mich. 1980), holding that a case at law can never be so complex as to override the right to jury trial. Judge Gilmore, who presided in this case, had such faith in juries that he also disapproved of court sponsored witnesses.

The trial court's granting of a motion to strike a jury demand was reversed in *Cotten v. Witco Chemical Corp.*, 651 F.2d 274 (5th Cir. 1981), holding that the mere fact that it would be "most difficult" for a jury to reach a verdict was not a sufficient reason to strike a demand for a jury. The court stated that before a motion to strike a jury demand could be granted for complexity, if it ever could, the case would have to be one where the jury ". . . could not render a rational decision. . . ." And in *City of New York v. Pullman Inc.*, 662 F2d 910 (2nd Cir. 1981), the court held that the case was not one where the issues were beyond the abilities of a jury where all the jury was asked to do was decide whether a group of non-scientists had acted in a rational manner.

One of the first commentators to pick up on the complexity idea was Edward J. Dewitt, Sr., Judge of the U.S. District Court for the District of Minnesota, whose article, "Should Jury Trial Be Required In Civil Cases? A Challenge to the Seventh Amendment," appeared in *The Journal of Air Law and Commerce*, Vol. 47, p. 495 (1981-82). In that article Judge Dewitt suggests that the Seventh Amendment ought to be abolished, not only in complex cases, but in all civil cases. The judge's feelings on the subject come as no shock since he had come to the same conclusion in 1974 and without using the *Ross* footnote as an excuse. "Federal Civil Juries Should be Abolished," Am. Bar Assoc. Jour., May 1974.

Professor Roger W. Kirst, Professor of Law at the University of Nebraska, discusses the complexity issue in "The Jury's Historic Domain In Complex Cases," 58 Wash. Law. Rev. 1 (1982). The professor stated that proponents of the complexity exception to jury trial have traditionally put forward three arguments, namely: (1) that a complex case is analogous to accounting actions over which equity had jurisdiction in 1791; (2) that equity had general jurisdiction over cases not suited for jury trial; and (3) that the chancellor had the power to control the flow of litigation and would have sent complex cases to equity if there had been any. Professor Kirst also notes and discusses the new constitutional argument put forward in *In Re Japanese Electronic Products Antitrust Litigation, supra,* to the effect that where complexity causes the Seventh Amendment right to a jury trial to come into conflict with the Fifth Amendment requirement of due process, the Fifth Amendment should override the Seventh.

Another article taking up this point is "Complex Jury Trials, Due Process, and the Doctrine of Unconstitutional Complexity," by David M. Nocenti, 18 Columbia Journal of L. and Soc. Problems 1

(1983). To the proponents of the complexity exception, Nocenti poses the following question: If a case is so complicated that a jury can't understand it with the help of lawyers, expert witnesses, auditors, visual aids, accounts, summaries and judges, how could a person whose conduct is sought to be controlled by the law at issue possibly have known what to do without that help?

The issue seems ripe for decision by the United States Supreme Court. The real solution seems not to dispense with juries, but to improve the trial procedures in ways suggested in some of the above cases and otherwise, such as by the use of summaries, masters, simplification of issues, trying one issue at a time, and avoiding joinder in complicated cases.

Meanwhile, pending any definitive ruling by the Supreme Court on the due process issue, the cases go on. One such case is *In Re Asbestos Litigation Coverage Cases,* Judicial Council Coordinated Proceeding No. 1072, which was scheduled to begin trial on March 4, 1985 in a remodeled San Francisco high school auditorium, Superior Court Judge Ira A. Brown, Jr. presiding. The case has 60,000 trial exhibits and approximately 2,000 deposition transcripts. Judge Brown plans to divide the trial into steps and have the jury decide one issue at a time. Another case which was scheduled to begin the week of March 25, 1985, Las Vegas, Nevada, is *MGM-Grand v. Frank B. Hall Inc.,* A-21-9970. This case has a least 50 lawyers. The daily cost of the trial, as estimated by Presiding Judge Paul S. Goldman, is approximately $342,000, including attorney fees. These two cases will be laboratories to determine if juries, judges and lawyers can get the job done in matters of this complexity.[28]

In Belleville, Illinois, as of March 3, 1986, a jury was in its 343rd day of trial. This case is to decide whether 69 people suffered injuries when a tank car derailed spilling chemicals.[29] A jury returned a verdict for $10.53 billion dollars in the case of *Pennzoil Co. v. Texaco Inc.* (Harris County Civil Court, Houston, Texas, 84-05905 (1985) in favor of Pennzoil after a 17 week trial.

19. Special Procedures

A person who believes what some of the courts have written about how much Americans value their right to jury trial might be tempted to say to an adverse party in a dispute, "Tell it to a jury." However, it is more likely than not that a jury would never have a right to judge the case. There are many issues tried to courts and administrative agencies in which the stakes are high but no right to jury trial exists. Representative and important examples of special proceedings and actions, both including and excluding the right of trial by jury, will be noted in this section.

a. Statutory Proceedings Unknown at Common Law and Rights Created by Statute

As we have seen, the right to trial by jury attaches primarily to actions at common law and their statutory successors. Thus, it is not surprising that the right does not exist in most statutory proceedings unknown at common law or actions to enforce rights created by statute, except where the action is essentially "legal" in character, or where the right is expressly or impliedly granted by the legislature.

Thus, money judgments awarded by the National Labor Relations Board against Jones & Laughlin Steel Corporation for discrimination against union members did not violate the Seventh Amendment. *National Labor Relations Board v. Jones & Laughlin Steel Corporation,* 301 U.S. 1 (1937). Where a black woman sued under § 812 of the Civil Rights Act of 1968, 42 U.S.C. § 3612, for damages, the defendant was entitled to a jury because the action was basically legal. Thus, even though the specific right was not in existence in 1791 and was a right created by Congress, the Seventh Amendment was applicable. *Curtis v. Loether,* 415 U.S. 189 (1974). And in a private civil action for lost wages under the Age Discrimination Act of 1976, the parties have a right to trial by jury because Congress used the words "legal relief." *Lorillard v. Pons,* 434 U.S. 575 (1978).

On the other hand, in an action under the Age Discrimination Act against the government for wages, the plaintiff was not entitled to trial by jury since the Seventh Amendment does not apply in actions against the United States Government. *Lehman v. Nakshian,* 453 U.S. 156 (1981). When the government sues to enforce public rights created by Congress, the facts can be adjudicated by an administrative agency. *Atlas Roofing Co., Inc., v. Occupational Safety and Health Review Commission,* 430 U.S. 442 (1977).

b. Eminent Domain

The procedure used to exercise the state's right of eminent domain is within the discretion of the legislature; thus the assessment of damages by a board of commissioners is permissible. *Secombe v. Railroad Company,* 90 U.S. 108 (1874). Land taken by the United States through delegation of authority to Wisconsin wherein the damages were assessed by a Board of Arbitrators was constitutional; all that is required under due process is a tribunal capable of estimating the value of the property. *United States v. Jones,* 109 U.S. 513 (1883). Just compensation for property taken under eminent domain does not have to be determined by a jury but can be entrusted by Congress to commissioners appointed by a court or executive authority, or by an inquest of more or fewer members than an ordinary jury. *Bauman v. Ross,* 167 U.S. 548 (1897). There is no constitutional right to a jury in eminent domain proceedings. *United States v. Reynolds,* 397 U.S. 14 (1970).

c. Bankruptcy

It is well established that the bankruptcy law does not unconstitutionally deprive litigants of the right to jury trial, since the Seventh Amendment does not apply to such proceedings. *Continental Bank v. Rock Island Ry.,* 294 U.S. 648 (1935). Moreover, the bankruptcy court has summary jurisdiction over the surrender of voidable preferences asserted and proved by a trustee as against a creditor who has received preference; the Seventh Amendment also has no application in such a case. *Katchen v. Landy,* 382 U.S. 323 (1966).

d. Court of Claims

In a suit against the United States or as to a counterclaim in such an action by the government, the plaintiff is not entitled to a jury trial in the Court of Claims. Under the principle of sovereign immunity the United States is immune from suit except under such conditions as it determines; thus, the government can make its own rules if it deigns to be sued. *McElrath v. United States,* 102 U.S. 426 (1880); *United States v. Sherwood,* 312 U.S. 350 (1962). This Congress has done in creating the Court of Claims pursuant to Article I,

Section 8 of the Constitution. In short, Congress is not required to provide jury trials for plaintiffs suing the government in the Court of Claims, and it has not done so. *Glidden v. Zdanok,* 370 U.S. 350 (1962).

e. Taxes

It is well established that the determination of tax deficiencies and penalties by an administrative agency does not violate the Seventh Amendment. *Helvering v. Mitchell,* 303 U.S. 391 (1937).

f. Anti-Trust

The case of *Fleitman v. Welsbach Street Lighting Company,* 240 U.S. 27 (1916) established early on that an action for treble damages under the federal anti-trust laws must be tried to a jury.

g. Rent Control

An Act of Congress creating a Commission to determine if rents are fair was constitutional even though there was no provision for jury trial. *Block v. Hirsh,* 156 U.S. 135 (1921).

h. Revocation of Professional Licenses

An attorney who was stripped of his right to practice law in a summary proceeding before a District Court because the District Court had knowledge of illegal activities by the attorney was not thereby deprived of his constitutional right to trial by jury; it is a mistaken idea that due process required a jury in all cases where property or personal rights are involved. *Ex Parte Wall,* 107 U.S. 265 (1882). And a proceeding before a state licensing board in a state court to revoke a physician's right to practice medicine does not violate due process, since what constitutes due process in state license violation proceedings is largely up to the states, subject to reasonable notice and an opportunity to be heard and present claims or defenses. *Missouri v. North,* 271 U.S. 40 (1926).

i. Matter Declared Obscene

Although the constitutional test for obscenity incorporates

reference to contemporary community standards, a state court in a civil proceeding may determine this issue without submitting the question to a jury. *Alexandria v. Virginia,* 413 U.S. 836 (1973).

j. Forcible Entry

A landlord's action to recover premises in the District of Columbia is essentially an ejectment action and the parties are entitled to trial by jury. The Seventh Amendment requires trial by jury in actions not known at common law if the actions involve rights of the sort traditionally enforced at law instead of equity or admiralty. A common law action in ejectment to recover possession involved a legal right, and was therefore tried to a jury. *Pernell v. Southall Realty,* 416 U.S. 363 (1974). Justice Thurgood Marshall, who wrote the opinion of the court stated, "Our courts were never intended to serve as rubber stamps for landlords seeking to evict their tenants, but rather to see that justice be done before a man is evicted from his home."

k. Imports

A board of appraisers has the power to fix the value of imports, subject only to the defense of fraud. This involves no deprivation of the right to trial by jury. *Passant v. United States* 148 U.S. 214 (1893).

20. Miscellaneous

The following miscellaneous points of law relating to the right to trial by jury are of sufficient interest to be worth noting.

A statutory procedure for assembling a jury venire does not bind the judge in regard to impressing talesmen. *Lovejoy v. United States,* 128 U.S. 171 (1888).

The verdict of a jury cannot be set aside because the jurors failed to follow the instructions of the court if the only basis of the claim is the testimony of jurors. In short, a verdict cannot be impeached solely upon the testimony of jurors. *Hyde v. United States,* 225 U.S. 347 (1912), *McDonald v. Pless,* 238 U.S. 264 (1918).

It has been held permissible for states to require fire insurance policies to provide for binding arbitration. The Fourteenth Amendment does not imply that all trials shall be by jury; no particular forum or method of state procedure is required thereby. *Hardware Dealers Mutual Fire Ins. Co. v. Glidden Co.,* 284 U.S. 151 (1931).

A juvenile has no right under the Fourteenth Amendment of the Federal Constitution to trial by jury in the adjudicative phase of a juvenile hearing even if he would be entitled to a jury trial if he had been an adult. *McKeiver v. Pennsylvania,* 403 U.S. 928 (1971).

The Ninth Circuit has recently held that states, as well as private business organizations, are entitled to the fundamental right of trial by jury in civil antitrust suits. *Standard Oil Co. of Cal. v. Arizona,* 738 Fed 1021 (9th Cir. 1984).

If young people (18-34) are significantly underrepresented in the jury venire, a criminal defendant is entitled to a new venire drawn from a fair cross section of the community. *Barber v. Ponte,* 772 Fed. 2d 982, at 994 (5th Cir. 1985).

21. Impact of The Jury in 1986

The impact of the jury process, from the point of view of numbers alone, is considerable. There are approximately 60,000 criminal jury trials in the United States every year and another 20,000 that are not carried to a verdict.[30] In the rest of the world there are about 10,000 jury trials a year with England and Wales accounting for half of that number. [31] In 1977, in England there were only 33 jury trials sought in the High Court.[32] In the United States there is a great diversity between states. Connecticut has three criminal jury trials a year per 100,000 persons of population and Georgia has 144, while the national average is 35.[33] In 1945, of all criminal felony charges, 75 percent of those charged pleaded guilty, 10 percent were tried to the bench and 15 percent were tried to a jury.[34] One seventh of all felony prosecutions end in a jury trial. The percentage of judge trials and guilty pleas is higher for misdemeanors.[35]

22. Innovations in Practice

The critical item in the trial lawyers' practice is anticipating what the jury will do. Behavioral scientists have introduced various techniques to aid the lawyer in this task including demographic surveys, retrial of actual cases to volunteer juries which are subjected to variety of variations the effect of which is carefully noted, phantom juries, and shadow juries. A phantom jury is one picked similarly to the real jury, approximating the same cross-section of the community. Attorneys utilizing this technique present both sides of the case to the phantom jury in an abbreviated form. A verdict is returned and questionaires are completed. Based on the results, adjustments are made for the real trial. The results can be helpful not only in the actual trial but in estimating the settlement value of a case.

Shadow juries are even newer and more interesting. Such a jury is picked as nearly as possible to mirror the background of the jury actually trying the real case. The shadow jurors sit in the courtroom and hear what the real jury hears. They are debriefed daily for their reactions to the testimony and rulings of the court. Such a jury was first used in a $300 million antitrust suit against International Business Machines Corp. (IBM). Although the court directed a verdict in favor of IBM in December of 1976, the defense team found the shadow jury very helpful.[36]

23. Civilians and the Military and the State Department

A military court sitting in Indiana had no jurisdiction to try a twenty year resident for charges that he conspired against the United States Government During the Civil War because the courts of Indiana had never been closed and the person charged was entitled to a jury trial. *Ex Parte Milligan,* 18 L.Ed. 281 (1886). A one-time court, a creature of the State Department of the United States, sitting in the United States sector of Berlin, Germany, in 1979 held that an east German man and his woman companion were entitled to trial by a jury of Berliner citizens on a charge of highjacking a Polish airline.[37] It was held in *Madsen v. Kinsella,* 72 S.Ct. 699 (1952), that a woman civilian could be tried in Germany before the United States Court of the Allied High Commission for Germany for the murder of her military husband in 1949 while living in military housing in Germany. There was no provision for the woman to have a jury trial.

24. Conclusion

In 1985, we find the jury is apparently well entrenched as a matter of right in criminal cases. In Federal Courts in criminal cases it will still be a 12 person jury with unanimity required for a verdict. In state cases the defendant in a non-petty criminal case will, at the least, have a right to a six person jury which must, if it is that size, render a unanimous verdict. If the state jury is larger than six persons in criminal cases, there are a number of variations which might very well survive the due process clause of the Fourteenth Amendment. In civil cases in Federal Courts, it is now a six person jury. Even this reduced right, at least in some circuits, has been eliminated in complex cases. In state courts, in the usual common law action for money and similar suits, most states (two or three excepted) offer some form of jury trial, but this is not a due process requirement. By and large, the jury is very much alive. The value of the jury to modern society in the United States will be our final consideration.

Chapter X Footnotes

1. *University of Michigan Journal of Law Reform*, Vol. 6, p. 671.

2. "A Jury of One's Peers", Faye A. Silas, 69 Am. Bar Assoc. J. 1609, (November, 1983)

3. The National Law Journal, April 16, 1984.

4. *Wigmore on Evidence*, Wigmore (Little, Brown and Co., Boston, 1904), Vol. IX-530.

5. *Democracy in America*, Alexis Cleral De Tocqueville, translated by Henry Reeves, Esq., revised by Francis Bowen, with further corrections by Phillips Bradley, originally published in Paris, 1835, Alfred A. Knopf, New York, 1972, Vol. I, p. 286

6. *Reports of Cases Argued In the Superior Court of Judicature of the Province of Massachusetts Bay, Between 1761-1772*, Josiah Quincy, Jr. (Little, Brown, and Co., Boston, 1865), p. 568.

7. "Juries as Judges of the Criminal Law," Mark DeWolfe Howe, 52 Harv.L.Rev. 582, 596 (1939).

8. Howe, *op. cit.* at note 7, at pp. 605-10.

9. Howe, *op. cit.* at note 7, at pp. 601-02.

10. Howe, *op. cit.* at note 7, at pp. 610-11.

11. Quincy, *op. cit.* at note 6, p. 568.

12. Howe, *op. cit.* at note 7, pp. 598-99.

13. Quincy, *op. cit.* at note 6, p. 568.

14. Howe, *op. cit.* at note 7, p. 496.

15. Howe, *op. cit.* at note 7, p. 593.

16. Howe, *op. cit.* at note 7, p. 595.

17. Quincy, *op. cit.* at note 6, p. 568.

18. Quincy, *op. cit.* at note 6, p. 569.

19. Quincy, *op. cit.* at note 6, pp. 569-70.

20. Howe, *op. cit.* at note 7, p. 597

21. Quincy, *op. cit.* at note 6, pp. 569-70.

22. Howe, *op. cit.* at note 7, p. 597.

23. Howe, *op. cit.* at note 7, p. 598.

24. *Constitutions of the United States, National and State,* For Legislative Research Fund of Columbia University (Dobbs-Terry, N.Y.) at Georgia constitution.

25. *Constitutions. . . , op. cit.* at Missouri constitution.

26. "The Functions of The Jury," Dale W. Broeder, 21 Univ. Chi. L. 386, 403.

27. "The Judge's Postmortem of the Sharon Libel Trial," David A. Kaplan, *The National Law Journal,* Vol. 7, No. 27, March 18, 1985.

28. "Megatrials," by Mary Ann Galante, *The National Law Journal,* Vol. 7, No. 28, March 25, 1985.

29. "Still Playing in Belleville," by Martha Middleton, *The National Law Journal,* Vol. 8, No. 25.

30. *The American Jury,* Harry Kalven, Jr. and Hans Zeisel (Little, Brown and Company, Boston, 1966), p. 12.

31. Kalven and Zeisel, *op. cit.* at note 30, at p. 13.

32. "The Decline of the English Jury," James Driscoll, 17 Am. Bus. Law Journal 99 (1979).

33. Kalven and Zeisel, *op. cit.* at note 30, at p. 16.

34. Kalven and Zeisel, *op. cit.* at note 30 at p. 18.

35. Kalven and Zeisel, *op. cit.* at note 30, at p. 17.

36. "Shadow Juries: Monitoring Jurors' Reactions," Donald E. Vinson, *Trial,* Vol. 19 No. 9, September, 1983, p. 75.

37. *Judgment in Berlin,* Herbert J. Stern (Universe Books, New York, 1984).

XI
Forensic Persuasion

"A word fitly spoken is like apples of gold in
pictures of silver." Prov. 25:11

1. Introduction

As a class, lawyers could stand a lot of improvement in their persuasive speaking. The reason so many slide by without trouble is because opposing counsel are equally inept. Law schools don't stress speaking. Lawyers generally make no special effort to improve their speaking ability, their efforts in this regard being limited to on-the-job experience and imitation of peers and of distinguished speakers at legal seminars.

Help is readily available. Classical works dating back to the fifth century B.C. give up-to-date advice on effective speaking. We will consider oratory the equivalent of forensic persuasion for purposes of this chapter.

Oratory was defined by Quintilian as ". . . the science of speaking well."[1] Marcus Cato said an orator was ". . . a good man skilled in speaking."[2] Plato, speaking on another level, said that rhetoric was the government of the souls of men.[3] Pascal wrote that eloquence was the portrait of thought.[4]

These eminent authorities notwithstanding, the art of speaking well has not received respect from some quarters. Gibbon said that persuasion was ". . . the resource of the feeble."[5] Thucydides said ". . . the strong do what they can and the weak suffer what they must."[6] There is some truth to what these observers of history said, but it is the entire purpose of the legal system to substitute legal persuasion, under law, for decisions by force. Even the inarticulate can hire a lawyer and manage on borrowed eloquence the same as Nero.[7]

As far as history is concerned, systematic oratory began with the Greeks at Syracuse in the fifth century, B.C. It was Corax who wrote the first book on rhetoric. His pupil Tisias built on this

195

foundation, stressing that argument is concerned with probability, not with truth.[8]

Aren't lawyers concerned with truth? Yes, if everyone agrees as to what the truth is. Then there would, indeed, be no need for eloquence. It is because truth is in dispute and will never be proved to a certainty that persuasion is necessary. The result of a trial is a verdict and judgment based on what the trier of the facts finds to be probable but not absolutely certain. Aristotle said, ". . . we seem only to deliberate about things which admit to issuing two ways . . . ."[9] Clients would often be better served if their lawyers would agree with Quintilian who said, "Where defeat is inevitable it is wisest to yield."[10] The Spartans at Thermopylea wouldn't have known what Quintilian was talking about, but lawyers are not warriors and would do better to look to Quintilian for wisdom.

These and the following pages are presented in the belief that Pericles, Demonsthenes and Cicero were effective speakers and that writers such as Aristotle and Quintilian told us why those men were effective. With this guidance from the ancients we will explore arrangement, analysis, figures, delivery and much else.

2. Arrangement

Quintilian said that the ". . . gift of arrangement is to oratory what generalship is to war."[11] He advises us generally to mass our facts in prosecution and to separate them in defense.[12]

In broad outline, the speech (that is, oral argument in the appellate courts, and opening statement and argument at the trial level) may be divided into various subdivisions for purposes of structuring and analyzing persuasion. One such analysis breaks the speech into five parts, namely, the exordium, the statement of facts (or the analysis), the proof, the refutation and the peroration.[13] Put in other words, the divisions are the opening, the overview, the main body with citation of authority or evidence, refutation of the opponent's position (either by way of anticipation or after the fact), and the wrap-up. A study of any long speech will show that the process can be much more complicated. For example, a lawyer may divide a long argument into three main divisions as to the factual material. Some cases are so simple, the issue so narrow, and time so limited, that the entire speech may consist of only a few sentences. The formal divisions of a speech are tags we use to talk about speeches; they are not barriers to creative presentation.

The exordium is the part of the presentation where most lawyers give their names, tell the jury that what they are going to say is not evidence, that the law will come to the jurors from the bench, that the lawyer is sorry that the jurors have had to be inconvenienced, and much more of the same deadly dull material which the jury has already heard or doesn't need to hear from the attorney. The opening sentences of the speech should set a serious tone and dispose the jury to receive what will follow.[14]

The words of Shakespeare are appropriate to the exordium where he said ". . . lend thy serious hearing to what I shall unfold."[15] Also, consider the passage from Isaiah, "Come now, and let us reason together, saith the Lord . . ."[16]

It is common for experienced trial lawyers to use an opening such as the following:

> For over a thousand years free people who speak English have submitted the most serious of their disputes between man and man or between a citizen and the state to a jury of fellow citizens. This right has been preserved in the Constitution of the United States and in the Constitution of this state because our heritage has taught us that there is no surer test of truth and justice than trial by jury.

This and similar openings emphasize the importance of the jury and the individual members of the jury. Flattering the jury this may be. Solon said that the tyrant Pisistratus found more credit when Pisistratus flattered the people than when Solon told them the truth.[17] Something of this sort also serves to get you settled down, and you speak your second sentence with less timidity.[18]

It is desirable to have the jury believe that you have undertaken the case reluctantly.[19] For example, a possible exordium in a criminal case:

> Members of the jury, it was only with the greatest reluctance that I undertook Clyde Martin's defense. If

you were fifty-five years old and had followed the practice of criminal justice for most of your years in the legal
profession, fully knowing that a criminal case—and all that
this implies—takes priority over every other consideration in both your private and your professional life, and
knowing that the case means sixteen-hour work days,
you can well believe that I undertook Clyde's case
reluctantly.

But when it was disclosed to me what has been disclosed to you through the evidence, that the police not
only didn't arrive at the scene until two hours after they
had been notified, that when they did arrive at the scene
their investigation was cursory at best and at worst one-
sided, that they did not even talk with Clyde before he
was charged although he was always willing to cooperate
with the authorities—you saw what an open and candid
testimony Clyde delivered to you under oath and during
a searching cross-examination—that when Clyde's alibi
checked out—you heard the witnesses—then you know
why I had to come to the courthouse one more time in a
criminal case. Someone had to present the facts of Clyde's
defense.

Reluctant, yes; ashamed, no. Another reason for being reluctant
is that the party and his legal representative are weak—not legally
or factually, of course—in terms of resources. You could begin like
this:

I had some reticence in undertaking Clyde's defense.
I'm sorry, but it's the truth. You've seen what we have
been up against. First the road officer did his thing. The
State wasn't satisfied with his story, so they brought in
the county detective bureau, then the state criminal
laboratory personnel, and finally the huge photographic
blow-ups you have seen. That's not to speak of all the
witnesses the State put up in the comfort and luxury that
our local hotels furnish. Clyde doesn't have those kinds of
resources. But, as you have seen during the presentation
of the evidence, he had the facts that prove his innocence
beyond any question.

If you're not old and tired or young and inexperienced, you might use the ugly nature of the charge as a reason for your reluctance to undertake the defense of a criminal case. Nobody is really thrilled about representing a rapist, a child abuser, or a person who has assaulted and robbed an elderly woman, but, if the defendant is innocent, he more desperately needs a defense than when the charge is not so ugly. So you undertake the case notwithstanding the public outrage at the crime, ignoring the effect that your heroic representation of the innocent defendant will have upon your personal and professional life. See what an admirable light that casts upon you.

The variations of the exordium are endless as are the variations of any art. The rule is to know your case, to look at the options, to think and to choose, not simply change the names and regurgitate your old clichés. Choose an opening that will gain the respectful attention of the jury without drawing a successful objection, and you will be well launched into your presentation.

Now that you have the jury listening, you proceed to the statement of facts, the analysis, outline or overview, as the next part of your presentation is variously known. This is the part of the speech where the trier of the facts is instructed as to the nature of the case.[20] This is not the place for fire but for analysis, which is perhaps the best name for this part of your speech. At this point you will want to tell the jury very briefly what the case is about, classify the factual divisions of the evidence in the order in which you intend to discuss them and set up the nature of your defense. The analysis is an outline of the proof which is to follow. You leave out matters here which will not be critical to the jury's decision. You don't need a flood of words. Hence, Shakespeare, "Sir, if you spend word for word with me, I shall make you bankrupt."[21] Quintilian helps you to cut it even finer. He said, "The point upon which above all the orator must make up his mind, even though he may be going to take up various lines of argument in support of his case, is this: what is it that he wishes most to impress upon the mind of the judge."[22] No more important point can be made.

There are times when the exigencies of the case make it prudent to dispense with the exordium altogether. One such opportunity is in a criminal case when the counsel have been introduced by the court, the lawyers have participated in voir dire and it is expected that the evidence will develop strong facts in favor of the defendant. The following opening was used by the writer in a felonious assault case:

> Randy is innocent. Five times in the last three years Brock, the thirty-year-old accuser, has assaulted Randy without provocation. On October 28, 1981, the date Randy is charged with felonious assault, Brock laid in wait for Randy at Randy's place of employment and assaulted him again. Randy once again used reasonable force to protect himself from this unprovoked attack.

In four sentences the case for the defense was capsulized. There was no pointless introduction, no small talk, no quoting of law or anticipation of instructions. Consider *The Second Book of Maccabees,* ". . . it is a foolish thing to make a long prologue and to be short in the story itself."[23] A statement of this type should be delivered in a firm clear voice, with the attorney standing still and his eyes meeting the eyes of the jurors.

In the *Apology,* Plato has Socrates follow an exordium, in which he praised the oratorical prowess of his opponents while being astonished with their misrepresentations, with a statement of facts in which Socrates divided the charges into two sets, the earlier charge being the slander that Socrates taught the weaker argument to appear the stronger and the more recent charges that Socrates corrupted the youth and believed in deities of his own invention instead of the deities recognized by the state.[24] This was Socrates' way of showing the motivation underlying the recent charges and of laying his entire life before the jury. Socrates' goal was not to save his life but to show that his life had been worth living.

Having gotten the interest of the jury, having given them the bare bones of your case, you put some meat on the skeleton. This is the part of the speech called the proof. By proof we mean legal evidence and the common experience of mankind that will persuade the jury toward the conclusion which you desire them to reach. Even speeches that are not given in a legal setting rely on proof, and most generally the proof in such a case is the common experience that the speaker shares with the members of the audience. In the famous funeral oration of Pericles, he wanted to assuage the grief of the audience and reinforce their patriotism. He referred to reverses they had suffered, both individually and as a people. He reminded them of the resources that remained and noted that they were the wonder of their own age and would be the wonder of future ages.[25]

Lawyers cannot argue outside the evidence, but, particularly during argument, they can make reference to the common experience much as a judge takes judicial notice of such items as geographic locations, dictionary definitions, who various public officials are and much else. There is much beyond this that the lawyer can argue, such as what would a normal six-year-old child do under certain circumstances, what would you expect out of a drunk, or the relative strength of a young man and an old man. Admissible evidence and fair conjecture in argument can vary, but the point is that hardly any legal argument is limited to the mere repeating of the testimony of witnesses without filling in the testimony with the lawyer's idea of the common experience of the jury trying the case.

During proof, the lawyer can arrange his material in many ways. The most ordinary way is for the lawyer to have a list of witnesses and discuss their testimony in the order of their appearance. That might be fine for some cases, especially if the lawyer had good control over the order of witnesses and if he has exercised that control so that the testimony was presented in a persuasive order. Most likely, however, discussing the evidence in the order of its presentation at trial is not the best way to discuss it. Usually, several witnesses have testified on a single point, and that testimony will not agree in all respects. It ought to be determined which witnesses testified on a point, and they should then be separated into groups of witnesses that agree with each other. Then the lawyer would discuss a particular point, citing first of all the testimony that supports the main thrust of his client's point of view, then touch upon contradictory testimony, and conclude that section of the speech by alluding to credibility difficulties that would tilt the balance in favor of his client's position.

Sometimes it is better to note a difficulty with the evidence and tell the jury that you will deal with it later, i.e., during your refutation. This should be done in a way that makes them interested in what you are eventually going to say. Some difficulties are so obvious that they must be dealt with at the outset in detail, such as a close-cut liability matter in a personal injury case. Then it might be best to convince the jury on the liability so they will be receptive to your comments on damages. On the other hand, the liability might be so weak, your client so credible, and the injuries so horrible that you will need all the sympathy that the injuries will elicit— never mind that the judge will tell the jurors that their verdict is not to be influenced by sympathy or prejudice. They will be so influenced and prejudiced.

During your proof another form of evidence you will use is physical items that have been introduced into the evidence, that is, you read from hospital reports, you summarize bills on charts, you work the action of the revolver, you display the colored pictures to the jury, but you don't do this ad nauseam. Some items are not only demonstrative evidence, they are real evidence, in the sense of being the promissory note in question, the damaged work of art, or the diamond ring which was stolen. But, even real evidence has to be authenticated as to ownership, presence, loss, responsibility, condition and value. An actual transcript of a critical testimony can be obtained during the trial, complete with the reporter's authentication, made into a transparency, red-lined and projected before the jury during your argument. This will do more to convince the jury as to what a witness said than your verbal recollection of that testimony. But, items of real and demonstrative evidence, projections of the testimony, charts and summaries will not substitute for effective oral presentation.

When I was in college I was told in psychology class that persons remember 80% of what they see and 15% of what they hear (the actual percentages don't matter, only that you are expected to remember what you see better than what you hear). Why then is eyewitness testimony responsible for more miscarriages of justice than any other type of testimony? It is because it is frequently mistaken but often believed. People often remember words that were spoken all their lives; for example, words of proposal received by a woman, the last words of a dying parent, the telephone call telling you that your wife is having an affair or that you have been indicted. A lot of people remember these items even though they weren't written on a chart in color.

Demonstrative aids can help in proof. They should be selected to emphasize and reinforce the critical areas of your case. They should not be a substitute for an effective oral presentation. Demonsthenes had a clerk read legal documents during his argument "On The Crown."[26] Cicero interrupted his argument in defense of Cleies to have a clerk read testimony.[27] These speakers wanted the real quality of the items presented, but they in no way allowed those extraneous items to impinge the quality of their oral delivery. Some lawyers are so frenetically running from counsel table to the evidence table to the chart board to the projector that the jury is so distracted they miss the point.

Refutation is where the lawyer deals with the evidence and arguments of the other side. Questions seldom get to court that don't have two sides. If the other side is ignored, the jury is most likely to conclude that you don't have any answers. If the other side opens and closes argument, it is necessary to refute what has been said earlier and what is to come. Refutation is a good place to show astonishment, incredulity and shock, if your evidence will stand it. Sometimes the liability in a negligence case is so weak it can't bear any more attention than what the other side has already given it, but this approach won't work if there are not strong sympathy elements in your favor. In such a case, it would be appropriate to deal briefly with the liability in opening and ignore it in the closing except to observe that the reason the defense spent so much time talking about liability was because of their desire to avoid responsibility for the grievous injuries the defendant had inflicted.

Of course the refutation must be internally organized according to the degree of complexies of the case, much as during the proof. In a case where the defendant in a personal injury or a criminal case has come off badly on the witness stand, you can point to him and, so to speak, make him a piece of real evidence as the person responsible for the injuries or crime as the case might be. It gives the jury something to focus on. Obviously you wouldn't use this tactic if the defendant in a personal injury case was a little old lady who never drove more than forty miles an hour. If the defendant testified to a series of matters that strung together strained credibility, you can comment on his "litany of lies." You would not use "lies", however, except in an extreme case where the lie was obvious. Otherwise, it would be better, much like Robert Ingersoll did in the last century, to suggest that, "The truth is easy to tell. A true fact will fit with everything else in the world except a lie. A lie won't fit with anything else except another lie. I hate to say the defendant lied, but it is difficult to fit anything he said with what anyone else said."

Shakespeare had some thoughts on this, for example, " 'He misses not much.' 'No: he doth but mistake the truth totally,' "[28] "You cram these words into mine ears, against the stomach of my sense."[29] Also, "The devil can cite scripture for his own purpose. An evil soul producing holy witness, Is like a villain's smiling cheek, a goodly apple rotten at the heart. O what a goodly outside falsehood hath,"[30] and ". . . malice bears down truth."[31] "Though I am not naturally honest, I am so sometimes by chance. . . ."[32] He ". . . will speak in a minute than he will stand to in a month."[33] He ". . . swore as many oathes, as I spake words, and broke them in the sweet face of Heaven."[34]

Other literature also helps us to deal with the lie. From James 3:5, ". . . the tongue's a little member and boasteth great things." From the Iliad, "I loathe like Hell's Gates the man who thinks one thing and says another."[35] Tolstoy, "It is very difficult to tell the truth, and young people are rarely capable of it."[36] Hermann Hesse, "It is very remarkable, all that man can swallow."[37] Cicero of the Greeks, ". . . fonder as they are of argument than of truth."[38] In reference to this last kind of thinking, some witnesses think that the admission of untruth by them on former occasions lends credibility to their present testimony.[39]

Others: Durant, ". . . eloquence is seldom accurate."[40] Shaw, ". . . if there was twenty ways of telling the truth and only one way of telling a lie, the Government would find it out."[41] Lincoln, "A specious and fantastic arrangement of words, by which a man can prove a horse-chestnut to be a chestnut horse."[42] Dostoevski, "You can travel to the end of the world on lies but they won't carry you back again. . . ."[43] Chekhov, "I shall say that lying is like a forest— the further one goes into it the more difficult it is to get out of it."[44]

In trials, it is in the peroration that the lawyer has his last direct and meaningful communication with the trier of the facts. Quintilian said that the peroration was the most important part of legal speaking,[45] and that it consisted mainly of appeals to the emotions.[46] He also said that it was in the peroration that, ". . . we must let loose the whole torrent of our eloquence."[47] The peroration in the style of the old lawyers can best be described by borrowing Shakespeare's words and say that they, ". . . tear a passion to tatters, to very rags, to split the ears of the groundlings."[48]

How long should the peroration be? It depends, naturally, upon the length of the entire presentation, but the actual peroration should generally not be longer than four or five paragraphs. It is not usually a time for the use of demonstrative aids because that would detract from bringing the whole force of the speaker's personality to bear upon the jury or the judge. Then, if anytime, it is desirable to have that one to one relationship (even with a jury of twelve), the individual eye contact and the rising emotion. When you're tearing a rag to tatters, you don't stop to pick up a picture.

But should the emotional delivery sustain itself until the very end of the speech? The answer is decidedly yes, but that does not mean that the volume either sustains itself at the highest level during the entire peroration or that the volume is highest at the very end of the peroration. It is better, even in the peroration, to build the volume to a peak and then to ease off and finish with a note of quiet intensity.

The peroration is no time for housekeeping, for tying together loose ends. It is the time when you isolate the two or three critical parts of the evidence. It may be the time for a well chosen metaphor. It may be the time for tears if they come naturally. Trying to bring yourself to that state is too much of an effort in a traffic case and will be thought ludicrous rather than infectious.

To end the peroration, you can ease to a stop while standing directly in front of the jury box and looking at the jury. Then solemnly walk back to your seat and sit down while your client reaches over and presses your hand (unless he was suffering from an injury to that part of his anatomy). Another ending would be to walk and stand behind your client, place your hands on his shoulders, and say, "George wanted me to personally thank each and every one of you for the attention you have given to his case during the past several days. He wouldn't have had it come to this except for the very serious nature of the injuries he has suffered. We both have the utmost confidence that you will abide by your oath, follow the credible evidence, and, pursuant to the court's instructions, bring back a just verdict."

Or, the writer has used a line similar to this, "Look deep into your hearts[49] before you sign the verdict and make sure you haven't cancelled George's life."[50] The reference and the phrasing can be either to the remainder of his life, such as in a personal injury case where a party's life would be meaningless if he lacked the financial resources to cope with his grievous injuries. On the other hand, the reference could be to all of the client's life up to the time of the slander in question, meaning that his life would, in effect, be canceled unless the jury's verdict erases the wrong done to your client.

In any event, you finally have to sit down. During the remainder of the trial, so long as you are in the presence of the jury or the judge (if the case is being tried to the court), be sure to maintain a demeanor in keeping with the tone of your closing argument, and be sure that your client does the same.

3. Delivery

Demosthenes said that the first principle of oratory was, "'Delivery,' the second 'delivery,' and the third 'delivery.'"[51] A story that illustrates the decisive difference that delivery makes is attributed to Aeschines, the great rival of Demosthenes. When Aeschines visited one of the Aegean islands, the inhabitants asked him to give one of his orations, which he did and which was warmly received. They then asked him if he would read to them one of Demosthenes' speeches. Aeschines accomodated them in this respect also. When he finished he was enthusiastically applauded. He said, "If you liked that, you should have heard Demosthenes deliver it." Cicero said and demonstrated that, "Delivery . . . is the dominant factor in oratory."[52] Chekhov wrote that ". . . books are the printed score, while talk is the singing."[53]

In delivery, many things are important, but a dignified, serious tone should generally pervade the presentation from start to finish. According to Pascal, "The tone of voice impresses the wisest among us, and can change a speech into an impromptu poem."[54] Quintilian claimed that a slow delivery evokes the greatest emotional power.[55] Demosthenes thought sincerity so important that he put the rhetorical question, "With what greater crime can one charge a man who is an orator than that of saying one thing and thinking another?"[56]

Any successful trial lawyer can tell you that tone is an ever present consideration. When you walk to the courthouse a juror may see you, not knowing who you are, but, later, during the course of a trial, he might remember you as the buffoon he saw earlier that day. This consideration applies to the client also. In a case in the United States District Court at Huntington, West Virginia, a client of the writer went outside the courthouse while the jury deliberated. When the jury was ready to report, the client was found in his automobile which was parked adjacent to the courthouse directly below the room where the jury had been deliberating. While waiting for the verdict, the client had killed a six-pack of beer in full view of the jury. Why they came back in his favor was never understood unless the jury thought he was trying to take the edge off the pain from his injury.

There are, naturally, different thoughts about the desired tone. Quintilian said that humble rank could be used for or against the accused.[57] Hugo describes a man who ". . . paid no attention to all those stumbling blocks which constitute obstacles in men's path known as conscience, sworn faith, justice and duty."[58] Trial lawyers are talking about tone when they advise you to, "Take charge of the courtroom." You are told to impose your presence. But,". . . an impudent, disorderly, or angry tone is always unseemly," according to Quintilian.[58a] Tone is only a part of "taking charge," but an important part. In passing, all the art you put into your presentation should be concealed, that is, the delivery should appear natural, spontaneous, to be from the heart. In the art of oratory, ". . . its highest expression will be in the concealment of its existence."[59]

A consideration in delivery is whether the speech should be presented without the aid of notes. A recent seminar speaker indicated that speaking without notes is preferable. No doubt this is true, but, interestingly enough, the speaker used notes during his presentation. Cicero cited at least three Roman orators who were able to speak without notes, word for word what they had prepared in writing.[60] Quintilian even gave instructions on how to remember our speeches. The speech should be divided into parts. Each part should be associated with a room of a familiar house. Thus, the content of the exordium should be associated with the foyer, and so on for each part of the speech.[61] Quintilian said that reducing a speech to writing gives only a "fancied security."[61a]

The present writer does not use notes in the usual way during voir dire, opening statement or summation. When representing the defendant it is easy, by concentration, to memorize the names of the jurors as they are called. Even when representing the plaintiff it can be done although there is not as much time for memorization. The task is made easier if you have studied the names before coming to the courthouse and if you have reviewed the information available concerning the jurors (jury questionnaires filled in by the jurors pursuant to court rule, the results of investigation into the jurors' backgrounds, and, in small counties, the knowledge the lawyer and his staff incidentally know—if nothing else is available, the name and the address of the juror can be significant). You will have to decide before the trial begins on an ideal juror profile for the particular case, and you will have to tentatively decide which jurors are desirable and which are not.

The information about the jurors can be put in a word processor, reduced to an abbreviated form and placed on individual cards for each juror (the card is about the size of a business card and the information is printed only on the top half of a long axis, the lower half being inserted into a slot on a cardboard panel). As each juror's name is called a member of the lawyer's support staff places the juror's card in the slot representing the juror's seat. The lawyer doing the voir dire pays the cards no mind until he comes to consideration of challenges. The support personnel update the cards with information elicited during voir dire. In this way critical information is at hand, and the critical decisions with reference to challenges can be accurately and swiftly made. More detailed information is usually kept at counsel table than can be put on the cards, but it is rarely necessary to refer to anything but the cards.

If you don't have the support staff or co-counsel available to handle the jurors' cards and update the information during voir dire, a client can handle this. The client must, however be trained for this task. Otherwise, confusion results.

The lawyer who conducts the voir dire should not, as the writer has seen some lawyers do, step before the jury box and call each of the jurors in turn by name. This appears strained and nothing more than an exercise in memory. A juror should be asked a question, using the juror's name. Then, another juror, also using this juror's name, should be asked if he agrees with the first juror. The lawyer should skip around, until all the jurors have been addressed by name.

Demonstrative aids, if used judiciously, can help in the recall of certain parts of your argument. For example, an elements chart will be useful to the jury and help you to keep in mind the divisions of your summation in relation to the proof as to each element. Likewise, transparencies (projected with an overhead projector) of key testimony will not only help you to remember that testimony, but they relieve the jury from having to accept your word as to what the witness said. The transparency does not give the appearance of a crutch to bolster your memory.

The writer's practice is to go over his opening statements and summations in his mind even before he has made a written outline. After the mental preparation is well along, a written outline is prepared and analyzed to make sure the arrangement and content are correct. Then, the presentation is again given mentally, not necessarily orally. Finally, certain passages may be written out word for word so that the language can be finely crafted. Once again, the statement or argument should be presented mentally, and finally, orally. When you make your courtroom delivery, you will remember because the reliance has not been on paper. The essential organization, wording and concept was conceived in the first instance mentally.

Not all hearings are suitable to proceeding without notes. English barristers have told the writer that complex cases being reviewed by the Law Lords are handled in a time-consuming presentation during which the bench and attorneys go from point to point and authority to authority, discussing each item in turn with frequent reference to pieces of evidence or leading cases. In such a proceeding, it would be imperative that counsel have a well organized file so that ready access could be had to the required material. At trial, such access should not take longer than fifteen seconds.

If you opt to use notes, your delivery can still be effective, although the notes will interfere with eye contact, with waking up a dozing juror, with reacting to the expression of jurors and with the handling of objections. Good arguments have been delivered from written notes. Don't feel bad just because Jesus and Socrates didn't use notes or that Plato cited the Egyptian gôd, Theuth, for authority that writing would, ". . . implant forgetfulness in their souls."[62] An ancient Chinese proverb says, "The paled ink is better than most retentive memory."[63]

Whether notes are used or not, the speed of delivery is worthy of consideration. Quintilian said, "Let not your tongue outrun your thought."[64] He also said, ". . . the slower the delivery the greater its emotional power."[65] John Kenneth Galbraith, however, remarked rather unkindly of John Foster Dulles that, "His speech was slow but it easily kept pace with his thought."[66]

A halting and hesitating delivery has no authority. Great speed of delivery should not be maintained throughout the speech. In fact, the best tone is often established by a friendly but controlled conversational style during voir dire, followed by a no-nonsense delivery of the opening statement. In the summation, the pace is gradually quickened until during the peroration the words flow quite rapidly and the emotional impact is unloaded upon the jury. As Quintilian put it, ". . . in any opening any preliminary appeal to the compassion must be made sparingly and with restraint, which in the peroration we may give full rein to our emotions."[67]

Speed of delivery is closely connected with emotional impact, and, as has been noted, it is not always the fastest delivery that results in the most effective emotional result. By the same token, the volume of delivery is important in relation to emotional effectiveness, and loudest is not necessarily best.

Victor Hugo advised caution, saying, "Let us not therefore carry flame where light alone will suffice."[68] But Quintilian said that, "Fire alone can kindle. . . ."[69] Gibbon said of Peter the Hermit that he possessed, ". . . that vehemence of speech /which/ seldom fails to impart the persuasion of the soul."[70] Cicero said that, ". . . the orator who inflames the court accomplishes far more than one who merely instructs it.[71] Hegel said, "It is passion that gives rise to language."[71a] The trial lawyer's modern equivalent of all this is the saying that, "They won't burn if there's no fire." Aristotle so far approves of this approach that he said, ". . . the hearer always sympathizes with one who speaks emotionally even though he says nothing."[72] A caution is, nonetheless, given by Quintilian who advises us that, ". . . it would be a mistake to cast any doubt upon its value /of certain music/ by showing an excessive zeal in its defense."[73]

There must be commitment on the part of the speaker if he is to be effective in conveying the credibility of his cause to the jury. A lawyer is no actor.[74] He must believe in his cause, "For if the trumpet give forth an uncertain sound, who shall prepare himself to the battle."[75] Quintilian agrees, saying, "The prime essential for stirring the emotions of others is . . . first to feel those emotions myself."[76]

There is some thinking among the bar and others that the lawyer has only an artificial connection with his client's cause, that he needs some special incentive to feel in his innermost being the truth of what he argues. Aristophanes understood the situation and said, ". . . there's no art where there's no fee."[77] Sometime later, Pascal said, ". . . how much juster an advocate who has been well paid in advance finds his client's cause."[78] A lawyer speaking on effective argument in drunk driving cases said, "When it is a close-cut thing, and you're down to the argument, you're not going to convince the jury if you don't believe in your client, and there's no way you're going to believe in that turkey if he still owes a thousand dollars on your fee."

Extravagant effects such as crying should be avoided. You wouldn't want it said of you that, "He has strangled his language in his tears."[79] Neither is "breath preaching" effective in the courtroom. It can be effective in a Freewell Baptist Church where the congregation is culturally attuned to receive the message from this type of delivery, and where the members feel free to participate with their "Amen Brother," but a jury will come from too diverse a background to be generally receptive to this style of delivery. Even the Baptist church member who was used to the style would think its use in the courtroom was an attempt to make fun of him and his church.

The words used in speaking must be carefully chosen. Cicero held that, ". . . the choice of language is the foundation of eloquence."[80] Quintilian said that, "The sole duty assigned to words by nature is to be the servant of thought."[81] The words chosen should be correct, lucid and eloquent,[82] and of these requirements, the most important is clearness.[83]

A key to what separates the great speakers from the good speakers can be found in this sentence from Corinthians, ". . . except ye utter by the tongue words easy to understand, how shall it be known what is spoken?"[84] In other words, speak in everyday language.[85] As Cicero said, ". . . in oratory the very cardinal sin is to depart from the language of every day life and the usage approved by the sense of the community."[86] Shakespeare wanted, "An honest speech plainly told."[87] Hamlet suggested that the players use, "More matter, with less art."[88] Confucius advised, "to stand up before men and pour forth a stream of glib words is generally to make yourself obnoxious to them."[89]

Aristophanes' comment could cure most anyone of inappropriately using big words, of which he said, ". . . winged words, tall as mountains, terrible scarers, which the spectator admired without understanding what they meant."[90] Pascal said you should not, ". . . use big words to say little things."[91] Merton, more movingly, said "It does no good to use big words to talk about Christ."[92] Terrence disapproved of a person, ". . . who is going to say with a great effort some very silly things."[93] Thucydides objected to the misuse of, ". . . fair phrases to arrive at guilty ends. . . ."[94]

Cicero said, ". . . language and delivery seem quite ridiculous when they are weightier than what the case can carry."[95] Shakespeare said, "Let proof speak."[96] A defense lawyer in Les Miserables seemed to be on the wrong road when he ". . . had begun expatiating on the theft of apples—a thing ill suited to lofty style."[97] This tells us that language appropriate in one case may not be appropriate in another. Style must adapt to cases.

Now consider some other thoughts on the choice of language. Quintilian preferred verbs for their strength.[98] Cicero was concerned that language might not appear overly correct to the point of being strained. He said, ". . . nobody ever admired an orator for correct grammar."[99] Quintilian, along the same line, said, ". . . it is one thing to speak Latin and another to speak grammar. . . ."[100]

Remember that every word will have several connotations to different persons and communities. Words once appropriate are less so now, for example, in many circumstances, the word "black" is now used where formerly one would have used the word "negro." The word "gold" might carry with it a feeling of the best in life to one person while to another it would conjure up images of the lazy rich. The only limit to the search for the right word is the imagination of the speaker.

Some cases are susceptible to the romantic style. The writer once defended a woman charged with killing the man who had sexually abused her twelve-year-old daughter. Such a case provided ample ground for lofty language. The average land appropriation case calls for a more pedestrian choice of words.

The length of the presentation depends on many factors, the most obvious of which are the requirements of particular courts. Frequently, appellate courts limit oral argument to thirty minutes to a side, with fifteen minutes not being unusual. Even then, counsel may be faced with the question from both appellate and trial benches, "Would counsel like to submit the case on the briefs?" (Or, "the evidence," as the case might be). Such judges obviously feel that there are no counsel in the entire world who could add any light whatsoever to the bright glow of knowledge already emanating from their minds. One appellate judge (who had been on the bench for at least six years) told the writer that he had never heard a memorable argument. There was difficulty in dealing with the subsequent depression suffered by the writer, who had argued many times before that judge.

On the flip side of this subject are courts such as the United States Court of Appeals for the Sixth Circuit where oral argument is encouraged, and there is lively participation by the bench with questions. Such questions should be answered immediately, directly and simply. The Sixth Circuit so much values oral argument that it will not permit assigned counsel in criminal cases to waive argument absent some compelling reason.

In jury trials, counsel will either be asked by the court, "How much time will you require for argument?" or "Counsel will have thirty minutes a side for argument. Does the Plaintiff wish to divide his time?" Many trial judges have told the writer that an argument that lasts more than a half hour hurts the speaker's cause. At seminars, it has been said that a peak of interest is reached and anything after that rapidly erodes whatever credibility had been established.

Can a long argument—for two or more hours—be of any worth? Of course it can. There must simply be enough issues needing to be discussed in a cause worthy of that type of consideration. But, the longer the argument the more skill that is required to keep the attention of the jurors. It is sometimes said that it is more difficult to compress words into a short, pithy statement, than it is to ramble at length. This is true, but speaking long is no excuse for rambling. In a long presentation, there must be changes of pace, of direction, of tone of voice, of volume, and the presentation must be decorated with suitable images. But no matter that the judge complains, that the reporter complains or others criticize, if a long argument is necessary to cover the waterfront, to explain a multiplicity of serious circumstances, then be as long as the rules permit; only don't put the jury to sleep. If you argue last, the jurors are ordinarily perking up because they think it is getting close to their time to go home.

The great writers have spoken on the subject of length of presentation. Shakespeare said, "Where words are scarce, they are seldom spent in vain. . . ."[101] And in Hamlet, ". . . brevitie is the soul of wit."[102] In Ecclesiastes it is said that, ". . . a fool's voice is known by a multitude of words."[103] Job was asked by one of his friends, "Should not the multitude of words be answered? and should a man full of talk be justified?"[104] Thomas a Kempis suggested, ". . . this is great wisdom, not to be moved by a wind of words."[105] Pascal agreed, saying, "Perpetual eloquence is wearisome. . . ."[106] The reason for brevity is given by Quintilian who said, ". . . every word that neither helps the sense nor the style is faulty."[107] The most extreme form of brevity is that advised by Tocqueville, who said, "To keep silence is the most useful service that an indifferent spokesman can render the commonwealth."[108]

There is a lobby for speaking at greater length. Tocqueville also asked, ". . . how can I be clear and at the same time be brief?"[109] Quintilian said, ". . . no one is ever contented with the simple truth."[110] Dr. Johnson said, "It is unjust to censure lawyers for multiplying words, when they argue; it is often necessary for them to multiply words."[111]

With this advice from the sages, now suggesting brevity and now suggesting multiplying words, what are lawyers to do? The authorities are not really in conflict. Short or long, every word must be intelligently chosen, and ". . . brevity must not be devoid of eloquence."[112]

As to repetition, as usual there are two points of view. Plato said that, ". . . there is no harm in hearing a thing several times."[113] Quintilian advised that, ". . . we may even at times go so far as to regard it as superfluous to plead the case at all."[114] In a personal injury case, the writer delivered the opening summation for the plaintiff. Defendant's counsel—apparently following Quintilian— waived summation. My partner, William J. Curry, a splendid trial lawyer, was to have done our closing. Instead, Curry did the white-knuckle argument from his chair. While we were waiting a verdict he told me, "Lloyd, we've lost." For once, Bill was wrong.

There is a lot of repetition in trials. The facts are alluded to in voir dire, anticipated in opening statements, made concrete by testimony, recalled by argument and structured by the judge. Notwithstanding all of this repetition, it would be an unusual case where counsel in his argument would not tell the jury what he was going to tell them, then tell them, and finally, tell them what he had told them. This repetition, however, must be for various specific purposes, namely, the preview, the proof and the heart-felt peroration that moves the jury to your position.

Sometimes actual lines are repeated, sometimes without intervention, for effect. For example, note a gift in a personal injury case in the form of testimony from the defendant trucker who said that he continued at thirty-five miles per hour through a fog bank because if everyone did that no one would get hit. That was worth coming back to in the closing at least three times.

Enumeration must be used with discretion. Cicero suggested that, ". . . care be taken in enumeration to avoid the appearance of childishness in embarking on a parade of one's power of memory.[115] This type of situation can come up in a domestic case where the lawyer recalls for the judge's benefit not only the major items of personal property but each knife and fork.

Gestures certainly can and should be used to aid persuasion. There are dangers. Cilon of Sparta said that, "Gesticulation should be avoided as a sign of insanity."[116] Gestures can be threatening. Actors and psychologists will tell you that you shouldn't thrust your finger at the jury when you are standing close to them. When the writer was a prosecuting attorney and presenting a case to the grand jury, a six foot four and two hundred fifty pound suspect, who was testifying at his request, when asked what had happened picked a pistol from the exhibit table, turned toward the jurors, pointed the gun at them and said "Bang!" That did intimidate a few jurors.

When defending a young woman accused of murdering her mother-in-law with a shotgun, the writer, not knowing anything about psychology or acting, took the club that the defendant claimed the deceased used to strike with and, during argument, banged it on a table in front of the jury. The jury hung ten to two for acquittal. One juror said afterwards that he wouldn't send a woman with four small children to the penitentiary no matter what. Another member of that jury said that he held out for a conviction because God had told him how to vote in a vision.

So, demonstrations and gestures can be used. What the effect is in a particular case is always a matter of speculation. A lawyer who wins will attribute the result to the brilliance of his argument, the lawyer who loses to the evidence, the judge to the law and the jurors to their sagacity. So long as you are a trial lawyer, however, you have to believe that you know some of the answers and that you can make a difference.

Quintilian believed that, "Changes of facial expression and glances of the eyes are most effective in pleading, but if the orator never ceases to distort his face with affected grimaces or to wag his head and roll his eyes, he becomes a laughing-stock."[117] Consideration can be given to not crossing your arms (shutting out the jury), gestures to the outside (friendly and inviting), in not weaving or pacing (distracting), in looking the jurors in the eyes (proof of sincerity), and in not talking with your back to the jury. Many lawyers have nervous habits such as playing with their wedding ring, brushing their hair, rolling the end of their moustache, and scratching their nose or worse. Still, in a hot courtroom, some mannerisms can contribute to persuasion. For example if someone left the air conditioner off, the lawyer can work himself into a sweat and use his handkerchief to effect, the same as many lawyers have affected poses using their glasses. In all such delivery techniques, ". . . care must be used to avoid anything, style of action or speaking, which can be made absurd by imitation."[118] When you speak last, you have a little more liberty in this regard.

Boasting by the lawyer is a mistake.[119] Humor is sometimes acceptable. When the writer was representing three young black men who had been charged with raping a teenaged white girl, a witness testified that he had seen the girl in an automobile with the defendants and that she appeared, ". . . well satisfied." The jury broke into laughter along with the audience, and the judge gavelled everyone back to silence. This testimony was used in argument along with the statement of the prosecuting witness that when she left the car of the defendants to go into her home she took a sixteen inch pizza with her because she thought she had, ". . . earned it." It was funny to the jury. If it hadn't been, it wouldn't have been used in argument. Quintilian said, ". . . one little breath of humor will sometimes turn the whole trend of opinion."[120] Humor may have saved those defendants from going to the penitentiary. Quintilian also said, "A foolish question makes for smart replies."[121]

Nietzsche said you should not extenuate the crime but glorify it.[122] You might not want to put it just that way, but even Quintilian believed that, ". . . there are some acts which require to be defended with no less boldness than was required for their commission."[123] Once, when representing a three hundred sixty pound leader of a motorcycle club (not a gang) against charges of felonious assault, carrying a concealed weapon and trafficking in drugs, testimony that he was ". . . not afraid of any man," that as to his girl friend throwing herself between the deputies' guns and himself, that he would, ". . . believe it when he saw it," and that "speed" was "going sixty in a fifty mile per hour zone." The jury acquitted the defendant on one count and hung on three counts. It wouldn't have done in that case to try and make a pussycat out of the defendant.

In the "old days" there were other persuasive techniques available. Shakespeare said, "Gold were as good as twenty orators!"[124] Epictetus said different men sell at different prices.[125] Although the bar and bench don't encourage that sort of thing, not a year will go by but what some client will allude to the possibility.

Victor Hugo refers to, "The wise man who knows when and how to stop."[126] Don't talk when you have nothing to say. Don't hesitate to take time to make clear what must be clear.

4. Figures

When a person thinks of something by himself, he is more likely to accept it as fact than if someone else explained it to him. Metaphors, similes, parables and allegories are ways of convincing persons to believe that they thought of something by themselves. Other words for these figures are "stories," "illustrations" and "anecdotes."

Many lawyers make the mistake of using a wonderful figure and then saying, "What I meant by that was . . ." This reminds one of the story, "The Reticence of Lady Anne," by Saki.[127] In matters of art, the characters in the story leaned toward the type of picture, ". . . that told its own story, with generous assistance from its title." They explained a painting ". . . to friends of duller intelligence."[128] Make your point clear, but don't say, "He knows where the hog ate the cabbage," or "He knows where the bodies are," and then explain, "What I meant by that is that the defendant was at his accomplice's apartment the night the plans were made to rob the bank."

Figures of speech are so important that Donald Traci, at a legal seminar, said that his senior partner, the nationally known Cleveland attorney, Craig Spangenburg, devotes as much as three days before an important trial to thinking of appropriate illustrations to aid in communicating the defendant's liability and the plaintiff's suffering to the jury. A seminar at Case Western College of Law referred to metaphor as the second strongest element in persuasion.

Animals are popularly used in figures of speech. Jesus used the camel figuratively at least twice. In Matthew 19:24, He said, "It is easier for a camel to go through the eye of the needle, than for a rich man to enter into the kingdom of God." He also accused the scribes and pharisees of straining at a gnat and swallowing a camel.[129] These illustrations not only don't need explanation, they are so familiar that most people who read will recognize the figures, know that they came from the Bible, and will congratulate themselves on being so knowledgeable.

Dogs are popularly used in illustrations both anciently and in the present day. How many prosecutors have used, ". . . a dog returneth to his vomit . . ."?[130] As to the opposing lawyer's tactic, say, "Try that bone on another dog."[131] Leon Uris, in *Trinity*,[132] said, "He's a dog with only one trick." Shakespeare said, "A staff is quickly found to beat a dog;"[133] and, "The cat will mew, and a dogge will have his day."[134]

Other animals are useful, especially the hog. It is suggested that you may find a way to use the following: "Graceful as a hog on ice," "Even a blind hog gets an acorn once in awhile," "Whole hog or nothing," "Root hog or die," and "Don't make a hog out of yourself."

Lincoln said, "Every man must skin his own skunk."[135] According to Aristotle, ". . . One swallow does not make a summer."[136] Dostoeysky said, "You can't take two skins off one ox."[137] He also said, "One reptile will devour the other."[138] Victor Hugo said, "The last thing owls wish is light."[139] Mario Pei said, "With so many roosters crowing the sun will never come up."[140] Shakespeare was on a roll when he had Edgar in *King Lear* describe himself as a ". . . hog in sloth, fox in stealth, wolf in greediness, dog in madness, lion in prey."[141] Shakespeare has Lady MacDuff say, "For the poor wren, The most diminutive of birds, will fight, Her young ones in her nest, against the owl."[142]

Inanimate objects can also make powerful figures. Saint Matthew said, the ". . . axe is laid to the root of the trees."[143] Tolstoy said, "When wood is chopped chips will fly."[144] Dostoevsky said,

"Water wears out a stone."[145] This line from Chekhov always reminds me of opposing counsel, ". . . the wind has broken loose from its chain."[146] Perlander, as to political opponents, said, "Cut the tall corn."[147] Consider Clare Boothe's great line on aging, "And that first gleam of white in your hair. It's the way you'd feel about autumn if you knew there'd never be another spring."[148] Alaric told the Roman senators who said that thousands of Romans stood ready to give their lives for their country, that, "The thicker the hay the easier it is mowed."[149] For a piece of advice to the jury, try *Job* where it is said, "Does not the ear try words as the palate tastes food?"[150]

One lawyer picked up a story from "Wild Kingdom" on television. He commented that much of television was a wasteland, but that, ". . . I really enjoy this program. One segment was about walruses and how they had been returning to the same islands in the North Atlantic to breed for centuries—maybe longer. Not only do they return to the same islands, each walrus returns to about the same spot. The old bull walruses stake out their territory. When a younger bull walrus tries to take over the turf of an old bull, there is a lot of groaning, butting and pushing around. There are even a few minor injuries, but not one of the walruses gets badly hurt. Even animals have rules." The reference is obviously to a defendant who had failed to follow a simple traffic rule which was aimed at preventing injury.

Another lawyer started his argument by saying, "The morning we began this trial I had to drop my daughter off at school. She's eight. On the way, she asked me what my case was about, I said my client entered into a contract with a builder to have a house built and that after the contractor was paid, the house began to leak, the furnace wouldn't work and the house was cold in winter because the contractor hadn't insulated it. My daughter asked, 'Is he going to get away with it?' I told her that the jury would have to answer that question." One lawyer said he wouldn't use this illustration. He didn't have a daughter.

The examples of figures are endless. Make them up, copy from others and lift them from literature. They will brighten your arguments and convince your jurors.

5. General Considerations

Standing is the most important element in persuasion. Standing is what Congressman Albert G. Riddle had in mind when he told Abraham Lincoln, "Your word, Mr. President, is the highest human evidence."[151]

There is local standing, celebrity standing, expert standing and no standing. The local lawyer, well-known and well liked in his own county has a heavy advantage over the unknown, visiting lawyer. On the other hand, let a Percy Forman, an F. Lee Bailey or a Melvin Belli come to town and they attract a kind of attention and consideration that can give them a commanding presence. Expertise, backed up with credentials as an author or a litigator in a specialized field gives standing within the limits of the specialty. Aristotle would have agreed with Congressman Riddle. He said, ". . . moral character constitutes the most effective means of proof."[152] Of the elements of persuasion, Quintillian gave first place to standing.[153]

Antithesis, asides and invective can add variety to your delivery, but these must be used thoughtfully, especially invective. This example of antithesis and invective combined, comes from Cicero, "I cannot but envy your master who received the huge fee I shall mention presently for his success in teaching you to be a fool."[154] Likewise is the line from Victor Hugo, "In a difficult situation he possessed all the essentials of stupidity; . . ."[155]

A memorable aside in a criminal defense came from Cicero, "/I/f I did not have cause of ill-feeling toward that woman's lover—I am sorry; I meant to say her brother. I am always making that slip."[156]

With these thoughts in mind, the young lawyer might ask, "What can I do to become more persuasive?" He can read good literature. He can practice speaking. An address to a local organization should be prepared as seriously as an argument in trial. The lawyer must treat even the simplest court appearance as an exercise in persuasion. Persuasion is a habit. You can't turn it off and on. It is habits of speech.

For serious trials, start thinking about your oral presentation long ahead of trial. Practice your opening statement and argument on video. Let your partner look at it and make suggestions. Don't video only your face. At least include from the waist up so you can see mannerisms and gestures.

How will you know when you are improving? There are lots of measures, but "The truth is that the orator who is approved by the multitude must inevitably be approved by the expert."[157] Quintilian said that the most coveted prize was, ". . . the applause of a large audience. . . ."[158] For a trial lawyer, the ultimate test of persuasion is either the judgment of the court or the verdict of the jury.

Chapter XI Footnotes

1. Marcus Fabius Quintilian, *Institutio Oratoria,* tr. H.E. Butler, Loeb Classical Library, 4 vols. (Cambridge, Mass., Harvard University Press, 1969, reprint of 1920-21), 1:317.

2. *Ibid.,* 4:355.

3. Plutarch, *The Lives of the Noble Grecians and Romans,* tr. John Dryden, rev'd Arthur Clough, The Modern Library (New York, Random House), 195.

4. Blaise, Pascal, *Les Pensees,* tr. Martin Turnell (Bloomfield, Conn., 1970): 174.

5. Edward Gibbon, *The Decline and Fall of the Roman Empire,* 3 vols. (New York, Random House), 3:451.

6. Thucydides, *The History of the Peloponnesian War,* tr. Richard Crawley, rev'd R.C. Feetham (Avon, Conn., The Limited Editions Club, 1974), 294.

7. Tacitus, *The Annals,* tr. John Jackson, Loeb Classical Library, 5 vols. (Cambridge, Mass., Harvard University Press, 1969, reprint of 1937), 5:7.

8. Aristotle, *Art of Rhetoric,* tr. John Henry Freese, Loeb Classical Library (Cambridge, Mass., Harvard University Press, 1967, reprint of 1926), viii-x.

9. *Ibid.,* 23.

10. Quintilian, *Institutio Oratoria, op. cit.* note 1, 2:511.

11. *Ibid.*

12. *Ibid.,* 23.

13. *Ibid.,* 1:515.

14. *Ibid.,* 2:9.

15. William Shakespeare, *Hamlet,* act 1, sc. 5, line 5.

16. Isa. 1:18.

17. Diogenes Laertius, *Lives of Eminent Philosophers*, tr. R.D. Hicks, Loeb Classical Library, 2 vols. (Cambridge, Mass., Harvard University Press, 1970, reprint of 1925), 1:67.

18. Quintilian, *Insitutio Oratoria, 4:269.*

19. *Ibid.*, 187.

20. *Ibid.*, 2:67.

21. William Shakespeare, *Two Gentlemen from Verona*, Act 2, sc. 4, line 41.

22. Quintilian, *Institutio Oratoria, op. cit.* note 1, 1:413-15.

23. 2 Macc. 2:32.

24. Plato, *Collected Dialogues*, Edited by Edith Hamilton and Huntington Cairns, tr. by Lane Cooper, *et al.*, Pantheon Books (New York, Random House, 1961), 4-5.

25. Thucydides, *The History of the Peloponnesian War, op. cit.* at note 6, 92.

26. Demonsthenes, *Public Orations*, tr. A. W. Pickard-Cambridge, Everyman's Library (New York, Dutton, 1963, reprint of 1906), 325, 328, 329, 337, 338, 339, and 341.

27. Cicero, *Orations and Essays*, tr. Palmer Bovie, et al. (Verona, Italy, The Limited Editions Club, 1972), 112.

28. William Shakespeare, *The Tempest*, act 2, sc. 1, line 57.

29. *Ibid.*, act 2, sc. 1, line 107.

30. William Shakespeare, *Merchant of Venice*, act 1, sc. 3, line 98.

31. *Ibid.*, act 4, sc. 1, line 214.

32. William Shakespeare, *The Winter's Tale*, act 4, sc. 4, line 712.

33. William Shakespeare, *Romeo and Juliet*, act 2, sc. 4, line 48.

34. William Shakespeare, *King Lear*, act 3, sc. 4, line 88.

35. Homer, *The Iliad*, tr. E. V. Rieu (London, The Folio Society, 1975), 133.

36. Leo Tolstoy, *War and Peace*, tr. Louise and Aylmer Maude (New York, Simon and Schuster, 1954, reprint of 1942), 260.

37. Hermann Hesse, *Steppenwolf*, tr. Basil Creighton, rev'd by Joseph Mileck and Horst Frenz (Westport, Conn., The Limited Editions Club, 1977), 28.

38. Cicero, *Cicero in Twenty-Eight Volumes*, Vol. 3, *De Oratore*, tr. E. W. Sutton, Loeb Classical Library (Cambridge, Mass., Harvard University, 1942, reprinted 1967), 3:37.

39. Gustave Flaubert, *Madame Bovary,* tr. Cleanor Marx Aveling, Modern Library (New York, Random House), 328.

40. Will Durant, *The Story of Civilization, The Age of Faith,* 11 vols. (New York, Simon and Schuster, 1950), 4:31.

41. Bernard Shaw, *Complete Plays With Prefaces,* 5 vols (New York, Dodd, Mead & Company, 1963), 5:143.

42. Carl Sandburg, *Abraham Lincoln, The Prairie Years,* 2 vols (New York, Harcourt, Brace & World, Inc., 1926), 2:158.

43. Fyodor Dostoevsky, *The Brothers Karamazov,* tr. Constance Garnett, rev'd Avraham Yarmolinsky (New York, The Heritage Press, 1949, reprint of 1933), 235.

44. Anton Chekov, *The Short Stories of Anton Chekhov,* tr. Constance Garnett (Avon, Conn., The Limited Editions Club, 1973), 198.

45. Quintilian, *Institutio Oratoria, op. cit.* at note 1, 2:21.

46. *Ibid.*

47. *Ibid.,* 45.

48. William Shakespeare, *Hamlet,* act 3, sc. 2, 11.

49. Robert Penn Warren, *All the King's Men,* Modern Library (New York, Random House, 1953, reprint of 1946), 155.

50. Quintilian, *Institutio Oratoria, op. cit.* at note 1, 4:161.

51. Cicero, *Cicero In Twenty-Eight Volumes,* Vol. 5, *Brutus,* tr. G. L. Hendrickson, and *Orator,* tr. H. M. Hubbell, Loeb Classical Library (Cambridge, Mass., Harvard University Press, 1971, reprint of 1939), 125.

52. *Ibid., De Oratore,* Vol. 3, tr. E. W. Sutton & H. Rackham (1968, reprint of 1942), 169.

53. Chekhov, *Short Stories, op. cit.* at note 44, 152.

54. Pascal, *Les Pensees, op. cit.* at note 4, 16.

55. Quintilian, *Institutio Oratoria, op. cit.* at note 1, 4:303.

56. Demosthenes, *Public Orations, op. cit.* at note 26, 397.

57. Quintilian, *Institutio Oratoria, op. cit.* at note 1, 3:67.

58. Victor Hugo, *Les Miserables,* tr. Charles E. Wilbour, The Modern Library (New York, Random House), 25.

58a. Quintilian, *Institutio Oratoria, op. cit.* at note 1, 4:171.

59. *Ibid.,* 1:185.

60. *Ibid.,* 4:131.

61. *Ibid.,* 4:221.

61a. *Ibid.,* 4:129.

62. Plato, *The Collected Dialogues of Plato,* Ed. by Edith Hamilton and Huntington Cairns, tr. by Lane Cooper, et al., Pantheon Books (New York, Random House, Inc., 1961), 520.

63. Mario Pei, *The Story of Language,* revised ed. (Philadelphia, J. B. Lippincott Company, 1965), 90.

64. Quintilian, *Institutio Oratoria, op. cit.* at note 1, 1:71.

65. *Ibid.,* 4:303.

66. John Kenneth Galbraith, *The Age of Uncertainty* (Boston, Houghton & Mifflin, 1977), 237.

67. Quintilian, *Institutio Oratoria, op. cit.* at note 1, 2:21.

68. Hugo, *Les Miserables, op. cit.* at note 98, 435.

69. Quintilian, *Institutio Oratoria, op. cit.* at note 1, 2:433.

70. Edward Gibbon, *The Decline and Fall of the Roman Empire,* The Modern Library, 3 vols (New York, Random House), 3:418.

71. Quintilian, *Institutio Oratoria, op. cit.* at note 1, 5:83.

71a. Page Smith, *A New Age Now Begins,* 2 vols (New York, McGraw-Hill Book Company, 1976), 2:1790.

72. Aristotle, *Art of Rhetoric, op. cit.* at note 8, 379.

73. Quintilian, *Institutio Oratoria, op. cit.* at note 1, 1:175.

74. Cicero, *Cicero In Twenty-Eight Volumes,* Vol. 4, *De Oratore,* tr. E. W. Sutton and H. Rackham, (1942, reprinted 1948), 4:171.

75. I Corin. 14:8.

76. Quintilian, *Institutio Oratoria, op. cit.* at note 1, 2:431.

77. Aristophanes, *The Eleven Comedies, Plutus,* Modern Library, 2 vols (New York, Random House) 2:436.

78. Pascal, *Les Pensees, op. cit.* at note 4, 19.

79. William Shakespeare, *King Henry the Eighth,* act 5, sc. 1., line 156.

80. Cicero, *Cicero In Twenty-Eight Volumes,* Vol. 4, *De Oratore, op. cit.* at note 38, 4:353.

81. Quintilian, *Institutio Oratoria, op. cit.* at note 1, 4:473.

82. *Ibid.,* 1:79

83. *Ibid.,* 221.

84. I Corin. 4:9.

85. Quintilian, *Institutio Oratoria, op. cit.* at note 1, 2:187.

86. Cicero, *Cicero In Twenty-Eight Volumes,* Vol. 3, *De Oratore, op. cit.* at note 38, 3:11.

87. William Shakespeare, *King Richard the Third,* act 4, sc. 4, line 358.

88. William Shakespeare, *Hamlet,* act 2, sc. 2, line 95.

89. Confucius, *The Wisdom of Confucius,* ed. by Epiphanius Wilson, tr. William Jennings (New York, Avenel Books, 1982), 125.

90. Aristophones, *The Eleven Comedies, The Frogs,* Modern Library, 2 vols (New York, Random House), 2:237.

91. Pascal, *Les Pensees, op. cit.* at note 4, 176.

92. Thomas Merton, *The Sign of Jonas* (Garden City, New York, Doubleday & Company, Inc.), 222.

93. Pascal, *Les Pensees, op. cit.* at note 4, 176.

94. Thycydides, *The History of the Peloponnesian War, op. cit.* at note 6, 169.

95. Cicero, *Cicero In Twenty-Eight Volumes,* Vol. 4, *De Oratore, op. cit.* at note 38, 4:353.

96. William Shakespeare, *The Tragedy of Cymbeline,* Act 3, sc. 1, Line 77.

97. Hugo, *Les Miserables, op. cit.* at note 98, 226.

98. Quintilian, *Institutio Oratoria, op. cit.* at note 1, 3:521.

99. Cicero, *Cicero In Twenty-Eight Volumes,* Vol. 4, *De Oratore, op. cit.* at note 38, 4:41.

100. Quintilian, *Institutio Oratoria, op. cit.* at note 1, 1:123. William Shakespeare, *Richard the Second,* act 2, sc. 1, line 7.

101. William Shakespeare, *Richard The Second,* Act 2, sc. 1, line 7.

102. William Shakespeare, *Hamlet,* Act 2, sc. 2, line 90.

103. Eccles., 5:3.

104. Job, 11:2.

105. Thomas a Kempis, *The Imitation of Christ,* rev'd tr., translator not listed, The Family Inspirational Library (New York, Grosset & Dunlap, 1974 printing), 163; also see, Eph., 4:14.

106. Pascal, *Les Pensees, op. cit.* at note 4, 179.

107. Quintilian, *Institutio Oratoria, op. cit.* at note 1, 3:241.

108. Alexis Tocqueville, *Democracy in America,* Henry Reeve text, rev'd by Francis Bowen and Phillips Bradley, 2 vols. (New York, Alfred A. Knopf, 1972), 2:90.

109. Tocqueville, *Democracy in America,* 1:139.

110. Quintilian, *Institutio Oratoria, op. cit.* at note 1, 3:345.

111. James Boswell, *The Life of Samuel Johnson, L.L.D.,* The Modern Library (New York, Random House), 958.

112. Quintilian, *Institutio Oratoria, op. cit.* at note 1, 1:75.

113. Plato, *Collected Dialogues, op. cit.* at note 62, "Phaedo," 86.

114. Quintilian, *Institutio Oratoria, op. cit.* at note 1, 2:61.

115. Cicero, *Cicero In Twenty-Eight Volumes, De Oratore, op. cit.* at note 38, 4:357.

116. Diogenes Laertius, *Lives of Eminent Philosophers,* tr. R. D. Hicks, Loeb Classical Library, 2 vols (Cambridge, Mass., Harvard University Press, 1970), 1:73.

117. Quintilian, *Institutio Oratoria, op. cit.* at note 1, 3:505.

118. Cicero, *Cicero In Twenty-Eight Volumes, Brutus, op. cit.* at note 38, 5:193.

119. Quintilian, *Institutio Oratoria, op. cit.* at note 1, 4:163.

120. *Ibid.,* 3:329.

121. *Ibid.,* 2:399.

122. Friedrich Nietzsche, *The Philosophy of Nietzsche,* tr. Thomas Common, Modern Library (New York, Random House, 1950), 459.

123. Quintilian, *Institutio Oratoria, op. cit.* at note 1, 2:405.

124. William Shakespeare, *Richard The Third,* act 4, sc. 2, line 38.

125. Epictetus, *The Discourses And Manual,* tr. P. E. Matheson, The Heritage Press (New York, The Limited Editions Club, 1968), 9.

126. Hugo, *Les Miserables, op. cit.* at note 58, 114.

127. Hector Hugh Munro, "Saki," *Saki, Short Stories* (London, The Folio Society, 1951), 19.

128. *Ibid.,* 20.

129. Matt., 23:24.

130. Prov., 26:11.

131. Miguel Cervantes Saavedra, *Don Quixote*, tr. John Ormsby, (New York, The Heritage Press, 1950), 228.

132. Leon Uris, *Trinity* (Garden City, New York, Doubleday & Company, Inc., 1976), 543.

133. William Shakespeare, *Richard The Second*, act 3, sc. 1, line 171.

134. William Shakespeare, *Hamlet*, act 5, sc. 1, line 292.

135. Sandburg, *Abraham Lincoln, The Prairie Years*, op. cit. at note 42, 1:296.

136. Aristotle, *Ethics*, tr. John Warrington, Everyman's Library (New York, Dutton, 1963), 13.

137. Dostoevsky, *The Brothers Karamazov*, op. cit. at note 43, 96.

138. *Ibid.*, 100.

139. Hugo, *Les Miserables*, op. cit. at note 58, 339.

140. Mario Pei, *The Story of Language*, op. cit. at note 63, 291.

141. William Shakespeare, *King Lear*, act 3, sc. 4, line 93.

142. William Shakespeare, *Macbeth*, act 4, sc. 2, line 93.

143. Matt., 3:10; see also, Luke, 3:9.

144. Tolstoy, *War and Peace*, op. cit. at note 36, 828.

145. Fyodor Dostoevsky, *Crime and Punishment*, tr. Constance Garnett (New York, 1927), 527.

146. Chekhov, *Short Stories*, op. cit. at note 44, 152.

147. Laertius, *Lives Of The Eminent Philosophers*, op. cit. at note 17, 1:105.

148. Bennett A. Cerf and Van H. Cartmell, Eds., *Sixteen Famous American Plays*, Clare Boothe, *The Woman*, The Modern Library (New York, Random House, 1941), 613.

149. Durant, *The Story of Civilization*, op. cit. at note 40, 4:31.

150. Job, 12:11.

151. Carl Sandburg, *Abraham Lincoln, The War Years*, 4 vols (New York, Harcourt, Brace & Company, 1939), 3:35.

152. Aristotle, *Art of Rhetoric*, op. cit. at note 8, 17.

153. Quintilian, *Institutio Oratoria*, op. cit. at note 1, 1:485.

154. Cicero, *The Basic Works of Cicero*, Ed. Moses Hadas, The Modern Library (New York, Random House, 1951), 343.

155. Hugo, *Les Miserables, op. cit.* at note 58, 590.

156. Cicero, *Orations and Essays, op. cit.* at note 27, 99.

157. Cicero, *Cicero In Twenty-Eight Volumes, Orator, op. cit.* at note 38, 5:157.

158. Quintilian, *Institutio Oratoria, op. cit.* at note 1, 1:263.

XII
The Summing Up

In an age when all things are subject to question, we should not be surprised to find that " . . . the market has turned against trial by jury."[1] Yet, considering the ancient origins of the jury, it seems only yesterday that legal opinion considered the jury to be the *sine qua non* for the trial of serious matters. Shortly before the turn of the century, Joseph H. Choate, in an address to the American Bar Association, could say with confidence, despite Mark Twain,* that:

> The truth is, however, that the jury system is so fixed as an essential part of our political institution. . . that there can be no substantial ground for fear that any of us will live to see the people consent to give it up.[2]

It is puzzling to observe the recent United States Supreme Court decisions which have transformed the concept of trial by jury into something entirely different than its original meaning, considering the extent of the respect that it held throughout United States history. In 1791, a party to a civil or a criminal case was entitled to a 12 member, male, white, unanimous jury. There has been substantial improvement in the respect that now there can be no systematic exclusion of jurors because of sex or race. On the other hand, blacks and women are less apt to be on federal civil juries and many state criminal juries because many of the juries have less than 12 members. In state criminal trials—even non-petty—there may be a jury of only six members. In state civil cases, the jury most often does not have to be unanimous. In federal civil cases, six person juries are the rule.

Justice Thurgood Marshall was understandably puzzled by the

---

*"The jury system puts a ban upon intelligence and honesty, and a premium upon ignorance, stupidity, and perjury. It is a shame that we must continue to use a worthless system because it *was* good a thousand years ago."*Roughing It,* Mark Twain (Limited Editions Club, New York, 1972, 1st printed Jan. 30, 1872), p. 247. Emphasis that of Mark Twain.

court's failure to maintain the principle of unanimity and a membership of 12 —features which had been central to jury trials for hundreds
of years. He said:

> We are asked to decide what is the nature of the 'jury' that is
> guaranteed by the Sixth Amendment. I would have thought
> that history provided the appropriate guide. . .[3]

Justice Marshall had good reason to be concerned about the future of
the jury. On January 1, 1971, less than two years after the Supreme
Court had held that the number 12 was a historical accident, the
Federal District Court of Minnesota adopted a rule that juries in civil
cases would consist of six jurors. By June of 1972, more than 40 of the
other 92 district courts had adopted similar rules.[4] All of this was
apparently based on the authority of *Williams* v. *Florida,* 399 U.S. 78 (1970).

Opinions which denigrate the value of jury trial are not a new
phenomenon. Justice Cardozo lent respectability to modern criticism
of trial by jury when he said, in *Connecticut v. U.S.,* 302 U.S. 319, 325
(1939):

> The right to trial by jury and the immunity to prosecution
> except as the result of an indictment may have value and
> importance. Even so, they are not of the very essence of a
> scheme of ordered liberty.

Perhaps the leading modern critic of trial by jury is Jerome Frank.
He said:

> I submit that the jury is the worst possible enemy of that
> ideal of the 'supremacy of law.' For jury-made law is par ex-
> cellence, capricious and arbitrary, yielding to the maximum
> in way of lack of uniformity, and of unknowability.[5]

More forceful yet is the criticism of Leon Sarky:

> Related to present day American life, civil jury trials
> represent the horse and buggy segment of American
> administration of justice, reflecting a judicial provincial-
> ism and a mid-Victorian drag on our judicial process,
> which calls for realistic treatment by way of reform.[6]

Balancing these adverse opinions is Thomas Jefferson who was
not bashful in his defense of the jury:

Were I called upon to decide, whether the people had best be omitted in the legislative or judicial department, I would say it is better to leave them out of the legislative. The execution of the laws is more important than the making of them.[7]

Justice White, when he wrote the opinion in *Duncan v. Louisiana,* 391 U.S. 145, 155 (1968), appeared to be a staunch friend of the jury. He said:

Providing an accused with the right to be tried by a jury of his peers gave him inestimable safeguard against the corrupt or overzealous prosecutor and against the compliant, biased, or eccentric judge.

Judges, the chief competition to the jury, have also been criticized, as the following samples will show. Jeremy Bentham's opinion of the judiciary (which, except at the lowest levels, is filled exclusively from the bar in England) is clear:

Filling the bench from no other fund than the bar, is it not exactly such a mode as if boarding-school-mistresses and governesses, were never to be chosen but from brothels?[8]

Less vehement but also expressing dissatisfaction with the judiciary was Charles Grove Haines:

The morality of courts may be higher than the morality of traders or of politicians, but it has, of course, often happened that the ideas entertained by the judges have fallen below the highest and most enlightened public opinion of a particular time.[9]

There can be no consensus as to the relative merits of a judge or jury trial, or, for that matter, other modes of trial. It is obviously impractical to sequester the critics in a room apart without food or drink until they come to a unanimous decision, and each critic will continue to be guided in large part by his own personal experience. Still, observations and analysis based on the authorities and the writer's experience in over 250 jury cases while prosecuting attorney, criminal defense attorney and an attorney in personal injury cases might prove helpful to those persons who are concerned with the preservation of trial by jury. It ought to be noted that the writer is solidly of the opinion that trial by jury ought to be pre-served with the common law features it possessed at the time of the adoption of the United States Constitution. Improvements will be suggested, but they will not relate to the essential features of the jury, such as the number of the jurors or unanimity of the verdict. In fact, the danger of even small changes was foreseen by Blackstone who wrote with reference to changes in the jury system:

> . . . though began in trifles, the precedent may gradually increase and spread to the utter disuse of juries in ques-tions of the most momentous concern.[10]

The rapid adoption of the minijuries is an apparent confirmation of Blackstone's fears.

There are certain disadvantages in trial by a judge alone as compared to trial by jury, which can be demonstrated by an exami-nation of the respective modes of trial apart from historical consid-erations. The disadvantages of a judge trial are due to the inherent features of this trial as compared to jury trial; for example, (1) the judge's period of service is long, while the jury's is short; (2) the judge can rule only by himself, whereas the jury has the added fairness of more members; (3) the identity of the judge is well known long in advance of trial, whereas the identity of jurors is learned shortly before trial; and (4) judges can be removed on motion of a client only upon demonstrating prejudice, while at least some jurors can be challenged without showing cause.

The judge's long tenure and wide acquaintance cause him to become suspected of favoritism regardless of his actions. It is often noted by members of the bar, and even by litigants themselves, that judges socialize with the members of the legal profession, and more often than not with only the most successful members. This is natural, though, and not the result of an evil plan to subvert justice.

It is common for a lawyer to be asked by clients, "Is there any way to get to the judge?" When it is explained that it is a criminal offense to try such an action, the clients have been known to say, "I didn't mean we would bribe him, but perhaps there is another lawyer who could help out who is close to the judge." After the case is tried, if the decision was unfavorable, the clients always suspect the judge of favoritism or dishonesty, and all the explanation in the world to the contrary falls on deaf ears. (If the decision were patently stupid, as occasionally happens, the lawyer himself cannot avoid secret imagination on the subject.)

On the other hand, litigants seldom suspect the jury, as they were picked by lot, investigated thoroughly and were subject to challenge. A client may say, "I was disappointed in Jones. I felt sure he would side with us," but he seldom suspects the entire jury of outright dishonesty. Even if he does believe the jury has been corrupted, he does not feel it would be futile to venture into court again, as he would have a new jury. Judges tend to hold office perpetually and, therefore, despite the honesty of a particular judge, a percentage of the people will inevitably come to believe that certain lawyers and interests obtain better results before one judge than before others. This is not to say, of course, that there are no dishonest judges, even on the much admired English bench.[11] Part of the problem with judges is inherent in the fact that a law suit almost always produces a loser and a winner. When parties go to court, they both believe that they have at least some portion of right on their side. To the extent that they lose this right, it does little to ease the hurt to be told the injustice was according to law.

The accumulation of frustration affects lawyers as well as clients. The writer has overheard a lawyer say, "I've never won a case tried before Judge N.T. sitting without a jury." This was a prosperous lawyer who had a large office practice, but who only occasionally ventured into court. His luck with the judge had been disastrous. His luck had not been altogether good with juries, but there he was consoled by the thought that there would be a new jury next time.

One lawyer in a southern Ohio county once won 15 jury cases in a row, both civil and criminal. If this had been accomplished before a judge, there would have been strong suspicion of corruption. It is just possible that the clients of this lawyer deserved to win all those cases; the jurors do not know the lawyers' specific record in this regard, but the judges do. Lawyers therefore suspect judges of compensating in one case for what a lawyer lost in a previous one. Jurors are not given this opportunity to trade justice, due to their short tenure.

Observation as a practicing lawyer provides more substantial evidence that some judges do not always conduct themselves according to the rules. For example, more than one judge has been known to attend legal seminars at the expense of counsel who practice before them. Generally, misdemeanors committed by lawyers and judges must be flagrant before they will be punished by the magistrates. This is particularly true with regard to violations relating to alcohol and automobiles.

This protection even extends to those associated with the bar. The writer once went to court with a distant relative who was charged with operating a motor vehicle under the influence of alcohol. Both parties had a valid case, and so a plea to reckless driving was accepted. After the hearing, the judge discovered that the client was a relative of mine and asked, "Why didn't you say something?" There was a clear implication that the relationship entitled the client to a different brand of justice. Judges have little compunction about levying heavy fines on persons with no community or political leverage, but hesitate to "ruin" the career of a doctor or lawyer with a compulsory sentence of three days in jail for drunken driving. These same judges will criticize a jury that acquits an industrial worker of the same charge.

A particular jury cannot continue its peculiar brand of injustice over a period of years. Judges, on the other hand, consciously or unconsciously, have a way of trading on judicial favors at election time. The writer has seldom met a judge of a magistrate court who was not guilty, at least unconsciously, of using his office for personal patronage by dispensing favors. A part of the problem seems to be that no matter how honest and careful the judge may be, he cannot avoid the suspicion of professional misconduct if he remains in office over a period of years.

An English barrister was heard extolling the virtues of the English judiciary who try most civil cases without juries. The writer asked him, "If the judges are so capable, why don't judges try all criminal cases without juries? After all, the very best tribunal ought to be used in cases of the highest importance where life and reputation are at stake." The barrister, surprisingly, said that judges sitting alone did not constitute a better tribunal for ascertaining truth than the jury, but only a more convenient tribunal. For the most serious matters he still preferred the jury. He was supported by no less an authority than Lord Denning who said, in 1967, that he still preferred juries for serious crimes, and that the jury was still " . . . one of the pillars of our freedom."[12] One cannot help but feel that some seemingly insignificant matters nonetheless could have a great impact on an individual's life. As Shakespeare's Shylock said in the *Merchant of Venice:*

> Nay, take my life and all; pardon not that:
> You take my house, when you do take the prop
> that doth sustain my house; you take my life,
> When you do take the means whereby I live. (IV.1.375)

Custody of children, invariably tried by judges in the United States, and damages in serious personal injury cases are only two common examples of civil litigation involving issues of the utmost importance. The argument that only criminal cases are important enough to justify the trouble of a jury trial is a specious argument found in the mouths of those who are not friendly to jury trial. This recalls what Repp said in 1832:

> Whatever some learned Judges may say in commendation of juries in their books, it would be difficult to find one friendly to that institution in practice, unless he happened to have Juries so well trained, that they conscientiously attend to every hint from the bench.[13]

Apart from real or imagined bias on the part of judges, it is thought by some authorities that the professionalism of the law is a lifetime process of degeneration into insensibility leaving judges unfit to solve the endless variety of disputes that come to the courts for resolution. Forsyth suggested that juries act as a check upon the "narrow subtlety" to which professional lawyers are subject.[14] In describing a judge trial without a jury, Holdsworth said, "One finds oneself in a rarified atmosphere of morality and respectability in which life is hardly possible.[15]

Devlin expressed this professional failing by saying, "The malady that sooner or later affects most men of a profession is that they tend to construct a mystique that cuts them off from common man."[16] The novelist, George Eliot, also diagnosed this ailment through the lips of Lydgate in *Middlemarch.* "In my opinion . . . , legal training only makes a man more incompetent in questions that require knowledge of another kind."[17]

As contrasted with the judge, the jury is alleged to be the depository of common sense. The types of cases appearing in court are as various as the backgrounds of the litigants. No single individual can be expected to view every case in court from the necessary points of view in order to properly understand it — no matter how much learning and good intentions he possesses. As Devlin said:

> I think it must be agreed that there are some determinations in which twelve minds are better than one, however skilled, and most people would accept that the determination whether a witness is telling the truth is one of them.[18]

A common practice is to base legal seminars on the theory that a lawyer is not capable of trying a particular lawsuit unless he has the specialized knowledge of a surgeon, a civil engineer, or a criminologist, as the case may require. Lawyers forget that at the basis of their knowledge should be an understanding of human nature. Lawyers must understand the witness to be able to examine him, while the technical knowledge for each trial can be learned or reviewed for each case. The tools acquired and retained by the lawyer during the course of his life enable him to handle the over-confident braggart, elicit believable truth from the introvert and bring down to earth the fantasy of a child. The lawyer must be able to extract from the evidence the essence of credibility and redeliver it during summation, using all his understanding of human nature and the art of persuasion.

The same persons who would reduce the personal injury lawyer to a medical technician would reduce the trial of injury cases to administrative procedures before a board of doctors, a process more out of touch with the human elements involved than judges are now. In short, judges, like all professionals, are apt to develop early "hardening of the categories,"[19] finding a category for a case whether it fits or not, while juries subordinate law to justice.[20]

Judges are considered to be subjected to more extra-judicial influence than juries. The most common example of this influence is the readiness of magistrates to accept police evidence. Williams insists that the jury is right to be slower than the judge in accepting the word of an officer against a defendant.[21] Cornish observed that those who regularly appeared in magistrate's courts were aware of the tendency to accept police evidence "without demur,"[22] and the danger is apparent when the judge claims, "I've heard that story before," although it is possible that the defendant may be innocent.[23] In one case, an English detective caused a series of unfounded prosecutions to be launched, although eventually he was found to be mentally ill.[24] No class of witnesses is so bound to the truth as to be worthy of belief in every instance, and juries are more cognizant of this than judges.

The jury was recognized by Forsyth as being a bulwark against arbitrary action on the part of the crown.[25] Devlin says that history shows that the executive branch of government has been more successful in finding judges who will bend to its will than it has been in finding juries with such amenable backbones.[26] Holdsworth touched on a different aspect of the same problem when he noted that juries kept the law in touch "with life."[27]

When Tocqueville visited America in 1831, it may have been that juries, far from being a cause of court congestion, expedited justice. At least that was the opinion of John C. Spencer, an American lawyer who wrote the preface and notes to the American edition to Tocqueville's *Democracy In America* which was first published in 1838. Spencer wrote, "By introducing the jury into the business of the courts you are enabled to diminish the number of judges; which is a very great advantage."[28] Now, though, it is is common for authorities to blame juries for the law's delay.

One authority, writing in 1962-63, said it took five and one-half years for jury trials to be tried in Nassau County in New York, while cases tried to judges sitting alone in Louisiana were tried within six months of a request for trial.[29] Cornish says that, " . . . trial by jury is a cumbersome and expensive method of trying a case; at the very least, this places the onus of proving its value on those who wish to see it continue."[30] He also claims judges work faster than juries.[31] Another authority claims jury trials are 60 percent longer than court trials.[32] Kalven and Zeisel note that juries cause delays in civil litigation and constitute an unfair tax on the time of underpaid jurors.[33]

Other authorities, claim jury trials take very little longer than judge trials if other factors not considered by other studies are taken into account.[34] These factors include the time it takes for a judge to deliberate and write his opinion. A study to determine the effect of the abolition of juries concluded that dispensing with jury trials would result in the saving of the time of 1.6 judges out of a total of 26.[35] In fact, it is possible that there would be no saving of time when all the factors are considered.[36]. On one occasion, for example, counsel had agreed to waive a jury and try a matter under the federal wage and hour law to the court. After the evidence was in and the case had been submitted, some weeks passed and no decision was forthcoming, and so, upon prompting of clients, inquiry was made and the judge replied that he would render a decision shortly. There were many inquiries and many promises. After about a year, the judge said he had decided to step aside and ask another judge to hear the case. This meant starting over.

In another case involving the title to a public cemetery, the case was argued and submitted. The court requested the reporter to prepare a transcript. Counsel also obtained copies to use in preparing briefs. The briefs were submitted and months passed. Inquiry was made by letter and phone over a period of months. The judge told counsel that he had been busy and that this case was next on his list. Nothing was said about a transcript in reply to any inquiries. More time elapsed, and one of the parties resorted to self-help which received wide newspaper coverage. This at least prompted action by the judge who then claimed the delay had been solely due to the fact that he had never been provided with a transcript. There was an implication that counsel had secreted the transcript in order to embarrass the court.

These examples, while extreme, are not isolated. Delays of up to one month between the submission of a case and the decision by the judge are common. Lawyers have been subjected to delays of weeks and months between submission of a case and a decision by the court.[37] Lawyers can not help thinking that the judge has forgotten the evidence by the time he writes his decision. No adequate remedy exists when there is an unreasonable delay on the part of a judge. He can be sued *in procedendo,* but this is expensive to the client and causes hard feelings on the part of the judge toward the lawyer handling the case. Repeated inquiries tend to irritate the judges, and thus lawyers and clients are reluctant to inqure about a decision for fear of irritating a judge and inducing an adverse decision. None of these problems arise when the case has been submitted to a jury.

The main claims are that a jury requires more time because: (1) the process of picking the jury (the *voir dire* examination of the jury) can be time consuming; (2) time is lost arguing over the admissibility of evidence which would not be required if the case were tried to a judge; and (3) final arguments by counsel are longer before juries than to judges. It has been suggested that the lawyers be limited in the questions they could ask jurors, and that most of the questioning should be done by the judge. This is the practice in many federal courts. The English practice is not to question jurors at all aside from those exceptional cases where there can be a preliminary showing of cause.

Any person who has observed the process of questioning jurors by skillful counsel cannot doubt the value of *voir dire* in eliminating the eccentric, prejudiced, and unqualified juror. Even prejudiced jurors who remain cannot help but be impressed with the fact that both sides are looking for fair and impartial jurors. Counsel who insist on wasting time should be brought into line by the court. The *voir dire* examination is often concluded within one-half hour and rarely exceeds two hours except in homicide cases. This is a small loss of time when the result is a fair jury. Kalven and Zeisel's work gave strong indications that *voir dire* was a valuable tool in obtaining a suitable jury.[38]

Time lost arguing over the evidence is mostly the fault of judges. Some judges keep a tighter rein on evidence during jury trials, thereby shortening the trial.[39] Most objections require no argument, and a simple ruling by the judge suffices. Unique and novel questions do require argument and authority, but this is true even when there is no jury. Generally these questions can be anticipated and briefed or even decided in advance. The writer observed few objections in trials by English counsel in London, and in the United States, the more experienced the counsel, the fewer the objections. Highly qualified counsel do not object to even erroneous matters unless the objection will aid his cause.

Devlin[40] and Williams[41] claim the arguments of counsel are longer to juries than to judges sitting alone. It is granted that the length of the argument should have a reasonable relation to the length of the trial, the difficulty of the issues and the importance of the case to the litigants. Again, most arguments, even when no time is set by the judge, are about one-half hour for each side. It is not unusual for the arguments to be as short as 15 minutes or as long as 45 minutes. The court ought to be permitted, within reason, to limit argument. Most critics of summation arguments claim that these arguments serve no real purpose, but in reality they serve to condense into a short time what has usually taken at least two days. Argument brings the issues clearly into focus immediately before the jury begins deliberation. Counsel may well touch on the very matters that are decisive of the case. Without this assistance the jury may well miss the crucial points.

More distressing than the length of argument to juries is the practical elimination of argument in many courts when cases are tried to a judge alone. It is common for judges at the conclusion of the evidence to lean across the bench and ask, "Is there any need for argument?" The obvious implication is that the counsel could not possibly say anything that could be of assistance in aiding the judge to reach a decision. The writer was once stopped by a judge from even presenting evidence. In a juvenile case, the judge, at the close of the state's evidence, directed this statement to the writer, "You can call your witnesses if you want to, but my mind's made up." The judge meant that his mind was made up in favor of the state without ever having heard the defense witnesses. The arrogance of judges in thinking that nothing can be said that will enlighten them is not mitigated by their supposition that juries share this obtuse quality.

The causes of court congestion are more deeply rooted than the delay inherent in a jury trial. Among the factors contributing to this congestion are increasing population, a greater frequency of accidents, and the failure of the public authorities to create new judgeships and court facilities.[42] Hung juries are often blamed for loss of time and delay, but inasmuch as it is usual for the cut and dried cases to be disposed of by settlement (in civil cases) and by guilty pleas (in criminal matters), it is not surprising to find that a large percentage of the more complex jury cases end in hung juries.[43] Generally juries are able to reach a decision. As early as 1852, Forsyth observed that hung juries were not much of a problem,[44] and at Old Bailey in 1965 only 4.1 percent of the juries failed to reach a verdict. At the London Sessions, the percentage was even lower.[45] The rate of hung juries in America, according to Kalven and Zeisel, is about 5 percent,[46] and the writer's experience confirms these conclusions. In approximately 250 jury trials in which the writer has acted as counsel, only nine ended in hung juries. All of these were criminal cases, six tried by the writer as defense counsel and three as prosecutor. Of the six tried as defense counsel, the only two retried ended in acquittals. Of the three in which the writer was prosecutor, two of the trials were the same case, and after two trials without a decision, the case was dismissed. In the other prosecution case, the defendant pleaded to a reduced charge. The group nature of decision-making by a jury tends to soften the effect of radical and eccentric views.[47]

It would be ill advised, especially in criminal cases, to weaken the principle of unanimity inherent in a jury verdict,[48] merely to avoid the small chance of a hung jury. The requirement of unanimity " . . . insures that the case is proved beyond a reasonable doubt,"[49] and a mistrial due to disagreement is a "safeguard to liberty."[50] When you add to that the protection unanimity gives to minorities and the assurance that all important aspects of the case receive ample consideration,[51] it seems clear that the principle ought to apply to civil trials as well. Bear in mind that most civil and criminal cases are disposed of before trial. The experience of the writer also illustrates that the principle of unanimity tends to require a higher quantum of proof for a conviction in a criminal case. In all nine hung juries in which the writer was a participant as a lawyer, the solitary conviction was obtained by a plea to a reduced charge.

It seems strange that judges themselves are not held to unanimity when trying cases in the first instance or on appeal. For instance, it is peculiar that an accused can be found to be guilty beyond a reasonable doubt by two judges when the third man holds him to be innocent. Those who believe judges are better able to correlate decisions with the true facts should become more aware of the disagreement among judges. The percentage of disagreement would no doubt run higher than the five percent rate of hung juries. This can be tested by thumbing through the decisions of the United States Supreme Court. *Johnson v. Louisiana,* 406 US 356, 92 Sup. Ct. 1620 (1972), is an outstanding example. This case produced seven different opinions, the majority opinion, two concurring opinions and four dissenting opinions. Chief Justice Vaughan commented on Bushell's case in 1670,"I would know whether anything be more common than for two students, barristers, or judges, to deduce contrary and opposite conclusions out of the same case in law."[52] As late as January, 1973, a prestigious New York Court held that a homosexual could be denied admission to the bar.[53] Where is the predictability in judge trial?

Some would try to save time by having smaller juries. One suggestion included the federal minijuries, noted earlier. The smaller jury diminishes the protection given to minorities, emphasizes the influence of a possible eccentric or dominant personality, and changes the nature of the decision-making process. Any change in number should also be avoided purely because popular opinion would be opposed to it. In addition, reducing the number of challenges goes hand in hand with the reduction of size. In 1972 when Ohio reduced civil juries from 12 members to 8, the number of challenges was also reduced from four to three. Working with the larger number of jurors and challenges, attorneys have a better chance of getting rid of jurors who may not be fair. When the size of the jury is reduced from 12 to 8, however, the likelihood of a minority racial group being represented is substantially reduced, while the chances of the majority being represented are hardly affected at all. In addition, a change in the number of persons constituting a jury without a compelling reason tends to lower confidence in the results. Criminal jury trials average less than 35 per 100,000 population a year,[54] and even if the total number of jury trials were much larger, the jury's advantages justify its retention and keeping the jury at its present size.

The serious claim is made that juries are prejudiced, irrational, and emotional. What trial lawyer would not occasionally find those same qualities in judges? It is said that male jurors favor a pretty woman; that juries will not convict for bootlegging, gambling and drunk driving; that they favor individuals over big corporations; and that they are prejudiced against minorities. Nearly all of these complaints have little significance when a jury is selected so as to be composed of both men and women, young and old and a true cross-section of the community. Generally, the jurors have no axe to grind, and certainly the more obvious cases of possible prejudice are eliminated during *voir dire* examination. An unfair juror who remains will, in a jury that is a true cross-section, be neutralized by a fair-minded majority.

As to the charge that juries nullify some laws and excercise the sovereign right of pardon, although having no explicit right to do so, the question must be asked whether this is not their real value. For example, although not all "drunks" are released, the jury may realize that alcoholism is not cured by a few days in jail, especially when this may result in the loss of the defendant's job. A partial answer to this and many other such situations may be to find a better remedy than jail.

An extreme example of the excercise of the power of pardon is a case in which the writer was defense counsel. The defendant was charged with armed robbery. He was arrested for a crime in one jurisdiction which was committed only a few days after a very similar crime had been committed in another area. For the second crime he pleaded guilty and served over four years at hard labor. He was released, returned to Ohio on his own, became gainfully empoyed and worked for one year before he was arrested on the earlier charge. The jury was unable to reach a verdict the first time the case was tried. By the time the second case came on for hearing, the defendant had been in jail for about one year. The second robbery was admitted into evidence as a similar crime, an accomplice turned state's evidence, and the license number (except one digit was not available) of the car used in the first robbery was identical with the license of the defendant's automobile. The defendant's only defense was his denial and the testimony of close friends that he was in another state at the time of the robbery.

The jury returned a verdict of acquittal after four hours of deliberation. Whether the man was guilty or not, the writer, as is often the case, could not know for certain, although the evidence against the defendant was overwhelming. The jury no doubt concluded that four years served for another crime plus the year spent awaiting trial for the first robbery was sufficient punishment. The judge, on the other hand, thought the verdict was a miscarriage of justice. The defendant returned to his employment and several years later was still making his living at legal employment. If the judge had had his way, the defendant would still be in a penitentiary.

Another charge against the jury is that it is unpredictable. This could be acceptable, especially in civil cases, if it is assumed the cases are capable of being decided either way. This is always the situation in civil cases, unless the situation is such that the judge directs a verdict.

It is claimed that as to damages in personal injury cases, the size of the verdicts is especially difficult to anticipate. In view of the wide differential of not only the injuries and their consequences but also the varying backgrounds of the different parties, wide variations in the amount of the verdicts are to be expected. No doubt a board of doctors or judges would be capable of reducing the whole procedure to a formula which would allow specified amounts for named injuries, with variations only within narrow limits, without any attempt to make full compensation. In such a case the injured party would bear the greater part of the consequence of his injuries himself. Counsel who handle a fair number of personal injury cases are able to predict within reasonable limits the verdicts of juries. There are publishing services which keep the lawyer informed of the latest results in personal injury cases, and, if the exceptional results are first eliminated, there is no undue variation. An examination of the exceptional cases often discloses exceptional circumstances which account for the results. On the other hand, you seldom hear that criminal cases are unpredictable. Experience seems to indicate that counsel can predict the jury's verdict about 90 percent of the time.

Another reason for preferring juries to judges is that, in criminal matters, juries really do require the state to prove their case beyond a reasonable doubt. This doubt is defined, in part, in some jurisdictions as an abiding conviction to a moral certainty of the truth of the charge. Kalven and Zeisel's study showed that the jury tolerates less doubt than judges. They concluded, "If society wishes to be serious about convicting only when the state has been put to proof beyond a reasonable doubt, it would be well advised to have a jury system."[55] A lower standard of proof could be adopted, but it would not seriously increase the total number which the judicial system holds responsible for crime. It must be remembered that the majority plead guilty. Many others are tried by judges who obviously do not use the reasonable doubt test, regardless of the law. Only a small percentage of all defendants are tried to juries, and some of these defendants are clearly innocent. Those who would lower the quantum of proof would do so for the sake of a few more convictions at the expense of some innocent persons being convicted.

Education of the public concerning the legal system is often listed as one of the advantages of the jury system.[56] Tocqueville said of the jury:

> It may be regarded as a gratuitous public school ever open, in which every juror learns to excercise his rights, enters into daily communication with the most learned and enlightened members of the upper classes, and becomes practically acquainted with the laws of his country, which are brought within the reach of his capacity by the efforts of the bar, the advice of the judge, and even by the passions of the parties.[57]

Some persons have been heard to complain that jurors should not be educated at the expense of the litigants. The same objection, however, could be made against letting the masses vote. Voters choose between candidates offering radically different programs to the electorate, but far from restricting the electorate to an intellectual elite, the tendency has been to further extend it until now in the United States almost any citizen of 18 or older can vote if he chooses. Our country has not suffered from widely based suffrage or trial by jury. It has been argued in the past and will continue to be argued that there are better methods of government, but the people nonetheless prefer to govern themselves, even if it results in a less efficient goverment.

The power of judgment has always been considered as a part of the sovereign power of a nation. In deciding questions between individuals, no more acceptable mode of decision has ever been found than the submission of disputes to jurors. Experts, boards, and judges are not the "people." The jury exercises a portion of the sovereign power.[58] It is ultimately a belief based on intuition and instinct which requires that the power of judgment in matters of the utmost consequence should be by one's peers. A decision that 12 fellow citizens are willing to live with has much to recommend it.

Jury trial ought, as a matter of policy, to be frequent enough so that it is looked upon as the usual and preferred mode of trial if not freely waived. If the jury is relegated to the trial of exceptional cases only, it will be looked upon as an anachronism instead of a necessity for the maintenance of justice and as a protection against arbitrary rule.[59] Frequency of service resulted in knowledgeable jurors in classical Greece, for example, and gave excellent results without setting undesirable precedents.[60] It is claimed that juries favor the poor,[61] but that is more desirable than the opposite alternative.

One line of criticism maintains that jury trial has a traumatic effect on some of the paticipants, particularly children who are parties or witnesses. There are children who have not obtained sufficient years to be capable of making coherent witnesses. There are even adults who are so emotionally disturbed as to be unable to deliver their testimony. For such instances, it ought to suffice to present their testimony by way of deposition. Actually, though, when children are too young to participate as a witness, their testimony will be of little value regardless of whether the trial is before a jury or a judge.

The stress of trial is an important ingredient in obtaining truth. Many glib liars have gone undetected in the calm of an office deposition only to be exposed on the witness stand before a jury in the charged atmosphere of the courtroom. The greater part of legal tension is not due to the jury or the courtroom setting but to the importance of the matters in issue. Critics of jury trial, for example, would prefer to isolate otherwise intelligent teenagers from the court proceedings. However, if he suffers no physical or mental disability, there is no reason why he should not be allowed to give testimony in cases which pertain to him personally. In such cases as attempted institutionalization or child custody matters, it is dishonest not to allow the child to give his opinion in court, rather than to be restricted to the judge's chambers. As a matter of fact, the writer has called the children of persons accused of homicide to testify on their behalf, not for the sympathy effect but because they had facts to offer. They would have always regretted not giving their testimony if they had not been called, and the jury was never an impediment to their testifying.

It is said by some that the jury is inefficient because of the nature of the proceeding, the claim being made that there is no logical order to the evidence, that there are constant interruptions by counsel, that the schedule is inflexible, note taking is not permitted, the counsel make deliberate appeals to passion, and the jury is pressed for time in making a decision and cannot deliberate in private.

It is simply not true that there is no logical order to the evidence. Jury cases are generally opened by both sides outlining their cases to the jury. Of necessity, evidence is presented one word at a time, witness by witness. No one witness can cover the whole case in a single sentence. The preview by counsel helps the jury to understand the importance and relationship of each piece of evidence. Counsel also give much thought both to the order of witnesses as well as to the order in which questions are asked. The order chosen takes into consideration interest, chronology, similarity of subject and other matters. The overall effect most often shows a strong sense of organization.

If interruptions are too frequent, it can usually be attributed to the inexperience of counsel or the failure of the judge to keep control of the trial. Interruptions are not caused by the jury. The trial of a case involves, apart from the jury, counsel and parties for both sides, the judge and a number of witnesses. If a relatively inflexible schedule is adhered to, this is more suitable to the expedient disposition of the litigation, whether a jury is present or not. Also, continuances and extended adjournments are more common when there is no jury. This causes additional and repeated inconveniences to the parties, lawyers, and witnesses, often for the mere personal convenience of the judge.

Some persons are convinced that note taking insures a better understanding of the evidence. On the other hand, someone once said that Cadmus (credited with importing 16 letters of the Greek alphabet from Phoenicia) did the human race a great wrong because reliance upon the written word weakens the powers of the mind. While this is an extreme view, observation of counsel tends to show that those who do not use notes make the most of effective presentations. Some counsel go to the extreme of writing down almost everything said at trial. When the time comes for them to deliver their arguments, their counsel table is a clutter of papers and they hold in their hand an elaborate outline of their argument. Much of the time is wasted looking through their outline or going through the stack of notes, often without finding what they are looking for. The best impressions of a trial are overall impressions. If particular testimony is desired, the court reporter's transcript or electronic recording is more accurate than a juror's notes. Another difficulty with notes is that a person has difficulty doing more than one thing at a time, and thus both counsel and jurors who take notes are apt to miss important points of testimony. If a juror wrote down one piece of evidence, for example, that portion would receive undue emphasis.

As far as the claim that counsel appeals to the emotions of jurors, such appeals are often justified, although at other times such appeals should be stopped by the judge. Emotions are neccessarily involved when livelihood, custody, freedom, reputation, and fortune are at stake. Parties, lawyers, and jurors and the law itself make a proper response to the emotions brought forth by the nature of the cause. It is passions which have nothing to do with the cause, such as racial prejudice, that should be stopped by the judge. Because of the emotional content necessary in a trial, the resolution of disputes can never be reduced to trial by computers.

If the jury was not pressed for a decision, they, like the judges, would procrastinate inordinately. Most cases are decided within a couple of hours, but when more time is required, jurors have enough fortitude and selflessness to take the time. As to deliberating in private, what is wanted is not 12 seperate impressions but a joint verdict which is partially the result of group pressure. Little headway would be made toward a group decision if the jurors deliberated in private. Solitary deliberation would deprive the jurors of the recollections and inferences of fellow jurors.

Jury trials are of a higher quality than judge trials. Counsel have cases better prepared when the presentation is to a jury.[62] The notorious tendency of judges to hold preconceived ideas and to be impatient at the length of trial causes the lawyers to unnecessarily limit not only their arguments but the number of witnesses called and their preparation generally. Lawyers are at their best for jury trials. The cross-examination is more effective and more trouble is taken to have highly qualified experts present. When the trial is before the judge alone, the lawyer is apt to assume, rightly or wrongly, that the judge is a self-appointed expert in all fields and immune to any attempts to influence or change him. It is therefore not difficult for judge trials to resolve themselves into formalized traffic courts.

Plea bargaining is an interesting aspect of criminal trials. Kalven and Zeisel found that expectation of a lesser sentence if convicted by a judge than by a jury was a prime reason for waiver of trial by jury.[63] They also found that the waiver of a jury in a capital case was often tantamount to excluding the death penalty.[64] Any lawyer could have told them this, but what lawyers could not tell them is why there should be different penalties for identical crimes. One factor is that judges, despite what they say, do not like jury trials, preferring to take all trials to themselves. Thus, the innocent person who stands charged with a crime may be told by competent counsel that he runs a serious risk of conviction in view of the evidence against him, whether he is tried by the judge or the jury. At this point, the person with a criminal past would be more apt to opt for a judge trial and take advantage of the probability of obtaining a lighter sentence. The innocent victim of circumstances with a blameless background is more apt to choose the jury, being told, no doubt, that the quantum of proof the jury will require for conviction is higher than that which the judge would require. Upon conviction, therefore, the innocent person suffers a greater penalty than the guilty but experienced criminal. This difference is totally the responsibility of judges who penalize litigants for choosing trial by jury.

The jury relieves the judge from the responsibility of judging the most difficult cases, thereby diverting criticism from himself and his office,[65] justified or otherwise. The jury's verdict ensures that the verdict will be acceptable to a substantial portion of the community. It gives all adult citizens an opportunity to be self-governing even in judgment. The people believe in the jury system.[66] On the top of all this, Kalven and Zeisel have shown that the jury does understand the cases submitted to it, and, when it differs from what the judge might have decided, it does so for reasons of ultimate justice.[67]

If the jury is to be replaced, judges are usuallly suggested as the alternative.[68] A few observations about the quality of judges as an institution for obtaining justice should be pertinent. Even Judge Frank admitted:

> . . . it is certain that we meet with judges who are at times harsher, more captious, more prone to convict, and at another more easy going, complaisant and more inclined to pardon.[69]

As a young lawyer, Judge Frank practiced before a distinguished judge who decided before hearing all of the evidence that a ". . . fine, hard working woman ought to win. . .," and so he ruled accordingly. This is not an uncommon example of a judge doing what juries are often accused of doing. At least in this case the jury would have been a representative portion of the sovereign.[70]

In many cases it has been found that judges do not follow the law if they can find a way to avoid it. Many jurisdictions formerly had statutory and constitutional provisions that permitted the jury to judge law as well as fact. Many judges paid scant attention to these enactments. An earlier author said of the judiciary's actions:

> What seems discreditable to the judiciary in the story which I have related is the fierce resolution and deceptive ingenuity with which the courts have refused to carry out the unqualified mandates of statutes and constitutional provisions.[71]

As far as the consistency of decisions by judges is concerned, the most damning study is that conducted under the direction of Charles Haines in 1915 and 1916 of the magistrates of New York City. According to his study, one judge, hearing cases of disorderly conduct, acquitted one defendant in 56.6 cases, while another acquited 18 percent of the defendants, and another 54 percent.[72] He concluded:

> The tabulations of the statistician was prepared in part to discover the personal equation in the administration of justice and they showed that the magistrates differed to an amazing degree in their treatment of similar classes of cases. The conclusion was inescapable that justice is a personal thing, reflecting the temperament, the personality, the education, environment, and personal traits of the magistrates. The results showing to what extent justice is affected by the personality of the judge were so startling and so disconcerting that it seemed advisable to discontinue the comparative tables of the records of the justices.[73]

A special commission of the New York Legislature was created to study the New York Court, and in 1973, according to press releases of January 6, it was found that there is still a great disparity in judicial decisions. For example, one judge might set bond at $500 in one case, while another judge would set bond at $5000 for an identical set of circumstances.

Lest the reader assume that the refusal of judges to follow the intent of legislative enactments is peculiar in America, attention is directed to the English courts. The Administration of Justice Act of 1933 provided:

> Save as aforesaid [personal injury actions were not excepted], any action to be tried in that division [Queen's Bench] may, in the discretion of the court or a judge, be ordered to be tried either with or without a jury.

In 1937, the English Court of Appeals ruled that this enactment conferred an unfettered discretion on the judge to order a jury as the court saw fit. In *Sims v. William Howard and Son, Ltd.*, 1964, 2 All English Reports 267, the same Court of Appeals held that the judges of the Queen's Bench had no discretion to order a jury trial in personal injury cases. Understandably, Justice Salmon, who concurred in *Watts* v. *Manning* 2 All English Reports 267, (1964), for reasons peculiar to the case, was unable to justify this strange reversal of a previous holding, especially in view of the clear language of the Act of Parliament.

These observations should be kept in mind by those who would eliminate the jury by creation of other tribunals or changing its basic nature. The only changes made in the jury system should be those which would strengthen its basic purposes. Computer selection of the panels chosen to report, programmed to give a true cross-section of the community, would be one such improvement. Also, this system could insure that jury service would be equitably spread among those available. The law ought to limit exemptions from duty to lawyers, judges, and court officials active in their profession and those with serious physical or mental disabilities. Excuses should be limited to those to whom jury service would be a real hardship, while those excused for a temporary reason should be reassigned to another panel.

In order to end a certain amount of hypocrisy in the system, a pamphlet ought to be given to all jurors setting forth their duties and a summary of the jury's history. In criminal cases the jury ought to be permitted to know what punishment the accused would be liable to upon a conviction. Even Judge Frank agrees that we should tell the jurors that they can decide contrary to the judge's charge if they find it necessary, even though the judge might not agree.[74] This has always been the practice in capital cases. In civil and criminal cases, jurors ought to be charged that under most circumstances they should take their law from the court but, in any event, they would not be required to return a verdict contrary to their consciences. The judge's charge ought to be brought into line with practice and theory. Frank looks upon the failure of the jury to follow the judge's charge as an act of legislation,[75] but in fact it is a solution suitable to a unique case. Legislation, on the other hand, applies generally to citizens and not to unique cases.

Other changes are also feasible to increase the effectiveness of the trial system. (1) Most civil cases should be tried to juries, including custody cases in divorce actions. Exceptions should be established for cases not having a certain jurisdictional amount, or, in the case of divorce, when there was no substantial property or custody question involved. (2) In complex cases the judge ought to be given authority to reduce the issue to a narrow one, capable of being resolved by a verdict in favor of one party or the other and/or for an amount of money. (3) There should be some adjustment from time to time in the jurisdictional amounts so that trials would be neither too burdensome nor too rare. (4) A citizen ought to be called for jury duty about every four years, and all cases should be concluded at the trial level within one year of filing and within two years at the appellate level. (5) Cases should be assigned according to specific criteria such as the order of filing. (6) The judge ought to deliver a brief and generalized statement on the law and facts about which the law suit revolves at the beginning of the trial. (7) Jurors should be paid at least the average wage in the community plus expenses. In addition, the jury's purpose and history ought to be taught in all primary and secondary schools, so that all citizens would be able to understand the purpose and functioning of the jury system. (8) Jurors should be excused after having sat on a case to a verdict.

In conclusion, it should be noted that the public has great confidence in the jury, at least in the United States. Jury trial insures the common citizen of receiving very nearly the same justice as the others in society. The changing composition of the jury's membership from one trial to another avoids the frustration complex to which defeated clients and lawyers are susceptible, and protects judges from unfair criticism. When the jury is fairly representative of the community, it is the best protection against judicial injustice. But, the overriding reason for retaining and expanding the jury system is the belief that, given the benefits and dangers of any possible system of justice, the sovereign power of judgment ought to be vested directly in the people. The words of Tocqueville are as true today as when they were written in the 1830's:

> He who punishes infractions of the law is therefore the real master of society. Now, the institution of the jury raises the people itself, or at least a class of citizens, to the bench of judicial authority. The institution of the jury consequently invests the people, or that class of citizens, with the direction of society.[76]

Chapter XII Footnotes

1. *Trial By Jury*, Sir Patrick Devlin (Stevens and Sons, 3rd ed., 1966), p. 147.

2. "Preservation of the Civil Jury," Stanley E. Sacks, 22 Wash. and Lee L. Rev. 76, 78 (1965).

3. *Johnson v. Louisiana*, 406 U.S. 356, 92 Sup. Ct. 1620, 1652 (1972).

4. "The New Minijuries: Panacea or Pandora's Box?", David J. Gibbons, 58 A.B.A.J. 594 (June 1972).

5. *Courts On Trial*, Jerome Frank (Princeton University Press, Princeton, New Jersey, 1949), p. 132.

6. "Civil Juries, Their Decline and Eventual Fall," Leon Sarky, 11 Loy. L. Rev. 243, 245 (1962-63).

7. "Juries as Judges of Criminal Law," Mark DeWolfe Howe, 52 Harv. L. Rev. 582 (1939).

8. *The Elements of the Art of Packing as Applied to Special Juries*, Jeremy Bentham (Effingham Wilson, London, 1821).

9. "General Observations on the Effect of Personal, Political, and Economic Influences In the Decisions of Judges," Charles Grove Haines, 17 Ill. Law. Rev. 96, 110 (1922).

10. *Commentaries On the Laws of England*, William Blackstone, Vol. 4 — 350 (1775).

11. *The Proof of Guilt, A Study of the English Criminal Trial*, Glanville Williams (Stevens and Sons, London, 3rd ed. 1963, 1st published 1955), p. 17.

12. "Address by the Right Honourable Lord Denning, Master of the Rolls," The Australian Law Journal, V 41, p. 224 (1967).

13. *A Historical Treatise On Trial By Jury*, Thorl. Gudn. Repp. (Thomas Clark, Edinburgh, 1832), p. 103.

14. *"History of Trial by Jury*, William Forsyth (John W. Parker, and Son, London, 1852), at p. 445.

15. *A History of English Law*, Sir William Holdsworth (Sweet and Maxwell, London, from 7th ed., 1956, reprinted 1966, 1st ed. 1903), V-1, p. 350.

16. Devlin, *op. cit.* at note 1, at p. 149.

17. *Middlemarch*, George Eliot (The Folio Society, London, 1972, first published 1871-2), p. 168.

18. Devlin, *op. cit.*, at note 1, at p. 149.

19. "The Case For The Retention Of The Unanimous Civil Jury," Howard Frank, 15 DePaul L. Rev. 403, 408 (1965).

20. "With Love In Their Hearts But Reform On Their Minds," 4 Col. J. of L. and Soc. Pro. 178, at 179 (1968).

21. *The Proof of Guilt, A Study of the English Criminal Trial,* Glanville Williams (Stevens and Sons, London, 3rd ed., 1963, 1st published, 1955), p. 325.

22. *The Jury,* W.R. Cornish (Penguin Press, London, 1968), p. 143.

23. *Id.* at p. 160.

24. Cornish, *op. cit.* at note 22, at p. 174.

25. Forsyth, *op. cit.* at note 14, at p. 426.

26. Devlin, *op. cit.* at note 1, at p. 159.

27. Holdsworth, *op. cit.* at note 15, at p. 349.

28. *Democracy In America,* Alexis Clerel DeTocqueville (George Adlard, New York, 3rd American Ed., 1839), footnote on p. 281.

29. Sarky, *op. cit.* at note 6, at pp. 243, 255.

30. Cornish, *op. cit.* at note 22, at p. 19.

31. Cornish, *op. cit.* at note 22, at p. 265.

32. "Abolition of the Civil Jury: Proposed Alternatives," Bruce Rashkow, 15 DePaul L. Rev. 417, 422 (1965).

33. *The American Jury,* Harry Kalven, Jr. and Hans Zeisel (Little, Brown and Company, Boston, 1960), p. 8.

34. Sacks, *op. cit.* at note 2, at p. 83.

35. Sacks, *op. cit.* at note 2, at p. 82.

36. Sacks, *op. cit.* at note 2, at p. 83.

37. Sacks, *op. cit.* at note 2, at pp. 83-84.

38. Kalven and Zeisel, *op. cit.* at note 33, at pp. 295-96.

39. Sacks, *op. cit.* at note 2, at pp. 83-4.

40. Devlin, *op. cit.* at note 1, at p. 145.

41. Williams, *op. cit.* at note 24, *op cit.* at note 11, at p. 279.

42. Sacks, *op. cit.* at note 2, at pp. 83-84.

43. Kalven and Zeisel, *op. cit.* at note 33, at p. 31; Cornish, *op. cit.* at note 22, at p. 31.

44. Forsyth, *op. cit.* at note 14, at p. 249.

45. Cornish, *op. cit.* at note 22, at p. 258.

46. Kalven and Zeisel, *op. cit.* at note 33, at p. 453.

47. Kalven and Zeisel, *op. cit.* at note 33, at p. 498.

48. Cornish, *op. cit.* at note 22, at p. 145.

49. Williams, *op. cit.* at note 21, *op. cit.* at note 11, at p. 315.

50. Kalven and Zeisel, *op. cit.* at note 33, at p. 454.

51. Forsyth, *op. cit.* at note 14, at p. 246.

52. *A Complete Collection of State Trials and Proceedings for High Treason,* Edited by T.B. Howell (T.C. Hansard, London, 1816), Vol. 6, p. 1006.

53. *The Wall Street Journal,* Editorial Page (January 19, 1973).

54. Kalven and Zeisel, *op. cit.* at note 33, at p. 498.

55. Kalven and Zeisel, *op. cit.* at note 33, at pp. 167, 181, 189.

56. Holdsworth, *op. cit.* at note 15, at p. 348; Cornish, *op. cit.* at note 22, at p. 255; Williams, *op. cit.* at note 11, at p. 282.

57. DeTocqueville, *op. cit.* at note 28, at p. 284.

58. DeTocqueville, *op. cit.* at note 28, at p. 283.

59. DeTocqueville, *op. cit.* at note 28, at p. 284.

60. Frank, *op. cit.* at note 5, at p. 221.

61. Devlin, *op. cit.* at note 1, at p. 155.

62. Rashkow, *op. cit.* at note 32, at p. 430.

63. Kalven and Zeisel, *op. cit.* at note 33, at p. 26.

64. Kalven and Zeisel, *op. cit.* at note 33, at p. 444.

65. Kalven and Zeisel, *op. cit.* at note 33, at p. 7.

66. "With Love In Their Hearts But Reform On Their Minds," *op. cit.* at note 20, at p. 188.

67. Kalven and Zeisel, *op. cit.* at note 33, at pp. 128, 495.

68. Kalven and Zeisel, *op. cit.* at note 33, at p. 9.

69. Frank, *op. cit.* at note 5, at p. 163.

70. Frank, *op. cit.* at note 5, at p. 168.

71. Howe, *op. cit.* at note 7, at p. 616.

72. Haines, *op. cit.* at note 9, at p. 105.

73. Haines, *op. cit.* at note 9, at p. 105.

74. Frank, *op. cit.* at note 5, at p. 137.

75. Frank, *op. cit.* at note 5, at p. 137.

76. DeTocqueville, *op. cit.* at note 28, at p. 282.

Appendix I.
Quotes on Justice and Juries from Decided Cases

The trial by jury is justly dear to the American People. It has always been an object of deep interest and solicitude, and every encroachment upon it has been watched with great jealousy.
Justice Joseph Story, *Parsons v. Bedford*, 28 U.S. 433 (1830).

It is the duty of the court in its relation to the jury to protect parties from unjust verdicts arising from ignorance of the rules of law and evidence, from impulses of passion or prejudice, or from any other violation of his lawful rights in the conduct of the trial.
Justice Samuel F. Miller, *Pleasants v. Fant* 89 U.S. 116 (1875).

The right to challenge is the right to reject, not to select.
Justice Stephen Johnson Field, *Hayes v. Missouri* 120 U.S. 68 (1887).

As the removal was upon the application of the appellees, they must cast in the costs.
Chief Justice Melville Weston Fuller, 149 U.S. 451 (1893).

Still it must be remembered that men may testify truthfully, although their lives hang in the balance.
Justice George Shiras, *Hicks v. United States*, 150 U.S. 442 (1893).

. . . The possession of a conscience void of offence toward God and men is not an indispensable prerequisite to justification of action in the fact of immediate and deadly peril . . . .
. . . argumentative matter of this sort should not be thrown into the scales of justice by the judicial officer who holds them.
Chief Justice Melville Weston Fuller, 153 U.S. 614 (1894).

Trial by jury has never been affirmed to be a necessary requisite of due process of law.
Justice John Marshal Harlan, in dissent, *Maxwell v. Dow*, 176 U.S. 581 (1900).

Even when persons are excluded, it is no ground for challenge

261

to an array if a sufficient number of unexceptional persons are present.

Justice Oliver Wendell Holmes, Jr., *Rawlins v. Georgia*, 201 U.S. 638 (1906).

. . . the law is full of instances where a man's fate depends on his estimating rightly, that is, as the jury subsequently estimates it, some matter of degree. If his judgment is wrong, not only may he incur a fine or a short imprisonment, as here; he may incur the penalty of death.

Justice Oliver Wendell Holmes, Jr., *Nash v. United States*, 229 U.S. 373 (1913).

A decided case is worth as much as it weighs in reason and righteousness, and no more.

Judge Wanamaker, *Adams Express Co., v. Beckworth*, 100 Ohio St. 348 (1919).

To uphold the voluntary reduction of a jury from twelve to eleven upon the ground that the reduction—though it destroys the jury of the Constitution—is only a slight reduction, is not to interpret that instrument but to disregard it.

Patton v. United States, 281 U.S. 276 (1930).

Consistently with /the Fourteenth/ amendment, trial by jury may be abolished.

Justice Benjamin Cardozo, *Snyder v. Commonwealth of Massachusetts*, 291 U.S. 97 (1934).

A fertile source of perversion in constitutional theory is the tyranny of labels.

Justice Benjamin Cardozo, *Snyder v. Commonwealth of Massachusetts*, 291 U.S. 97 (1934).

With, perhaps, some exceptions, trial by jury has always been, and still is, generally regarded as the normal and preferred mode of disposing of issues of fact in civil cases at law as well as in criminal cases.

Justice Sutherland, *Dunick v. Schiedt*, 293 U.S. 474 (1935).

The right to trial by jury and the immunity from prosecution except as the result of an indictment may have value and importance. Even so, they are not of the very essence of a scheme of

ordered liberty. To abolish them is not to violate a principle of justice so rooted in the traditions as to be ranked as fundamental.
Justice Benjamin Cardozo, *Palko v. Connecticut*, 302 U.S. 319 (1937).

If there has been discrimination, whether accomplished ingeniously or ingenuously, the conviction cannot stand.
Justice Hugo Black, *Smith v. Texas*, 311 U.S. 128 (1940).

/The defendant/ has no constitutional right to friends on the jury.
Justice Robert H. Jackson, *Fay v. New York*, 332 U.S. 621 (1947).

England, from whom the Western World has largely taken its concept of individual liberty and of the dignity and worth of every man has bequeathed to us safeguards for their preservation, the most priceless of which is that of trial by jury.
Justice Tom C. Clark, *Irvin v. Dowd*, 366 U.S. 717 (1961).

A defendant's only Constitutional right concerning the method of trial is to an impartial trial by jury.
Chief Justice Warren, *Singer v. United States*, 380 U.S. 24 (1965).

Whatever else might be said of capital punishment, it is at least clear that its imposition by a hanging jury cannot be squared with the Constitution.
Justice Stewart, *Witherspoon v. Illinois*, 391 U.S. 510 (1968).

. . . the primary purpose of the jury is to prevent the possibility of oppression by the Government.
Justice White, *Baldwin v. New York*, 399 U.S. 66 (1970).

A requirement of unanimity, however, does not materially contribute to the exercise of the commonsense judgment.
Justice White, *Apodaca v. Oregon*, 406 U.S. 404 (1972).

Because juries frequently face complex problems laden with value choices, the benefits are important and should be retained.
Justice Blackmun, *Ballew v. Georgia*, 435 U.S. 223 (1978).

It is inevitable that lines must be drawn somewhere if the substance of jury trial is to be preserved.
Justice Rehnquist, *Burch v. Louisiana*, 441 U.S. 130 (1979).

If you can find a jury that's both a computer technician, a

lawyer, an economist, knows all that stuff, I think you could have a qualified jury, but we don't know anything about that.

(This was the answer of a juror to a judge after a mistrial had been declared, to the question as to whether jurors were capable of handling a complex case), *ILC Peripherals v. International Business Machines*, 458 F. Supp. 423 (1978).

. . . to hold that a jury trial is required in this case would be to hold that the Seventh Amendment gives a single party at its choice the right to an irrational verdict.

Berstein v. Universal Pictures, 79 FRD 59 (1978).

First, those who would dispense with juries in complex cases overlook the fact that the alternative to a lay jury is a lay judge.

Judge Edward R. Becker, *Zenith Radio Corporation v. Matsushita Electric Industrial, Co., Ltd., et. al.*, 478 F. Supp. 889 (1979).

One unique virtue of the jury is its 'black box' function; it gives results without reasons.

Judge Edward R. Becker, *Zenith Radio Corporation, supra.*

We have no real assurance, however, of objective truth whether the trial is to the court or to a jury.

Judge John J. Gibbons, dissent, *In re Japanese Electronic Products Antitrust Litigation*, 631 F2d 1069 (1980).

Appendix II.
Chronology of Significant Jury Dates

B.C.

Unknown   According to Greek Mythology, The God Ares was acquitted by a 6-6 verdict of 12 Gods for the murder of the son of Poseidon.

2,000   An eight person jury existed in Egypt.

1,250   Orestes was acquitted of matricide by the vote of Pallas Athena after a jury of 12 Athenians had hung 6-6.

451-50   Athenian jury brought to Rome.

450   In Athens the Assembly of Citizens supreme in civil and criminal legal disputes. Size of the Assembly ranged from 200 to 2,000 plus one for a tie breaker.

399   Socrates found guilty and sentenced to death by Athenian Assembly.

122   Membership in the Roman jury transferred from the Senatorial class to the Equestrian class.

70   Membership in the Roman jury restored to the Senatorial class.

A.D.

41-50   Roman form of jury brought to England under Claudius.

410-448   Romans abandon England.

400-500   Burgundians in what is now southeast France had the Roman form of jury.

430   Anglos and Saxons began to migrate to England.

568-615   Saxons tried by members of Tithing for crimes under reign of Ethelbert.

780   Frankish inquisitio, a form of jury, established.

800   Form of jury in existence in Scandinavia.

866-71   Under reign of Aethelred, 12 or more freemen met twice a year and judged in each county.

871-99   King Alfred reigned and had a form of jury.

997   Aethelred II promulgated a form of jury in the Danish district of England.

1024-66 Under Edward the Confessor, boundary disputes submitted to a group of neighbors.

1066   Norman invasion of England, bringing with them remnants of the Frankish form of jury.

1099   A form of jury established in Jerusalem by French crusaders.

1166   Under the Grand Assize of Henry II, a person in possession of land had a right to trial by jury if a person challenged his title.

1215   Magna Carta, often cited as authority for right to jury trial.

1367   From this time until modern times an English jury had to return a unanimous verdict.

1400   From this time until modern times, jury trial was the dominant mode of trial in England.

1606   Jury trial introduced into the Colony of Virginia.

1628   Jury trial introduced into the Massachusetts Bay Colony.

1664   Jury trial introduced into New York.

1665   Jury used in Sweden.

1670   William Penn and William Mead acquitted by jury at Old Bailey.

1681   Counsel permitted to argue law in English trials, but could not argue to the jury.

1688   The Seven Bishops Trial at Westminster Hall.

1772   *Peine forte et dure* abolished by statute in England.

1774   Declaration of Rights of the First Continental Congress included the right to trial by jury.

1775   The First Session of the American Stamp Act Congress listed trial by jury as an essential right.

1776   June 29, The Constitution of Virginia adopted. It was the first modern constitution in a republic to contain a guaranty of trial by jury.

1776   July 4, The Declaration of Independence which complained of the deprivation of trial by jury.

1787   The Ordinance for the Government of the United States Territory Northwest of the Ohio River provided for trial by jury.

1789   The Constitution of the United States was adopted.

1789   The Judiciary Act adopted which provided that suits in equity were not to be maintained where there was a plain and adequate remedy at law, that is, in a trial before a jury.

1791   The Bill of Rights, the first ten amendments to the Constitution adopted including guaranties of trial by jury.

1791   French Constituent Assembly adopted trial by jury in criminal cases.

1794   The case of *Georgia v. Brailsford,* 3 U.S. 1 (1794), decided by the United States Supreme Court and seemed to say that juries had the power to decide both law and fact.

1807   Aaron Burr found not guilty of treason by a jury. John Marshall presided.

1808   The Code Napoleon adopted in France and provided for trial by jury in criminal cases.

1812   A fact determined by a jury not to be re-examined by a court of the United States except by a new trial granted for good cause shown or by the award of a *facias de novo* awarded when a case is reversed on appeal. *United*

States v. Wonson, 28 Fed. Cases 745 (Cir. Ct. Dist. Mass. 1812).

1828   A federal court judge can sum up law and facts and express his opinion on the facts, but not in absolute terms. *M'Lanahan v. Universal Insurance Company,* 26 U.S. 170 (1828).

1835   When there is no evidence on a point, the court can so instruct the jury. *Greenleaf v. Birth,* 34 U.S. 292 (1835).

1848   Various German states had trial by jury.

1868   The Fourteenth Amendment adopted, guaranteeing citizens of the various states equal protection and due process.

1879   A violation of the Fourteenth Amendment to exclude persons from grand and petit juries because of race. *Strauder v. West Virginia,* 100 U.S. 303 (1879).

1897   The Constitution secured to United States citizens the right to a unanimous jury in suits in federal courts *American Publishing Company v. Fisher,* 166 U.S. 464 (1879).

1900   Fourteenth Amendment does not require states to have a 12 person jury in criminal cases. *Maxwell v. Dow,* 176 U.S. 581 (1900).

1909   It is the duty of the jury to accept the law as declared by the court. *Hepner v. United States,* 213 U.S. 103 (1909).

1920   The Nineteenth Amendment was adopted, giving women the right to vote.

1924   Germany dispensed with trial by jury.

1938   Federal Rules of Civil Procedure effective, providing for one cause of action, a "civil action", merging law and equity.

1942   In a federal criminal trial, even a defendant without counsel can waive trial by jury. *Adams v. United States,* 317 U.S. 269 (1942).

1946   Wage earners cannot be systematically excluded from jury duty, *Thiel v. Southern Pacific Co.*, 328 U.S. 217 (1946), and women cannot be systematically excluded from jury duty, *Ballard v. United States*, 329 U.S. 187 (1946).

1968   Denial by the state of jury trial in non-petty criminal cases violates the due process clause of the Fourteenth Amendment. *Duncan v. Louisiana*, 391 U.S. 145 (1968).

1970   A six person jury in state, non-petty criminal case, must be unanimous. *Williams v. Florida*, 399 U.S. 78 (1970).

1972   State court convictions for felonies by 11-1 and 10-2 jury verdicts do not violate the Fourteenth Amendment. *Apodaca v. Oregon*, 406 U.S. 404 (1972).

1973   Six person juries in civil cases in federal courts do not violate the Seventh Amendment. *Colgrove v. Battin*, 413 U.S. 149 (1973).

1978   A five person jury in a state criminal case violates the due process clause of the Fourteenth Amendment. *Ballew v. Georgia*, 435 U.S. 223 (1978).

1979   A non-unanimous verdict by a six person jury in a state criminal proceeding violated the Fourteenth Amendment. *Burch v. Louisianna*, 441 U.S. 130 (1979).

1985   A Houston Texas jury returned a verdict in favor of Pennzoil and against Texaco Co. for 10.53 billion dollars for the largest jury verdict in history.

1986   The Fourteenth Amendment is violated when the prosecution systematically uses peremptory challenges to exclude blacks. *Batson v. Kentucky*, 476 U.S. 106 S.Ct 1712 (1986).

1987   A jury in Belleville, Illinois returned a verdict of 16.2 million dollars against Monsanto Co. in the case of *Kemper v. Monsanto Co.* The case had lasted over three and one-half years, making it the longest lasting jury trial in history.

INDEX

All cases are indexed under the case name if cited in the text. Under the entry "Jury" are various subentries to aid in finding precise items. References are to page numbers.